Taste of Home's
Favorite Brand Name Recipes
2006

Taste of Home Books

Editor: Heidi Reuter Lloyd
Food Editor: Janaan Cunningham
Associate Food Editor: Diane Werner
Senior Home Economist: Patricia Schmeling
Senior Recipe Editor: Sue A. Jurack

Front cover photography by Reiman Publications
Photographer: Dan Roberts

Pictured on the front cover *(clockwise from top right):* Chocolate Orange Marble Chiffon Cake *(page 186),* Basil Vinaigrette *(page 37)* and Harvest Pot Roast *(page 158).*

Pictured on the back cover *(clockwise from top):* Heartwarming Beef Stew Skillet *(page 140),* Herbed Green Bean Casserole *(page 54)* and Libby's® Pumpkin Roll *(page 198).*

ISBN: 1-4127-2369-8

ISSN: 1554-0111

Manufactured in China.

8 7 6 5 4 3 2 1

Microwave Cooking: Microwave ovens vary in wattage. Use the cooking times as guidelines and check for doneness before adding more time.

Taste of Home's Favorite Brand Name Recipes 2006

A Collection of Favorite Recipes From America's Most Trusted Brands

WE TAKE trust seriously at *Taste of Home,* the No. 1 cooking magazine in America. This exciting new book, *Taste of Home's Favorite Brand Name Recipes 2006,* has earned your trust in two ways.

First, all 352 down-home recipes were hand-picked by the home economists at *Taste of Home.* Second, every recipe features name-brand foods you've used with confidence (and had great results with) for years.

The best part is that you don't have to worry if the foods will taste good or the recipes will turn out. They will.

Chosen From the Best

This book is filled with family-favorite recipes. We've spent a year sifting through hundreds of name-brand favorites to create a collection that will make your taste buds tingle and your mouth water. And we went right to the source. For instance:

• When we wanted a refreshing beverage to cool you off on those hot summer days, we chose Fresh Fruit Lemonade from Sunkist (see page 8 in the Appetizers & Snacks chapter).

• When we wanted to kick a plain salad up a notch, we opted for Chicken, Tomato and Avocado Pasta Salad from Hunt's (see page 36 in the Salads chapter).

• When we decided we needed a side dish that was pure comfort food, we picked Golden Corn Pudding from Del Monte (see page 60 in the Side Dishes chapter).

• And when we wanted a main dish that was perfect for a hearty Sunday dinner, we chose Southwestern Beef Stew from Lipton (see page 162 in the Main Dishes chapter).

You'll also find enough desserts to keep your sweet tooth happy for months sampling dozens of delicious cakes, cookies, pies, bars and cobblers in a multitude of flavors.

Chicken Corn Chowder with Cheese

Picture-Perfect Foods

We packed over 300 recipes into the 224 pages of this useful book. Many of the recipes include photographs, so you'll be able to see what you're making and how wonderful the finished product will look.

The photos are large; in fact a number are full-page. You'll count more than 150 photographs.

This book will take you from the start of a family meal to the finish, giving you plenty of choices for appealing appetizers, delicious desserts and everything in between—soups, salads, entrees, side dishes and breads.

You won't have to worry about running out of clever combinations. You can mix and match to your heart's content. And your family will be happy, too, because every single recipe has been kitchen-tested and approved by *Taste of Home* food editors.

Chocolate Almond Biscotti

Warm Ginger Almond Chicken Salad

How to Find a Recipe

This book is indexed in two helpful ways. The general index, beginning on page 213, lists every recipe by food category, major ingredient and/or cooking style.

For example, if you know you want to serve chicken tonight, turn to "chicken" in the general index and ponder the many tasty options. You can also look under general categories such as "oven entrees," "skillet dishes" and "grilled and broiled."

The alphabetical index starts on page 221, so once you and your family have discovered a few favorites, it's a snap to find them by name when you're ready to make them again.

We hope you enjoy using *Taste of Home's Favorite Brand Name Recipes 2006* as much as we enjoyed making it.

Appetizers & Snacks

Artichoke Frittata

(Pictured at left)

1 can (14 ounces) artichoke hearts, drained
3 teaspoons olive oil, divided
1/2 cup minced green onions
5 eggs
1/2 cup (2 ounces) shredded Swiss cheese
2 tablespoons grated Parmesan cheese
1 tablespoon minced fresh parsley
1 teaspoon salt
Pepper

1. Chop artichoke hearts; set aside.

2. Heat 2 teaspoons oil in 10-inch skillet over medium heat. Add green onions; cook and stir until tender. Remove from skillet.

3. Beat eggs in medium bowl until light. Stir in artichokes, green onions, cheeses, parsley, salt and pepper to taste.

4. Heat remaining 1 teaspoon oil in same skillet over medium heat. Pour egg mixture into skillet. Cook 4 to 5 minutes or until bottom is lightly browned. Place large plate over skillet; invert frittata onto plate. Return frittata, uncooked side down, to skillet. Cook about 4 minutes more or until center is just set. Cut into small wedges.   *Makes 12 to 16 appetizer servings*

Clockwise from top left: *Olive Tapenade Dip (p. 14), Tomato and Bacon Quesadillas (p. 20), Mariachi Chicken (p. 18) and Artichoke Frittata*

Home-Style Corn Cakes

(Pictured at right)

    1 cup yellow cornmeal
    1/2 cup all-purpose flour
    1/2 teaspoon baking powder
    1/2 teaspoon baking soda
    1 envelope LIPTON® RECIPE SECRETS®
        Onion Soup Mix*
    3/4 cup buttermilk
    1 egg, beaten
    1 can (14-3/4 ounces) cream-style corn
    2 ounces roasted red peppers, chopped
        (about 1/4 cup)
    I CAN'T BELIEVE IT'S NOT BUTTER!® Spread

*Or, substitute Lipton® RECIPE SECRETS® Golden Onion Soup Mix.

In large bowl, combine cornmeal, flour, baking powder and baking soda. Blend soup mix with buttermilk, egg, corn and roasted red peppers; stir into cornmeal mixture.

In 12-inch nonstick skillet or on griddle, melt 1/2 teaspoon Spread over medium heat. Drop 1/4 cup batter for each corn cake and cook, turning once, 5 minutes or until cooked through and golden brown. Remove to serving platter and keep warm. Repeat with remaining batter and additional I Can't Believe It's Not Butter!® Spread if needed. Serve with sour cream and prepared salsa, if desired.

Makes about 18 corn cakes

Tip: Leftover corn cakes may be wrapped and frozen. Remove from wrapping and reheat straight from freezer in preheated 350°F oven for 15 minutes.

Fresh Fruit Lemonade

    1 to 1-1/2 cups sliced ripe strawberries, whole
        raspberries or blueberries
    Juice of 6 SUNKIST® lemons (1 cup)
    1 cup sugar
    4 cups cold water
    1 fresh SUNKIST® lemon, unpeeled, cut into
        cartwheel slices
    Ice cubes

In blender or food processor, combine berries, lemon juice and sugar; blend until smooth. Pour into large pitcher. Add cold water, lemon cartwheel slices and ice; stir well. Garnish each serving with additional fruit and/or fresh mint leaves, if desired.

Makes about 6 (8-ounce) servings

Roasted Red Potato Bites

    1-1/2 pounds red potatoes (about 15 small)
        1 cup shredded cheddar cheese (about 4 ounces)
    1/2 cup HELLMANN'S® or BEST FOODS®
        Real Mayonnaise
    1/2 cup sliced green onions
        2 tablespoons chopped fresh basil leaves
        (optional)
    10 slices bacon, crisp-cooked and crumbled

1. Preheat oven to 400°F. On large baking sheet, arrange potatoes and bake 35 minutes or until tender. Let cool to handle.

2. Cut each potato in half, then cut thin slice from bottom of each potato half. With small melon baller or spoon, scoop pulp from potatoes leaving 1/4-inch shell. Set aside shells and reserve pulp.

3. In medium bowl, lightly mash reserved pulp. Stir in remaining ingredients. Spoon or pipe potato filling into potato shells.

4. Arrange filled shells on baking sheet and broil 3 minutes or until golden and heated through.

Makes 30 bites

Ham and Cherry Roll-Ups

    1 package (8 ounces) cream cheese, softened
    1/2 cup sliced green onions
    1/2 cup chopped toasted walnuts
    1/4 cup cherry preserves
    1 pound sliced deli ham (16 to 20 slices)

In small bowl, stir together all ingredients except ham. Spread rounded tablespoon cream cheese mixture on each ham slice. Roll up; cut each roll in half. Secure rolls with wooden picks. Refrigerate, covered, until serving time.

Makes 32 to 40 appetizers.

Tip: Prepare and refrigerate these easy appetizers up to 1 day ahead.

Favorite recipe from **National Pork Board**

Home-Style Corn Cakes

Spicy Roasted Chick-Peas

Spicy Roasted Chick-Peas

(pictured above)

> 1 can (about 15 ounces) chick-peas
> 3 tablespoons olive oil
> 1/2 teaspoon salt
> 1/2 teaspoon black pepper
> 3/4 to 1 tablespoon chili powder
> 1/8 to 1/4 teaspoon cayenne pepper
> 1 lime, cut into wedges

1. Preheat oven to 400°F. Rinse chick-peas in colander; drain well, shaking colander to remove as much water as possible.

2. Combine chick-peas, olive oil, salt and black pepper in baking pan large enough to hold chick-peas in single layer. Bake 15 minutes or until chick-peas begin to brown, shaking pan twice to brown evenly.

3. Add chili powder and cayenne pepper to taste; bake an additional 5 minutes or until dark golden-red. Serve with lime wedges.

Makes about 2 cups

Zesty Party Snack Mix

> 4 cups oven-toasted corn cereal squares
> 2 cans (1-1/2 ounces each) *French's®* Potato Sticks
> 1 cup honey-roasted peanuts
> 3 tablespoons melted butter or vegetable oil
> 2 tablespoons *French's®* Worcestershire Sauce
> 2 tablespoons *Frank's® RedHot®* Original Cayenne Pepper Sauce
> 1/2 teaspoon seasoned salt

1. Place cereal, potato sticks and peanuts in 3-quart microwavable bowl. Combine melted butter, Worcestershire, ***Frank's RedHot*** Sauce and seasoned salt in small bowl; mix well. Pour butter mixture over cereal mixture. Toss to coat evenly.

2. Microwave, uncovered, on HIGH 6 minutes, stirring well every 2 minutes. Transfer to paper towels; cool completely. *Makes about 6 cups*

Tex-Mex Snack Mix: Add 1 teaspoon each chili powder and ground cumin to butter mixture. Substitute 1 cup regular peanuts for honey-roasted nuts. Prepare as directed.

Italian Snack Mix: Add 1-1/2 teaspoons Italian seasoning and 1/2 teaspoon garlic powder to butter mixture. Substitute 1/2 cup grated Parmesan cheese and 1/2 cup sliced almonds for honey-roasted nuts. Prepare as directed.

Indian Snack Mix: Omit seasoned salt. Add 2 teaspoons each sesame seeds and curry powder and 1/4 teaspoon garlic salt to butter mixture. Substitute 1 cup cashews for honey-roasted nuts. Prepare as directed.

Nacho Popcorn

> 3 quarts popped JOLLY TIME® Pop Corn
> 2 cups corn chips
> 1/4 cup butter or margarine
> 1-1/2 teaspoons Mexican seasoning
> 3/4 cup shredded taco cheese

Preheat oven to 300°F. Spread popped popcorn and corn chips in shallow baking pan lined with foil. Melt butter in small pan. Stir in Mexican seasoning. Pour over popcorn mixture and toss well. Sprinkle with cheese and toss to mix. Bake 5 to 7 minutes or until cheese is melted. Serve immediately.

Makes about 3-1/2 quarts

Sausage-Stuffed Mushrooms

(pictured below)

4 ounces uncooked bulk turkey Italian sausage
2 tablespoons bread crumbs
4 medium portobello mushroom caps
1 tablespoon olive oil
1/4 cup shredded Asiago cheese

1. Preheat oven to 325°F. Crumble sausage into small skillet. Cook over medium-high heat until no longer pink; drain fat. Remove from heat and stir in bread crumbs.

2. Brush both sides of mushroom caps lightly with oil. Spoon sausage stuffing into caps, dividing evenly among mushrooms.

3. Place mushrooms, stuffing-side up, on baking sheet. Sprinkle 1 tablespoon cheese over each mushroom. Bake 15 minutes or until cheese melts and mushrooms are tender.   *Makes 4 servings*

Tip: Avoid heating up your kitchen on hot summer days by using your toaster oven. Many appetizers and side dishes can be made in this smaller appliance.

Franks Under Wraps

1/2 package PEPPERIDGE FARM® Frozen Puff
        Pastry Sheets (1 sheet)
1 egg
1 tablespoon water
10 frankfurters, cut crosswise into halves

1. **THAW** pastry sheet at room temperature 30 minutes. Preheat oven to 400°F. Mix egg and water.

2. **UNFOLD** pastry on lightly floured surface. Cut into 20 (1/2-inch) strips. Wrap pastry strips around frankfurters, pressing gently to seal. Place 2 inches apart on baking sheet. Brush with egg mixture.

3. **BAKE** 15 minutes or until golden. Serve with mustard for dipping.   *Makes 20 appetizers*

Variation: For a holiday twist, use 5 frankfurters and cut each into quarters lengthwise, then cut in half crosswise. Twist pastry strips while wrapping around 2 frankfurter pieces. Press gently to seal.

Sausage-Stuffed Mushrooms

Mexican Salsa

(pictured at right)

1 can (14.5 ounces) HUNT'S® Petite Diced
    Tomatoes, undrained
1/4 cup chopped onion
1 small jalapeño pepper, seeded and chopped
2 tablespoons chopped fresh cilantro
1 clove garlic, minced
1/2 teaspoon granulated sugar
1/4 teaspoon salt
1/4 teaspoon ground black pepper

COMBINE all ingredients in small bowl.

COVER and refrigerate 2 hours prior to serving.
Makes 2 cups

Hints from Hunt's®: This salsa is great for a simple
snack with chips, served over potatoes or rice, or
as a zesty condiment for Mexican dishes.

Mediterranean Sausage and Spinach Tartlets

1 (16-ounce) package PERDUE® Fresh Seasoned
    Lean Turkey Sausage, Sweet Italian
1/2 cup frozen chopped spinach, thawed and
    squeezed dry
1 cup crumbled feta cheese
2 green onions, minced
1-1/2 teaspoons fresh oregano, chopped
    Salt and pepper, to taste
2 (2.1-ounce) packages mini fillo dough shells
15 pitted kalamata olives, halved

Preheat oven to 375°F.

Remove sausage from casing and place in a large,
nonstick skillet over high heat. Sauté until cooked
through, breaking up sausage with a wooden spoon
as it cooks. Stir in spinach until hot. Turn off heat;
stir in feta, green onions, oregano and salt and
pepper to taste.

Set fillo cups on a baking sheet and bake them until
crisp and hot, about 4 minutes. Fill each cup with
sausage mixture and top with an olive half. Serve
immediately. *Makes 30 appetizers*

Parmesan-Pepper Crisps

2 cups (4 ounces) loosely packed coarsely grated
    Parmesan cheese
2 teaspoons pepper

Preheat oven to 400°F. Line wire racks with paper
towels.

Place heaping teaspoonfuls of cheese 2 inches apart
on ungreased nonstick baking sheet. Flatten cheese
mounds slightly with back of spoon. Sprinkle each
mound with pinch of pepper.

Bake 15 to 20 minutes or until crisps are very lightly
browned. (Watch closely—crisps burn easily.) Let
cool on baking sheet 2 minutes; carefully remove
with spatula to prepared racks. Store in airtight
container in refrigerator up to 3 days.
Makes about 26 crisps

Salsa Party Meatballs

2-1/2 pounds ground beef *or* ground meat loaf mix
    (beef, pork, veal)
6 tablespoons dry bread crumbs
1/4 cup milk
2 eggs
1 teaspoon garlic powder
4 green onions, chopped
1 cup shredded Cheddar cheese
2 tablespoons olive or vegetable oil
2 jars (16 ounces each) PACE® Chunky Salsa

MIX beef, bread crumbs, milk, eggs, garlic powder,
green onions and **2 tablespoons** cheese. Form into
60 (1-1/2-inch) meatballs.

HEAT 1 tablespoon oil in large nonstick skillet and
cook meatballs in batches until browned, using
remaining oil as needed.

STIR meatballs and salsa together in skillet and heat
to a boil. Cover and simmer for 8 minutes. Stir in
remaining cheese and cook for 1 minute or until
cheese melts. Sprinkle with additional chopped
green onions if desired. Serve with toothpicks.
Makes 60 appetizers

Serving Suggestion: Serve with tortilla chips for
dipping in salsa mixture.

Quick Sausage Appetizers

    1/2 pound BOB EVANS® Italian Roll Sausage
    1/3 cup mozzarella cheese
    1/4 cup sour cream
      3 tablespoons mayonnaise
      2 tablespoons chopped green onion
    1/2 teaspoon Worcestershire sauce
     10 slices white bread*

Party rye or thinly sliced French bread can be used instead of white bread. Double recipe to have enough sausage mixture.

Preheat broiler. Crumble and cook sausage in medium skillet until browned. Drain on paper towels. Transfer sausage to small bowl; stir in cheese, sour cream, mayonnaise, green onion and Worcestershire. Cut crusts from bread. Cut each slice into 4 squares; spread about 1 teaspoon sausage mixture onto each square. Arrange squares on ungreased baking sheet; place under hot broiler just until cheese melts and topping bubbles. (Be careful not to burn corners and edges.) Serve hot.

Makes 40 appetizer squares

Note: Quick Sausage Appetizers may be made ahead and refrigerated overnight or frozen up to 1 month before broiling.

Olive Tapenade Dip

(pictured on page 6)

    1-1/2 cups (10-ounce jar) pitted kalamata olives
      3 tablespoons olive oil
      3 tablespoons *French's*® Bold n' Spicy Brown Mustard
      1 tablespoon minced fresh rosemary leaves or 1 teaspoon dried rosemary leaves
      1 teaspoon minced garlic

1. Place all ingredients in food processor. Process until puréed.

2. Serve with vegetable crudités or pita chips.

Makes 4 (1/4-cup) servings

Tip: To pit olives, place in plastic bag. Gently tap with wooden mallet or rolling pin until olives split open. Remove pits.

Mushroom Parmesan Crostini

      1 tablespoon olive oil
      1 clove garlic, finely chopped
      1 cup chopped mushrooms
      1 loaf Italian or French bread (about 12 inches long), cut into 12 slices and toasted
    3/4 cup RAGÚ® Pizza Quick® Snack Sauce
    1/4 cup grated Parmesan cheese
      1 tablespoon finely chopped fresh basil leaves or 1 teaspoon dried basil leaves

Preheat oven to 375°F. In 8-inch nonstick skillet, heat olive oil over medium heat and cook garlic 30 seconds. Add mushrooms and cook, stirring occasionally, 2 minutes or until liquid evaporates.

On baking sheet, arrange bread slices. Evenly spread Ragú Pizza Quick Snack Sauce on bread slices, then top with mushroom mixture, cheese and basil. Bake 15 minutes or until heated through.

Makes 12 crostini

Tip: Many varieties of mushrooms are available in supermarkets and specialty grocery stores. Shiitake, portobello and cremini mushrooms all have excellent flavor.

Red Hot Pepper Wings

(pictured at right)

     28 chicken wing drumettes (2-1/4 to 3 pounds)
      2 tablespoons olive oil
        Salt and black pepper
    1/4 to 1/2 cup hot pepper sauce
      2 tablespoons melted butter
      1 teaspoon sugar

Brush chicken with oil; sprinkle with salt and pepper. Grill chicken on covered grill over medium KINGSFORD® Briquets about 20 minutes until juices run clear, turning every 5 minutes. Combine pepper sauce, butter and sugar in large bowl; add chicken and toss to coat. Serve hot or cold.

Makes 7 servings

Easy Spinach Appetizer

Easy Spinach Appetizer

(pictured above)

2 tablespoons butter
3 eggs
1 cup milk
1 cup all-purpose flour
1 teaspoon baking powder
1 teaspoon salt
2 packages (10 ounces each) frozen chopped
   spinach, thawed and well drained
4 cups (16 ounces) shredded Monterey Jack
   cheese
1/2 cup diced red bell pepper

Preheat oven to 350°F. Melt butter in 13×9-inch baking dish.

Beat eggs in medium bowl. Add milk, flour, baking powder and salt; beat until well blended. Stir in spinach, cheese and bell pepper; mix well. Spread mixture over melted butter in pan.

Bake 40 to 45 minutes or until set. Let stand 10 minutes before cutting into triangles or squares.
Makes 2 to 4 dozen pieces

Tip: Easy Spinach Appetizer can also be made ahead, frozen and reheated. After baking, cool completely and cut into squares. Transfer squares to cookie sheet; place cookie sheet in freezer until squares are frozen solid. Transfer to resealable food storage bag. To serve, reheat squares in preheated 325°F oven for 15 minutes.

Creamy Hot Reuben Dip

4 tablespoons CRISCO® Butter Flavor Stick
   or 4 tablespoons CRISCO® Butter Flavor
   Shortening
1 large onion, finely diced
1/2 pound corned beef, sliced and shredded
1 (8-ounce) package cream cheese, cubed
2 cups grated Swiss cheese
1-1/2 cups sauerkraut, drained and chopped
1/2 cup mayonnaise
1/2 cup ketchup
2 tablespoons sweet pickle relish
2 tablespoons dill pickle relish

Melt shortening in heavy 4-quart saucepan. Add onion and cook until golden brown. Add corned beef; cook over medium heat 3 minutes, stirring often. Drain fat.

Add cream cheese, 1 cube at a time, stirring after each addition. Add cheese, sauerkraut, mayonnaise, ketchup and pickle relish.

Stir until cheeses are melted and ingredients are well blended. Serve in fondue pot or chafing dish with toasted mini rye triangles. *Makes 6 to 8 servings*

Roasted Red Pepper Spread

1 cup roasted red peppers, rinsed and drained
1 package (8 ounces) cream cheese, softened
1 packet (1 ounce) HIDDEN VALLEY®
   The Original Ranch® Salad Dressing &
   Seasoning Mix
Baguette slices and sliced ripe olives (optional)

Blot dry red peppers. In a food processor fitted with a metal blade, combine peppers, cream cheese and salad dressing & seasoning mix; process until smooth. Spread on baguette slices and garnish with olives, if desired. *Makes 2 cups*

Hearty Calico Bean Dip

(pictured below)

3/4 pound ground beef
1/2 pound sliced bacon, crisp-cooked and crumbled
1 can (16 ounces) baked beans
1 can (15 ounces) great northern beans, rinsed and drained
1 can (15 ounces) kidney beans, rinsed and drained
1 small onion, chopped
1/2 cup packed brown sugar
1/2 cup ketchup
1 tablespoon cider vinegar
1 teaspoon prepared yellow mustard
Tortilla chips

SLOW COOKER DIRECTIONS

Brown ground beef in large nonstick skillet, stirring to separate meat. Drain and discard fat. Spoon meat into slow cooker.

Add bacon, beans, onion, brown sugar, ketchup, vinegar and mustard to slow cooker; mix well.

Cover; cook on LOW 4 hours or on HIGH 2 hours. Serve with tortilla chips. *Makes 12 servings*

Turkey Bacon Biscuits

5 JENNIE-O TURKEY STORE® Turkey Bacon slices, cooked, crumbled, divided
1 (8-ounce) package cream cheese, softened
2 eggs
2 tablespoons milk
1/2 cup shredded Swiss cheese
2 tablespoons chopped green onion
1 (10-ounce) can refrigerated flaky biscuits

Heat oven to 375°F. Grease 10 muffin cups. Cook bacon according to package directions. In small bowl, beat cream cheese, eggs and milk with electric mixer at low speed until smooth. Stir in Swiss cheese and green onion. Separate dough into 10 biscuits. Place 1 biscuit in each greased muffin cup; firmly press in bottom and up sides, forming 1/4-inch rim. Place half of bacon in bottom of dough-lined muffin cups. Spoon cheese mixture over bacon. Bake 20 to 25 minutes or until filling is set and biscuits are golden brown. Sprinkle each cup with remaining bacon; lightly press into filling. Remove from pan. *Makes 10 servings*

Hearty Calico Bean Dip

Tomato Pesto Tart

(pictured at right)

1 sheet puff pastry, thawed according to package
    directions
    PAM® No Stick Cooking Spray
1/2 cup prepared pesto
1 cup (4 ounces) shredded mozzarella cheese,
    divided
1 can (14.5 ounces) HUNT'S® Whole Tomatoes,
    sliced

UNFOLD puff pastry on a floured surface. Cut off
1/2- to 3/4-inch strips from each side. Place pastry
square on a baking sheet sprayed with cooking
spray. Wet edges of pastry square lightly with water.
Lay strips of pastry on top of pastry square, forming
a pastry shell with raised edges. Press strips lightly
to seal to pastry shell.

SPREAD pesto evenly across bottom of pastry shell;
sprinkle with 1/2 cup cheese, tomato slices and
remaining 1/2 cup cheese.

BAKE in preheated 400°F oven for 17 to 20 minutes
or until golden brown. Serve immediately.
Makes 9 servings

Hints from Hunt's®: No need to fear working
with puff pastry. It is easy to thaw and use. Do
not confuse puff pastry with phyllo pastry,
which is more delicate.

Mariachi Chicken

(pictured on page 6)

1-1/4 cups crushed tortilla chips
1 package (1 ounce) LAWRY'S® Taco Spices &
    Seasonings
2 dozen chicken drummettes or 1 pound
    boneless chicken breasts
    Salsa and sour cream (optional)

In large resealable plastic bag, combine chips and
Taco Spices & Seasonings. Dampen chicken with
water; shake off excess. Place a few pieces at a
time in bag; seal and shake to coat with chips.
Arrange in greased shallow baking pan. Bake,
uncovered, in preheated 350°F oven for 40 to
45 minutes, until chicken is thoroughly cooked.
Serve with salsa and sour cream, if desired.
Makes 24 appetizers or 4 main-dish servings

Nachos à la Ortega®

1 can (16 ounces) ORTEGA® Refried Beans,
    warmed
4 cups baked tortilla chips
1-1/2 cups (6 ounces) shredded Monterey Jack
    cheese
2 tablespoons ORTEGA® Jalapeños, sliced
SUGGESTED TOPPINGS
    ORTEGA® Salsa-Thick & Chunky, sour cream,
    guacamole, sliced ripe olives, chopped green
    onions, chopped fresh cilantro (optional)

PREHEAT broiler.

SPREAD beans over bottom of large ovenproof
platter or 15×10-inch jelly-roll pan. Arrange chips
over beans. Top with cheese and jalapeños.

BROIL for 1 to 1-1/2 minutes or until cheese is
melted. Top with desired toppings.
Makes 4 to 6 servings

Zesty Bruschetta

1 baguette French bread, cut into 1-inch slices
1 cup diced plum tomatoes, drained of excess
    juice
1 (4-ounce) package feta cheese, crumbled
2 to 3 green onions, chopped
1/4 cup chopped black olives
2 tablespoons finely chopped fresh basil
1 teaspoon olive oil
1/2 teaspoon TABASCO® brand Pepper Sauce
    Salt to taste
    Fresh basil sprigs (optional)

Preheat broiler. Place bread slices on broiling pan
and broil each side until lightly toasted. Set aside.

Gently combine remaining ingredients except basil
sprigs in medium bowl until well blended. Top each
bread slice generously with tomato mixture. Serve
bruschetta on platter; garnish with basil sprigs, if
desired.
Makes 20 to 24 pieces

Hot French Onion Dip

(pictured at right)

**1 envelope LIPTON® RECIPE SECRETS®
    Onion Soup Mix
1 container (16 ounces) sour cream
2 cups shredded Swiss cheese (about 8 ounces)
1/4 cup HELLMANN'S® or BEST FOODS® Real
    Mayonnaise**

1. Preheat oven to 375°F. In 1-quart casserole, combine soup mix, sour cream, 1-3/4 cups Swiss cheese and mayonnaise.

2. Bake uncovered 20 minutes or until heated through. Sprinkle with remaining 1/4 cup cheese.

3. Serve, if desired, with sliced French bread or your favorite dippers. *Makes 2 cups dip*

Parmesan Cheese Twists

**1/2 package PEPPERIDGE FARM® Frozen Puff
    Pastry Sheets (1 sheet)
1 egg
1 tablespoon water
1/4 cup grated Parmesan cheese
1 tablespoon chopped fresh parsley
1/2 teaspoon dried oregano leaves, crushed**

1. **THAW** pastry sheet at room temperature 30 minutes. Preheat oven to 400°F. Mix egg and water. Mix cheese, parsley and oregano.

2. **UNFOLD** pastry on lightly floured surface. Roll into 14×10-inch rectangle. Cut in half lengthwise. Brush both halves with egg mixture. Top 1 rectangle with cheese mixture. Place remaining rectangle over cheese-topped rectangle, egg-side down. Roll gently with rolling pin to seal.

3. **CUT** crosswise into 28 (1/2-inch) strips. Twist strips and place 2 inches apart on greased baking sheet, pressing down ends. Brush with egg mixture.

4. **BAKE** 10 minutes or until golden. Serve warm or at room temperature. *Makes 28 appetizers*

Tip: To make ahead, twist strips. Place on baking sheet and brush with egg mixture. Freeze. When frozen, store in plastic bag for up to 1 month. To bake, preheat oven to 400°F. Place frozen strips on greased baking sheet. Bake 15 minutes or until golden.

Tomato and Bacon Quesadillas

(pictured on page 6)

**8 flour tortillas (8-inch soft taco size)
2 cups shredded Mexican cheese blend
1 can (14.5 ounces) HUNT'S® Petite Diced
    Tomatoes, drained
8 strips bacon, cooked, crumbled
1/2 cup loosely packed chopped fresh basil
    WESSON® Vegetable Oil
    Sour cream (optional)**

LAYER over half of each tortilla: 1/4 cup cheese, 2 tablespoons tomatoes, 1 tablespoon bacon and 1 tablespoon basil. Fold each tortilla over to form a half-circle.

COAT a large nonstick skillet or griddle lightly with oil. Cook each quesadilla, over medium-low heat, about 1-1/2 minutes on each side until cheese is melted and the tortilla is lightly browned.

CUT each quesadilla into 4 wedges. Serve with sour cream, if desired. *Makes 8 servings*

Cheese Straws

**1/2 cup (1 stick) butter, softened
1/8 teaspoon salt
    Dash ground red pepper
1 pound sharp Cheddar cheese, shredded,
    at room temperature
2 cups self-rising flour**

1. Heat oven to 350°F. In mixer bowl, beat butter, salt and pepper until creamy. Add cheese; mix well. Gradually add flour, mixing until dough begins to form a ball. Form dough into ball with hands. Fit cookie press with small star plate; fill with dough according to manufacturer's directions. Press dough onto cookie sheets in 3-inch-long strips (or desired shapes).

2. Bake 12 minutes or just until lightly browned. Cool completely on wire rack. Store tightly covered. *Makes about 10 dozen*

Favorite recipe from **Southeast United Dairy Industry Association, Inc.**

Hot French Onion Dip

Salads

Field Green Salad with Balsamic Vinaigrette

(Pictured at left)

6 cups field greens (spring mix)
1 cup thinly sliced mushrooms
1/2 medium cucumber, thinly sliced
1/2 sweet onion, thinly sliced
   Balsamic Vinaigrette (recipe follows)
   Freshly grated Parmesan cheese to taste

Toss greens with mushrooms, cucumber and onion in large serving bowl. Dress with Balsamic Vinaigrette as desired. Divide salad among 4 salad plates; garnish with Parmesan cheese. Serve immediately. Refrigerate any remaining dressing. *Makes 4 servings*

Balsamic Vinaigrette

1/4 cup balsamic vinegar
1 tablespoon Dijon mustard
1/4 teaspoon sugar
1/4 teaspoon salt
1/8 teaspoon pepper
3/4 cup CRISCO® Canola Oil*

*Or use your favorite Crisco Oil.

Combine all ingredients except oil in small plastic container with tight-fitting lid; shake well. Pour in oil and shake until well blended. *Makes 4 servings*

Helpful Hint

Balsamic vinegar is an Italian aged vinegar with a distinctive mellow flavor. Its dark brown color is derived from the wood barrels in which it is aged.

Clockwise from top left: *Best 'Cue Coleslaw (p. 28), German Potato Salad with Grilled Sausage (p. 36), Field Green Salad with Balsamic Vinaigrette and Spicy Peanut Noodle Salad (p. 40)*

Southwestern Chicken Taco Salad

(Pictured at right)

Aluminum foil
Nonstick cooking spray
6 (8-inch) plain or flavored flour tortillas
2 (10-ounce) cans HORMEL® chunk breast of
    chicken, drained and flaked
2 tablespoons water
1 tablespoon taco seasoning mix
1 (15-ounce) can red kidney beans, drained and
    rinsed
1 (11-ounce) can whole kernel Mexican corn,
    drained
6 cups shredded lettuce, divided
1 cup shredded cheddar cheese
1 tomato, diced
1 avocado, diced
1 cup salsa, drained
1/2 cup sour cream

Preheat oven to 350°F. Make six 2-1/2-inch balls of foil by slightly crushing six 12×12-inch pieces of foil. Lightly spray one side of each flour tortilla and inside of 6 (10-ounce) custard or small baking dishes with nonstick cooking spray. Gently press tortillas, sprayed sides up, into custard cups; folding edges to fit as necessary. Place ball of foil in center of each cup. Place cups on baking sheet. Bake tortilla shells 10 minutes; remove from oven and remove foil balls. Return to oven and continue baking an additional 3 to 5 minutes or until shells are crisp and edges are lightly browned. Meanwhile, combine chunk chicken, water and taco seasoning mix in skillet. Simmer over low heat 3 to 5 minutes. Add beans and corn. Heat until warmed through. Place 1 cup shredded lettuce into each tortilla shell. Fill with meat mixture. Top with cheese, tomato and avocado. In small bowl, combine salsa and sour cream. Drizzle dressing over salad and serve.

Makes 6 servings

Easy Pineapple Slaw

1 can (15-1/4 ounces) DEL MONTE® Pineapple
    Tidbits In Its Own Juice
1/3 cup mayonnaise
2 tablespoons vinegar
6 cups coleslaw mix or shredded cabbage

1. Drain pineapple, reserving 3 tablespoons juice.

2. Combine reserved juice, mayonnaise and vinegar; toss with pineapple and coleslaw mix. Season with salt and pepper to taste, if desired.

Makes 4 to 6 servings

Warm Ginger Almond Chicken Salad

DRESSING
1/3 cup GRANDMA'S® Molasses
1/4 cup oil
1/4 cup cider vinegar
1 teaspoon finely chopped ginger root *or*
    1/2 teaspoon ground ginger
1 teaspoon soy sauce
1/2 teaspoon salt
    Dash hot pepper sauce

SALAD
1 pound boneless, skinless chicken breasts,
    cut into thin strips
4 cups torn mixed greens
1 cup (2 medium) shredded carrots
1/4 cup chopped green onions
1 tablespoon cornstarch
2 tablespoons water
1/4 cup sliced almonds, toasted

1. In medium bowl, combine all dressing ingredients. Add chicken strips; blend well. Cover; refrigerate 1 to 2 hours. In serving bowl, combine greens, carrots and green onions. Refrigerate.

2. In large skillet, combine chicken and dressing. Bring to a boil, cooking and stirring until chicken is no longer pink in center, about 3 to 5 minutes. In small bowl, combine cornstarch and water; blend well. Stir into chicken mixture. Cook until mixture thickens, stirring constantly. Spoon hot chicken mixture over vegetables; toss to combine. Sprinkle with almonds. Serve immediately.

Makes 4 servings

Southwestern Chicken Taco Salad

Spinach & Grapefruit Salad

  1 bag (10 ounces) spinach, washed, stemmed and torn
  2 cups sliced mushrooms
1/2 red onion, sliced into thin wedges
  6 slices uncooked bacon, cut into thin strips
1/2 cup water
  2 teaspoons cornstarch
1/2 cup cider vinegar
  3 tablespoons sugar
  3 tablespoons *French's®* Bold n' Spicy Brown Mustard
  1 teaspoon *French's®* Worcestershire Sauce
  2 pink grapefruits, peeled and cut into sections

1. Place spinach in large salad bowl. Add mushrooms and onion; set aside. Cook bacon in large nonstick skillet over medium-high heat until bacon is crisp. Set bacon aside on paper towels. Drain drippings, reserving 2 tablespoons drippings in pan.

2. Combine water and cornstarch in 2-cup measure until blended. Stir in vinegar, sugar, mustard and Worcestershire. Pour into skillet with bacon drippings. Bring to a boil; simmer 2 minutes or until thickened, whisking constantly. Cool slightly. Top salad with bacon and grapefruit. Pour dressing over salad; toss well to coat evenly. Serve immediately. *Makes 6 to 8 servings*

Breakfast Salad

  1 apple, diced (with peel)
  1 banana, sliced
1/2 cup sunflower kernels
1/2 cup raisins
1/4 cup chopped dates
  2 tablespoons honey
  1 tablespoon orange juice
  1 teaspoon WATKINS® Vanilla
1/2 teaspoon WATKINS® Ground Cinnamon
  1 cup cottage cheese
  4 melon halves

Combine apple, banana, sunflower kernels, raisins, dates, honey, orange juice, vanilla and cinnamon in medium bowl; toss to blend. Spoon cottage cheese evenly into melon halves; top with fruit mixture.
Makes 4 servings

Easy Tossed Niçoise with Garlic and Cheese Dressing

(Pictured at right)

1-1/2 pounds steamed red potatoes, cut into small chunks
  1 package (10 ounces) frozen Italian green beans, thawed and drained
3/4 cup Niçoise or pitted ripe olives, sliced
1/2 red onion, slivered
1/2 red bell pepper, slivered
1/2 green bell pepper, slivered
1/4 cup coarsely chopped green onions, including tops
1-1/2 cups Garlic and Cheese Dressing (recipe follows)
  1 (7-ounce) pouch of STARKIST Flavor Fresh Pouch® Albacore Tuna
1/2 cup minced fresh parsley
    Whole romaine leaves, washed and dried
    Freshly ground black pepper (optional)
    Grated Parmesan cheese (optional)

In large bowl, combine potatoes, beans, olives, red onion, bell peppers and green onions; toss with Garlic and Cheese Dressing. Refrigerate. Just before serving, add tuna and parsley. Line plates with lettuce; spoon salad onto leaves. Serve with black pepper and cheese, if desired.
Makes 6 to 8 servings

Garlic and Cheese Dressing

1/4 cup wine vinegar
  2 tablespoons lemon juice
  1 to 2 cloves garlic, minced or pressed
  1 tablespoon Dijon-style mustard
    Salt and pepper to taste
  1 cup olive oil
1/2 cup grated Parmesan cheese

In small bowl, whisk together vinegar, lemon juice, garlic, mustard, salt and pepper. Slowly add olive oil, whisking until all oil is added and dressing is thickened. Stir in cheese.

Easy Tossed Niçoise with Garlic and Cheese Dressing

Panzanella

(Pictured below)

1 package KNORR® Recipe Classics™ Tomato
    with Basil Soup, Dip and Recipe Mix
1/2 cup BERTOLLI® CLASSICO™ Olive Oil
1/2 cup red wine vinegar
1 package (16 ounces) frozen tortellini, cooked
    and drained (reserve 1/4 cup pasta water)
3 cups day-old or toasted bread cubes
1 cup sliced pepperoni (4 ounces)
4 ounces provolone cheese, cut into 1/2-inch
    cubes (about 1 cup)
1/3 cup pitted Kalamata olives, sliced
1/4 cup thinly sliced red onion

In large bowl, combine recipe mix, olive oil, vinegar
and pasta water.

Add remaining ingredients; toss to coat. Chill
2 hours.   *Makes 6 servings*

Note: Panzanella is an Italian salad traditionally
made with chunks of bread, tomatoes, onion,
olive oil, vinegar and seasonings.

Panzanella

Best 'Cue Coleslaw

(Pictured on page 22)

1/3 cup dill pickle relish
1/3 cup vegetable oil
3 tablespoons lime juice
2 tablespoons honey
1 teaspoon salt
1 teaspoon ground cumin
1 teaspoon cayenne pepper
1 teaspoon black pepper
1 small head green cabbage, rinsed and very
    thinly sliced
2 large carrots, shredded
1 bunch green onions, sliced
5 radishes, sliced

1. Combine relish, oil, lime juice, honey, salt, cumin,
cayenne pepper and black pepper in large bowl.

2. Add cabbage, carrots, green onions and radishes;
stir until well combined. Chill at least 1 hour before
serving.   *Makes 6 to 8 servings*

Tip: For an even sweeter taste, add slivered apples
instead of the dill pickle relish.

Chicken Salad Canton

1 cup fresh Chinese snow peas *or* 1 package
    (6 ounces) frozen snow peas, thawed
1 can (14-1/2 ounces) DEL MONTE® Stewed
    Tomatoes - Original Recipe
3 tablespoons vegetable oil
3 tablespoons cider vinegar
1 tablespoon soy sauce
4 cups shredded cabbage or iceberg lettuce
1 cup cubed cooked chicken
1/3 cup packed cilantro, chopped *or* 1/3 cup
    sliced green onions

1. Dip fresh snow peas in boiling water 30 seconds
(do not dip frozen snow peas); cool.

2. Drain tomatoes, reserving 1/4 cup liquid.
Combine reserved liquid with oil, vinegar
and soy sauce.

3. Toss soy dressing and tomatoes with remaining
ingredients. Season to taste with pepper, if desired.
Garnish with sliced green onions and toasted
sesame seeds, if desired.

Makes 2 main-dish servings
(4 side-dish servings)

Salsa Beef Salad

Salsa Beef Salad

(Pictured above)

1 pound ground beef
1 can (15-1/2 ounces) pinto beans, rinsed and drained
2 jalapeño peppers,* seeded and chopped
2 tablespoons chili powder
1/2 teaspoon ground cumin
 Salt and pepper
1 head iceberg lettuce, shredded
2 medium tomatoes, diced
1/2 cup shredded pepper Jack cheese
1/4 cup chopped fresh cilantro
1/2 cup chopped green onions
 Juice of 1 lime
1 cup salsa
1 package (12 ounces) corn tortilla chips, broken
 Sour cream (optional)

*Jalapeño peppers can sting and irritate the skin; wear rubber gloves when handling peppers and do not touch eyes. Wash hands after handling.

1. Cook and stir ground beef in large skillet over medium-high heat until browned. Drain.

2. Add beans, jalapeños, chili powder, cumin, salt and pepper to skillet. Cook and stir 5 minutes or until heated through. Set aside to cool.

3. Combine lettuce, tomatoes, cheese and cilantro in large bowl. Top with ground beef mixture, green onions and lime juice. Serve with salsa, chips and sour cream, if desired. *Makes 4 to 6 servings*

Helpful Hint

Choose green onions that have firm white bases and crisp, bright green tops. Store them in a plastic bag in the refrigerator (preferably in the vegetable crisper) for up to five days.

Citrus-Berry Chicken Salad

(Pictured at right)

4 boneless skinless chicken breast halves
1/2 cup *French's®* Sweet & Tangy Honey Mustard,
   divided
1/3 cup canola oil
2 tablespoons raspberry vinegar or balsamic
   vinegar
1/4 teaspoon each salt and black pepper
8 cups mixed salad greens, washed and torn
1 cup sliced strawberries or raspberries
1 orange, cut into sections

1. Coat chicken with *1/4 cup* mustard. Broil or grill 10 to 15 minutes or until chicken is no longer pink in center. Cut diagonally into slices.

2. In small bowl, whisk together remaining *1/4 cup* mustard, oil, vinegar and salt and pepper.

3. Arrange salad greens and fruit on serving plates. Top with chicken. Drizzle with dressing just before serving. *Makes 4 servings*

Sesame Pork Salad

3 cups cooked rice
1-1/2 cups slivered cooked pork*
1/4 pound fresh snow peas, trimmed and julienned
1 medium cucumber, peeled, seeded and
   julienned
1 medium red bell pepper, julienned
1/2 cup sliced green onions
2 tablespoons sesame seeds, toasted (optional)
1/4 cup chicken broth
3 tablespoons rice or white wine vinegar
3 tablespoons soy sauce
1 tablespoon peanut oil
1 teaspoon sesame oil

Substitute 1-1/2 cups slivered cooked chicken for pork, if desired.

Combine rice, pork, snow peas, cucumber, bell pepper, onions and sesame seeds in large bowl. Combine broth, vinegar, soy sauce and oils in small jar with lid; shake well. Pour over rice mixture; toss lightly. Serve at room temperature or slightly chilled. *Makes 6 servings*

Favorite recipe from **USA Rice**

Seafood Salad

4 tablespoons olive oil, divided
1/2 cup diced onion
2 cloves garlic, minced
8 ounces medium shrimp, peeled, deveined
8 ounces medium scallops
1/4 teaspoon salt
1/4 teaspoon ground black pepper
1 cup Italian bread cubes
1 can (14.5 ounces) CONTADINA® Recipe Ready
   Diced Tomatoes, drained
2 cups torn salad greens
1 cup yellow bell pepper strips
2 tablespoons chopped fresh Italian parsley
1 tablespoon white wine vinegar

1. Heat 1 tablespoon oil in medium skillet. Add onion and garlic; sauté for 1 minute.

2. Add shrimp, scallops, salt and black pepper; sauté for 3 minutes. Remove from heat.

3. Heat 1 tablespoon oil in small skillet. Add bread cubes; sauté until golden brown.

4. Toss seafood mixture, tomatoes, greens, bell pepper, parsley, remaining oil and vinegar in large bowl. Top with bread cubes. *Makes 6 servings*

Ranch Tuna Stuffed Tomatoes

1 can (6 ounces) solid white tuna, drained
1 can (8 ounces) kidney beans, rinsed and drained
1 can (8 ounces) corn, drained
1 cup (4 ounces) shredded mild Cheddar cheese
2/3 cup HIDDEN VALLEY® The Original Ranch®
   Dressing
1/4 cup chopped green onions
4 large fresh tomatoes (at least 8 ounces each)

Flake tuna and combine with beans, corn, cheese, dressing and onions in a medium bowl. Cover and chill 1 hour. Just before serving, core each tomato and carefully scoop out center to within 1/4 inch of edge forming a bowl; discard flesh and seeds. Drain tomatoes upside down on paper towels. Cut each tomato into 5 or 6 wedges, leaving the bottom intact. Gently open each tomato to support the salad. Arrange tuna mixture on top of the tomatoes. *Makes 4 servings*

Caesar Salad in Crouton Cups

(Pictured at right)

    CRISCO® No-Stick Butter Flavor Spray
12 slices white bread
  1 teaspoon garlic salt
  1 teaspoon dried thyme
  1 teaspoon dried rosemary, crushed
1/2 teaspoon cracked pepper
  4 cups romaine lettuce, finely sliced into
      1/8-inch strips
  2 green onions, thinly sliced, plus additional
      for garnish
      Purchased Caesar dressing, to taste
      Shredded Parmesan cheese

Preheat oven to 350°F.

Spray 12-muffin pan with cooking spray. Trim crusts off bread; spray both sides of bread with cooking spray.

Mix together garlic salt, thyme, rosemary and cracked pepper in small bowl. Lightly sprinkle mixture over both sides of bread.

Use rolling pin to slightly flatten and press spice mixture into bread. Press each slice into muffin cup, allowing edges to hang over cup.

Bake for 12 to 15 minutes or until golden brown and crisp. Remove from oven and cool. Toss lettuce and green onions with dressing. Spoon salad into crouton cups. Garnish with shredded Parmesan and green onion slices. Serve immediately.

Makes 12 appetizer servings

Lamb Salad with Tomatoes and Feta

3/4 pound boneless lamb chops (1 inch thick)
  3 tablespoons olive oil
  1 can (14-1/2 ounces) DEL MONTE® Diced
      Tomatoes with Garlic & Onion
  3 tablespoons red wine vinegar
  2 to 3 tablespoons minced fresh mint *or*
      1/2 teaspoon dried mint
1/2 medium red onion, thinly sliced
      Shredded lettuce
1/2 cup crumbled feta cheese

1. Season meat with salt and pepper, if desired.

2. Heat 1 tablespoon oil over medium-high heat in large skillet. Add meat; cook about 4 minutes on each side or until desired doneness. Cut meat crosswise into thin slices.

3. Drain tomatoes, reserving 1/3 cup liquid. Combine reserved liquid with vinegar, mint and remaining 2 tablespoons oil.

4. Toss meat slices, tomatoes and onion with dressing. Arrange over lettuce; top with cheese. Garnish, if desired. *Makes 4 servings*

Variation: Grill lamb over hot coals instead of pan-frying.

Marinated Grilled Beef and Pepper Salad

  1 bottle (12 ounces) LAWRY'S® Herb & Garlic
      Marinade With Lemon Juice, divided
  1 pound beef loin, sirloin or tri-tip roast
  1 EACH: red, yellow and green bell pepper,
      halved
1-1/2 pounds cooked baby red potatoes, quartered
  1 tablespoon BERTOLLI® Olive Oil
  1 tablespoon balsamic vinegar
  1 teaspoon sugar

In large resealable plastic bag, combine 2/3 cup Herb & Garlic Marinade with beef; seal bag. Marinate in refrigerator for at least 30 minutes. Meanwhile, grill peppers and potatoes, brushing often with 1/4 cup Marinade. When potatoes are lightly charred, remove from grill. When peppers are tender and charred, remove from grill and slice into 1/2-inch strips. In small bowl, thoroughly whisk together 1/3 cup Marinade with oil, vinegar and sugar; set aside. Remove beef from bag, discarding used marinade. Grill beef to desired doneness. Cool slightly and slice into thin strips. In large salad bowl, combine beef, vegetables and dressing; toss to mix and coat. Serve slightly warm or chill before serving. *Makes 4 main dish salads*

Hint: For a timesaver, potatoes may be pierced and microwaved to cook before finishing on the grill.

Caesar Salad in Crouton Cups

Pasta Salad with Pesto

(Pictured at right)

1 package BOB EVANS® Italian Grillin' Sausage
   (approximately 5 links)
1 pound uncooked penne pasta
1 tablespoon butter or margarine
2 cloves garlic, peeled
2 cups fresh basil leaves
1/2 cup fresh parsley leaves
2 tablespoons pine nuts
1/2 cup olive oil
1/4 cup freshly grated Parmesan cheese
1/4 teaspoon black pepper
2 cups seeded and diced Roma tomatoes
1 small green bell pepper, chopped
1 cup whole ripe olives
1 cup (4 ounces) cubed mozzarella cheese
   Red leaf lettuce for garnish (optional)

Cook sausage in large skillet or on grill until browned; let cool. Cut in half lengthwise; cut each half into 1/4-inch slices and set aside. Cook penne according to package directions; drain. Toss in large bowl with butter to prevent sticking.

To prepare pesto sauce, place garlic cloves in food processor with metal blade or in blender; process until smooth. Add basil and parsley; process until finely chopped. Add pine nuts; process until finely chopped. With motor running, slowly add olive oil in fine, steady stream. Add Parmesan cheese and black pepper; process until well blended, scraping down side as needed.

To assemble salad, toss sausage, tomatoes, bell pepper, olives and mozzarella cheese with penne. Gradually stir in pesto until salad is moist but not saturated. Serve salad on lettuce-lined platter, if desired. Refrigerate leftovers. *Makes 8 servings*

Beet and Pear Salad

1 can (15-1/4 ounces) DEL MONTE® Bartlett
   Pear Halves
1 can (14-1/2 ounces) DEL MONTE® Sliced
   Beets, drained
1/2 cup thinly sliced red onion, separated into
   rings
2 tablespoons vegetable oil
1 tablespoon white wine vinegar
1/3 cup crumbled blue cheese
   Lettuce leaves, optional

1. Drain pears, reserving 1 tablespoon syrup.

2. Cut pears in half lengthwise.

3. Place pears, beets and onion in medium bowl.

4. Whisk together oil, vinegar and reserved syrup. Pour over salad; toss gently.

5. Just before serving, add cheese and toss. Serve on bed of lettuce leaves, if desired.
Makes 4 to 6 servings

Walnut Sweet Potato Salad

2 pounds sweet potatoes or yams, boiled just
   until tender and drained
1/3 cup vegetable oil
2 tablespoons cider vinegar
1 tablespoon soy sauce
1 teaspoon finely grated fresh ginger
1 small clove garlic, minced
1 large red apple, cored and sliced
1/2 cup sliced green onions
2/3 cup toasted California walnut pieces
   Black pepper to taste
   Butter lettuce

Cool potatoes completely; set aside. Meanwhile, whisk together oil, vinegar, soy sauce, ginger and garlic in large bowl. Add apple and onions; toss. Peel and cut sweet potatoes into 1/4-inch-thick slices; add with walnuts to apple mixture. Toss gently. Season with pepper. Arrange lettuce on serving platter. Spoon potato mixture onto lettuce. Garnish with additional apple slices, if desired. Serve at room temperature. *Makes 6 servings*

Favorite recipe from **Walnut Marketing Board**

Helpful Hint

For fresh grated ginger, first peel away the rough outer skin, then grate the flesh on a ginger grater (sold in many Asian markets) or another fine grater.

Pasta Salad with Pesto

Provençal Bean & Tomato Salad

1/4 cup chopped fresh basil
  3 tablespoons *Frank's® RedHot®* Original
    Cayenne Pepper Sauce
  2 tablespoons olive oil
  1 tablespoon lemon juice
1/4 teaspoon salt
  2 cans (15 ounces each) small white kidney
    beans, drained and rinsed
  1 red onion, finely chopped
  1 cup cherry tomatoes, quartered

1. Whisk basil, **Frank's RedHot** Sauce, oil, lemon juice and salt in large bowl. Stir in beans, onion and tomatoes; toss to coat evenly.

2. Cover; refrigerate 1 hour. Toss just before serving.

Makes 8 servings (about 4 cups)

German Potato Salad with Grilled Sausage

(Pictured on page 22)

2/3 cup prepared vinaigrette salad dressing
1/4 cup *French's®* Bold n' Spicy Brown Mustard
    or *French's®* Honey Dijon Mustard
  1 tablespoon sugar
1-1/2 pounds red or other boiling potatoes,
    cut into 3/4-inch cubes
  1 teaspoon salt
  1 cup chopped green bell pepper
  1 cup chopped celery
1/2 cup chopped onion
1/2 pound kielbasa or smoked sausage, split
    lengthwise

1. Combine salad dressing, mustard and sugar in large bowl; set aside.

2. Place potatoes in large saucepan. Add salt and enough water to cover potatoes. Heat to boiling. Cook 10 to 15 minutes until potatoes are tender. Drain and transfer to bowl. Add bell pepper, celery and onion. Set aside.

3. Grill sausage over medium-high heat until lightly browned and heated through. Cut into small cubes. Add to bowl with potatoes. Toss well to coat evenly. Serve warm. *Makes 6 to 8 servings*

Chicken, Tomato and Avocado Pasta Salad

Chicken, Tomato and Avocado Pasta Salad

(Pictured above)

  2 cans (14.5 ounces each) HUNT'S® Diced
    Tomatoes with Balsamic Vinegar,
    Basil & Olive Oil, undrained
  4 cups shredded cooked chicken
  2 medium avocados, pitted, diced
  4 green onions, sliced
  1 box (16 ounces) uncooked farfalle pasta,
    cooked according to package directions,
    drained, kept warm
1/4 cup finely chopped walnuts (optional)

COMBINE tomatoes, chicken, avocados, and onions in a medium saucepan; simmer 10 minutes.

TOSS tomato mixture with warm pasta in a large serving dish.

SPRINKLE with walnuts, if desired.

Makes 6 to 8 servings

Salmon Salad with Basil Vinaigrette

(Pictured below)

1 pound asparagus
1-1/4 teaspoons salt, divided
1 pound salmon fillets
1-1/2 teaspoons olive oil
1/4 teaspoon pepper
Basil Vinaigrette (recipe follows)
4 lemon wedges

1. Prepare Basil Vinaigrette. Preheat oven to 400°F or preheat grill to medium-hot. Snap tough ends off asparagus. Place in pot with 1 teaspoon salt and water to cover. Bring to boil over medium-high heat. Boil 10 minutes or until asparagus is fork-tender. Plunge into bowl of cold water to stop cooking; drain and set aside on serving plate.

2. Brush salmon with olive oil. Season with remaining 1/4 teaspoon salt and pepper. If roasting, place fish in shallow pan and cook 11 to 13 minutes or until fork inserted near center of fillet shows fish is cooked all the way through. If grilling, grill on well-oiled grid over medium-high heat 8 to 10 minutes (4 or 5 minutes per side) or until cooked through.

3. Remove cooked salmon from heat and peel skin. Break salmon up into bite-size pieces and sprinkle over asparagus. Spoon Basil Vinaigrette over salmon. Serve with lemon wedges.   *Makes 4 serving*

Basil Vinaigrette

(Pictured on front cover)

3 tablespoons extra-virgin olive oil
1 tablespoon white wine vinegar
1 tablespoon minced fresh basil
1 small garlic clove, minced
1 teaspoon minced chives
1/4 teaspoon pepper
1/8 teaspoon salt

Combine all ingredients in small bowl and mix well.
Makes 4 servings

Tip: Basil Vinaigrette is a versatile dressing; it can be used on vegetable, potato and mixed green salads.

Salmon Salad with Basil Vinaigrette

Near East Steak Salad

(Pictured at right)

2/3 cup *French's*® Honey Dijon Mustard
1/2 cup water
1/4 cup teriyaki sauce
 2 tablespoons grated peeled ginger
 1 teaspoon minced garlic
 1 pound boneless sirloin or flank steak
 (1 inch thick)
 8 cups mixed salad greens, washed and torn
 1 medium yellow or orange bell pepper, thinly
 sliced
 2 green onions, thinly shredded
1/4 cup chopped dry roasted peanuts

1. Combine mustard, water, teriyaki sauce, ginger and garlic in small bowl. Pour 1 cup dressing into small serving bowl.

2. Broil or grill steak 10 minutes or until desired doneness, basting with remaining 1/2 cup dressing. Let stand 5 minutes.

3. Thinly slice steak. Serve over salad greens. Top with bell pepper, green onions and peanuts. Drizzle with reserved dressing.   *Makes 4 servings*

Artichoke and Olive Salad

 1 pound dry rotini pasta
 2 cans (14.5 ounces each) CONTADINA® Recipe
 Ready Diced Tomatoes with Roasted Garlic,
 undrained
 1 jar (6 ounces) artichoke hearts, packed in
 water, drained, sliced
1/2 cup Italian dressing
 1 can (2.25 ounces) sliced pitted ripe olives,
 drained
1/4 cup chopped fresh parsley *or* 2 teaspoons
 dried parsley flakes, crushed
1/4 cup sliced green onions
1/2 cup sliced almonds, toasted

1. Cook pasta according to package directions; drain and rinse in cold water.

2. Combine pasta, undrained tomatoes, artichoke hearts, dressing, olives, parsley and green onions in large bowl; toss well.

3. Cover. Chill before serving. Sprinkle with almonds just before serving.   *Makes 10 servings*

Chopped Mesquite Chicken Salad

 2 (6-ounce) boneless, skinless chicken breasts
 2 tablespoons olive oil, divided
 3 tablespoons MRS. DASH® MESQUITE
 GRILLING BLENDS™
 1 head red cabbage
 1 cup frozen corn kernels, thawed
 1 cup black beans, rinsed and drained
 1 avocado, diced into 1/4-inch cubes
1/2 cup diced red onion
1/2 cup lightly packed chopped cilantro leaves,
 stems discarded
 2 tablespoons freshly squeezed lime juice

Brush chicken breasts with 1 tablespoon olive oil, then sprinkle both sides with Mrs. Dash® Mesquite Grilling Blends™.

Grill or broil chicken about 5 minutes per side or until no longer pink in center. Let cool, then cut into 1/4-inch cubes.

Cut core out of cabbage using paring knife. Carefully peel off whole outer leaves and set aside 6 to use as serving bowls. Thinly slice 1-1/2 cups inner part of cabbage; transfer to large bowl.

Add chicken, corn, beans, avocado, onion, cilantro, lime juice and remaining 1 tablespoon oil to sliced cabbage. Toss thoroughly and serve in red cabbage bowls.   *Makes 6 servings*

Pineapple Lime Mold

 1 can (20 ounces) DOLE® Pineapple Chunks
 2 packages (3 ounces each) lime gelatin
 2 cups boiling water
 1 cup sour cream
1/2 cup chopped walnuts
1/2 cup chopped DOLE® Celery

Drain pineapple chunks; reserve syrup. Dissolve gelatin in boiling water. Add sour cream and reserved syrup. Chill until slightly thickened. Stir in pineapple chunks, walnuts and celery. Pour into 7-cup mold. Chill until set.   *Makes 8 servings*

Italian Antipasto Salad

(Pictured at right)

1 box (9 ounces) BIRDS EYE® frozen Deluxe
    Artichoke Heart Halves
1 box (9 ounces) BIRDS EYE® frozen Deluxe
    Whole Green Beans
12 lettuce leaves
1 pound salami, cut into 3/4-inch cubes
3/4 pound provolone cheese, cut into 3/4-inch
    cubes
1 jar (7 ounces) roasted red peppers*
1/3 cup Italian salad dressing

Or, substitute pimientos, drained and cut into thin strips.

In large saucepan, cook artichokes and green
beans according to package directions; drain.
Rinse under cold water to cool; drain again.

Place lettuce on serving platter. Arrange cooked
vegetables, salami, cheese and peppers in separate
piles.

Drizzle with dressing just before serving.

Makes 6 servings

Serving Suggestion: Add pitted ripe olives and
jarred pepperoncini, if desired.

Spicy Peanut Noodle Salad

(Pictured on page 22)

1/3 cup *French's*® Honey Dijon Mustard
1/3 cup chicken broth
1/3 cup peanut butter
2 tablespoons teriyaki sauce
2 tablespoons *Frank's*® *RedHot*® Cayenne Pepper
    Sauce, or more to taste
2 cups thinly sliced vegetables, such as green
    onion, snow peas, cucumber or bell peppers
4 ounces thin spaghetti, cooked and drained
    (1-1/2 cups cooked)

1. Combine mustard, chicken broth, peanut butter,
teriyaki sauce and *Frank's*® *RedHot*® Sauce in large
bowl; whisk until blended.

2. Add remaining ingredients; toss to coat. Serve
immediately. If desired, serve on salad greens.

Makes 4 servings

Tip: To serve as a main dish, add 2 cups diced
cooked turkey.

Grilled Potato Salad

1 envelope LIPTON® RECIPE SECRETS®
    Onion Soup Mix*
1/3 cup BERTOLLI® Olive Oil
2 tablespoons red wine vinegar
1 clove garlic, finely chopped
2 pounds small red or all-purpose potatoes,
    cut into 1-inch cubes
1 tablespoon fresh basil, chopped *or* 1 teaspoon
    dried basil leaves, crushed
Freshly ground black pepper

*Also terrific with LIPTON® RECIPE SECRETS® Onion Mushroom or
Golden Onion Soup Mix.*

1. In large bowl, blend soup mix, oil, vinegar and
garlic; stir in potatoes.

2. Grease 30×18-inch sheet of heavy-duty aluminum
foil; top with potato mixture. Wrap foil loosely
around mixture, sealing edges airtight with double
fold. Place on another 30×18-inch sheet of foil; seal
edges airtight with double fold in opposite
direction.

3. Grill, shaking package occasionally and turning
package once, 40 minutes or until potatoes are
tender. Spoon into serving bowl and toss with
basil and pepper. Serve slightly warm or at room
temperature. *Makes 4 servings*

Oven Method: Preheat oven to 450°F. Prepare foil
packet as above. Place in large baking pan on
bottom rack and bake, turning packet once,
40 minutes or until potatoes are tender. Toss
and serve as above.

Honey-Herb Salad Dressing

1/4 cup white wine vinegar
1/4 cup honey
2 tablespoons chopped fresh basil or mint
1 tablespoon minced green onion
Salt and pepper to taste

Combine all ingredients in small bowl; mix well.

Makes 1/2 cup

Favorite recipe from **National Honey Board**

Italian Antipasto Salad

Balsamic Chicken Salad

(Pictured at right)

1/3 cup olive oil
1/4 cup *French's*® Sweet & Tangy Honey Mustard
2 tablespoons balsamic or red wine vinegar
2 tablespoons water
1 teaspoon minced shallots or onion
1/8 teaspoon salt
8 cups mixed salad greens, washed and torn
1 package (10 ounces) fully cooked carved chicken breasts
1 package (4 ounces) goat or Feta cheese, crumbled
1 cup croutons

1. Whisk together oil, mustard, vinegar, shallots, water and salt.

2. Arrange salad greens, chicken, cheese and croutons on serving plates. Serve with dressing.

Makes 4 servings

Mediterranean Orzo Salad

SALAD

1 cup orzo pasta
1 cup diced red bell pepper
1/2 cup crumbled feta cheese
1 can (2-1/4 ounces) sliced ripe olives, rinsed and drained
1/4 cup chopped fresh basil *or* 1/2 teaspoon dried basil
Fresh basil leaves or parsley sprigs, for garnish (optional)

DRESSING

1 packet (1 ounce) HIDDEN VALLEY® The Original Ranch® Salad Dressing & Seasoning Mix
3 tablespoons olive oil
3 tablespoons red wine vinegar
1 teaspoon sugar

Cook orzo according to package directions, omitting salt. Rinse with cold water and drain well. Mix orzo, bell pepper, cheese, olives and chopped fresh basil in a large bowl. (If using dried basil, add to dressing.) Whisk together salad dressing & seasoning mix, oil, vinegar and sugar. Stir dressing into orzo mixture. Cover and refrigerate at least 2 hours. Garnish with basil leaves before serving, if desired.

Makes 4 to 6 servings

Brown Rice Salad

2-1/2 cups water
1 cup uncooked brown rice
3/4 cup SMUCKER'S® Grape Jelly
1/2 cup fresh lemon juice
1/4 cup olive oil
2 tablespoons dried mint leaves
1/2 teaspoon salt
1 cup chopped fresh parsley
2 cucumbers, peeled, halved, seeded and diced
1 cup chopped red radishes
1/2 cup chopped green onions

In medium saucepan, bring water to a boil. Add rice. Cover and cook over low heat for about 45 minutes or until water is absorbed and rice is tender. Cool.

In blender container, combine jelly, lemon juice, oil, mint and salt; cover and blend until smooth.

In straight-sided 1-1/2-quart glass bowl or soufflé dish, layer rice, parsley and half of cucumbers. Pour half of dressing over layers. Add radishes, remaining cucumbers, green onions and remaining dressing. Refrigerate several hours or overnight. Toss before serving.

Makes 6 to 8 servings

Note: To make a bulgur salad, omit the rice (and water). Cook 1 cup of bulgur in 2 cups of boiling water until tender, about 15 minutes. Continue as directed above.

Piquant Pasta Toss

3 cups cooked tri-color rotini pasta, drained
2 cups broccoli florets
1 cup grated Parmesan cheese
1 bottle (8 ounces) Italian salad dressing
1 package (6 ounces) HILLSHIRE FARM® Hard Salami, cubed
1/2 cup chopped red bell pepper
1/2 cup black olives
1/3 cup sliced red onion

Combine all ingredients in large bowl until well blended. Refrigerate before serving.

Makes 4 to 6 servings

Balsamic Chicken Salad

Side Dishes

Baked Sweet Potato Fries with Spicy Apricot Dipping Sauce

(Pictured at left)

3 sweet potatoes (12 to 14 ounces each), peeled,
  cut into narrow wedges
2 tablespoons vegetable oil
1-1/2 teaspoons kosher salt
1/4 teaspoon pepper
  Spicy Apricot Dipping Sauce (recipe follows)

Heat oven to 450°F. Gently toss potatoes, oil, salt and pepper in large bowl until potatoes are evenly coated. Divide potatoes between two large baking sheets or jelly-roll pans. Bake 30 minutes or until lightly browned. Serve hot with sauce. *Makes 6 servings*

Spicy Apricot Dipping Sauce

1 cup apricot jam
1/4 cup orange juice
1 tablespoon prepared mustard
1/4 teaspoon ground red pepper

Melt jam in small saucepan over medium-high heat. Whisk in orange juice, mustard and red pepper. Purée sauce in food processor. *Makes 6 servings*

Tip: The sauce can be also served with chicken, either as a dipping sauce or brushed over cooked chicken and browned briefly under the broiler for a tasty glaze. Or, try the sauce with pork—brush it on grilled pork chops or pork tenderloin towards the end of the cooking time.

Clockwise from top left: *Couscous Provençal (p. 52), Baked Sweet Potato Fries with Spicy Apricot Dipping Sauce, Golden Mushroom Risotto (p. 50) and Sesame Snow Peas (p. 60)*

Ratatouille Rice

(Pictured at right)

2 bags SUCCESS® Brown Rice
1 tablespoon olive oil
1 medium onion, chopped
2 cloves garlic, minced
1 small eggplant (about 1/2 pound), unpeeled,
   cut into 1/2-inch cubes
1/4 pound fresh mushrooms, sliced
1 large green pepper, chopped
1 can (15 ounces) tomato sauce
1/2 cup chicken broth
1-1/4 teaspoons dried thyme leaves, crushed

Prepare rice as directed on package.

Heat oil in medium skillet over medium heat. Add
onion and garlic; cook and stir until tender. Add
vegetables; cook, stirring constantly, until liquid
is evaporated, about 5 minutes. Stir in tomato
sauce, broth and thyme. Reduce heat to low;
simmer 10 minutes. Add rice; heat thoroughly,
stirring occasionally.   *Makes 8 servings*

Hot and Spicy Cabbage Medley

1 teaspoon CRISCO® Oil*
2 ounces smoked ham, chopped
1/2 cup chopped green bell pepper
1/2 cup chopped onion
1 can (10 ounces) tomatoes with green chilies,
   undrained and chopped
1/2 teaspoon sugar
4 cups sliced cabbage
1/8 teaspoon black pepper
1/8 teaspoon hot pepper sauce

Use your favorite Crisco Oil.

1. Heat oil in large skillet over medium heat. Add
ham, green pepper and onion. Cook and stir until
vegetables are crisp-tender. Add tomatoes and
sugar. Simmer 3 minutes.

2. Add cabbage, black pepper and hot pepper sauce.
Simmer 15 minutes, stirring occasionally.
                                  Makes 8 servings

Two-Toned Stuffed Potatoes

3 large baking potatoes (12 ounces each)
2 large sweet potatoes (12 ounces each), dark
   flesh preferred
3 slices thick-cut bacon, cut in half widthwise
   on a diagonal
2 cups coarsely chopped onions
2/3 cup buttermilk
1/4 cup (1/2 stick) butter, cut into small pieces
3/4 teaspoon salt, divided

1. Preheat oven to 450°F. Pierce potatoes with fork
in several places. Bake directly on rack 45 minutes
or until fork-tender. Reduce oven to 350°F.

2. Meanwhile, cook bacon in medium skillet over
medium-high heat 6 to 8 minutes or until crisp.
Remove from heat; transfer bacon to paper towels
with slotted spoon.

3. Add onions to bacon fat in skillet; cook about
12 minutes over medium-high heat or until golden
brown. Remove onions from skillet; set aside. Stir
buttermilk into skillet, scraping up any browned bits
from bottom of pan. Add butter, swirling until
melted.

4. Cut baking potatoes in half lengthwise with
serrated knife; carefully scoop out flesh into large
bowl. Reserve skins. Add 3/4 of buttermilk mixture,
1/2 teaspoon salt and 3/4 of cooked onion. Mash
with potato masher until smooth.

5. Cut sweet potatoes in half lengthwise with
serrated knife; scoop out flesh into medium bowl.
Discard skins. Add remaining buttermilk mixture,
1/4 teaspoon salt and remaining cooked onion.
Mash with potato masher until smooth.

6. Fill half of each reserved potato skin horizontally,
vertically or diagonally with baked potato mixture,
using spoon. Fill other half with sweet potato
mixture. Top each stuffed potato half with half
slice of bacon. Transfer stuffed potatoes to baking
sheet; bake 15 minutes or until heated through.
                                  Makes 6 servings

Tip: Stuffed potatoes can be made weeks in advance
and frozen. Reheat frozen potatoes in a 350°F oven
for 75 to 90 minutes. If made ahead and refrigerated
for a few days, reheat in a 350°F oven for 25 minutes.

Carrie's Sweet Potato Casserole

(Pictured below)

Topping (recipe follows)
3 pounds sweet potatoes, cooked and peeled*
1/2 cup (1 stick) butter, softened
1/2 cup sugar
2 eggs, beaten
1/2 cup evaporated milk
1 teaspoon vanilla extract
1 cup chopped pecans

For faster preparation, substitute canned sweet potatoes.

1. Prepare Topping; set aside. Preheat oven to 350°F. Grease eight 6-ounce ovenproof ramekins.

2. Mash sweet potatoes with butter in large bowl. Beat with electric mixer until light and fluffy. One at a time, add sugar, eggs, evaporated milk and vanilla, beating after each addition.

3. Spoon mixture into prepared dishes, filling almost to top. Spoon Topping over potatoes and sprinkle with pecans. Bake 25 minutes or until set.

Makes 8 servings

Topping: Combine 1 cup packed light brown sugar, 1/2 cup all-purpose flour and 1/3 cup melted butter in medium bowl.

Carrie's Sweet Potato Casserole

Hint: This casserole can also be baked in a greased 13×9-inch baking dish. Bake 20 minutes or until set.

Sautéed Snow Peas & Baby Carrots

1 tablespoon I CAN'T BELIEVE IT'S NOT BUTTER!® Spread
2 tablespoons chopped shallots or onion
5 ounces frozen whole baby carrots, partially thawed
4 ounces snow peas (about 1 cup)
2 teaspoons chopped fresh parsley (optional)

In 12-inch nonstick skillet, melt I Can't Believe It's Not Butter!® Spread over medium heat and cook shallots, stirring occasionally, 1 minute or until almost tender. Add carrots and snow peas and cook, stirring occasionally, 4 minutes or until crisp-tender. Stir in parsley, if desired, and heat through.

Makes 2 servings

Note: Recipe can be doubled.

Beefy Barbecued Onions

1 envelope LIPTON® RECIPE SECRETS® Beefy Mushroom Soup Mix*
2 tablespoons firmly packed brown sugar
2 tablespoons vegetable oil
2 tablespoons ketchup
4 large onions (about 2 pounds), thinly sliced
1 extra-heavy-duty foil bag, regular size

Also terrific with LIPTON® RECIPE SECRETS® Savory Herb with Garlic Soup Mix.

1. In large bowl, combine soup mix, brown sugar, oil and ketchup. Add onions; toss to coat. Turn into foil bag. Double-fold open end of bag to seal.

2. Grill over medium heat, turning bag over halfway through cooking, 25 minutes or until onions are tender. Serve on hot dogs, hamburgers, sausage or steak.

Makes 2-1/2 cups onions

Oven Method: Preheat oven to 450°F. Place foil bag on large baking pan on bottom rack of oven and bake, turning bag over halfway through cooking, 45 minutes or until onions are tender.

Cranberry-Pumpkin Spoonbread

Cranberry-Pumpkin Spoonbread

(Pictured above)

    3 cups milk
    1 cup cornmeal
    6 tablespoons butter
    2 tablespoons packed light brown sugar
1-1/4 teaspoons pumpkin pie spice
    1 teaspoon baking powder
  3/4 teaspoon salt
    1 can (15 ounces) solid-pack pumpkin
    4 eggs, separated
    1 cup dried cranberries, coarsely chopped*

You can substitute 1 cup of any dried fruits, such as blueberries, strawberries, chopped apricots, mangos or a combination.

1. Preheat oven to 350°F. Grease 11×7-inch baking pan. Bring milk to a simmer in medium saucepan over medium-high heat. Slowly whisk in cornmeal, stirring until thickened. Remove from heat and stir in butter.

2. Whisk brown sugar, pumpkin pie spice, baking powder and salt to blend. Stir into cornmeal mixture until well blended; cool. Stir in pumpkin, egg yolks and cranberries until well blended.

3. Beat egg whites until stiff peaks form. Fold whites into cornmeal mixture in three stages, adding about 1/3 each time. Spoon into prepared pan. Bake 35 minutes or until puffed and golden. Serve warm. *Makes 8 servings*

Helpful Hint

Stock up on dried cranberries when they're on sale at the supermarket. They add great flavor and color to a wide variety of side dishes, salads and desserts. They will keep up to a year when stored in an airtight container or sealed plastic bag.

Rosemary Roasted Oven Fries

(Pictured at right)

CRISCO® No-Stick Cooking Spray
3 large baking potatoes
1/4 cup CRISCO® Vegetable Oil*
2 teaspoons dried rosemary
1 teaspoon salt
1/8 teaspoon pepper
1/4 cup grated Parmesan cheese
Ranch or blue cheese dressing for dipping
(optional)

Or use your favorite Crisco Oil.

Preheat oven to 450°F. Spray baking sheet with cooking spray; set aside.

Slice potatoes into 1/2-inch wedges; rinse with cold water and pat dry.

Whisk together oil, rosemary, salt and pepper in medium bowl. Add potato wedges; toss to coat. Place potato wedges on prepared baking sheet; bake 45 minutes, turning every 15 minutes. Sprinkle with Parmesan cheese.

Serve immediately with your choice of dressing for dipping. *Makes 4 to 6 servings*

Golden Mushroom Risotto

(Pictured on page 44)

1 package boil-in-bag rice (2 cups cooked)
1 tablespoon vegetable oil
8 ounces mushrooms, wiped clean and sliced
(3 cups)
1 can (10-3/4 ounces) condensed golden
mushroom soup
3/4 cup water
1/2 cup grated Parmesan cheese
1-1/3 cups *French's*® French Fried Onions, divided
2 tablespoons chopped fresh parsley

Cook rice according to package directions. Drain; set aside.

Heat oil in medium saucepan. Add mushrooms; cook and stir until golden brown. Stir in hot rice, soup, water, cheese and *2/3 cup* French Fried Onions. Cook until heated through, stirring often.

Sprinkle with remaining *2/3 cup* onions and parsley before serving. *Makes 6 servings*

White Rice Turkish Style

1 tablespoon FILIPPO BERIO® Olive Oil
1 small onion, sliced
1/2 green bell pepper, seeded and cut into
thin strips
2 cups chicken broth, beef broth or water
1 (2-ounce) jar sliced pimientos, drained
1 cup uncooked long-grain rice
1 (8-1/2-ounce) can small peas, drained
Salt

In 3-quart saucepan, heat olive oil over medium heat until hot. Add onion and green pepper; cook and stir 5 to 7 minutes or until tender. Add chicken broth and pimientos. Reduce heat to low; simmer 5 minutes. Stir in rice. Cover; simmer 15 minutes or until rice is tender and liquid is absorbed. Remove from heat; let stand, covered, 5 to 10 minutes. Stir in peas. Season to taste with salt.

Makes 4 to 6 servings

Spring Spinach Sauté

1 tablespoon butter
1 large sweet onion, halved and thinly sliced
2 cloves garlic, sliced
2 large tomatoes, seeded and chopped
3/4 cup SWANSON® Chicken Broth *or* NATURAL
GOODNESS™ Chicken Broth
1 bag (11 ounces) baby spinach
2 ounces crumbled blue cheese (optional)
2 tablespoons chopped walnuts, toasted
(optional)

MELT butter in large nonstick skillet. Add onion and garlic and cook until tender.

ADD tomatoes, broth and spinach. Cook for 2 minutes or until spinach wilts. Season with salt and pepper.

SPRINKLE with cheese and walnuts if desired.

Makes 6 servings

Stovetop Summer Squash

(Pictured at right)

1-2/3 cups water
   1 package (6 ounces) stuffing mix with herb seasoning packet
   3 tablespoons butter
   1 cup chopped onion
   1 cup chopped red bell pepper
   2 cups sliced yellow squash
   2 cups sliced zucchini
   1 teaspoon minced fresh basil

1. Bring water to a boil in 2-quart saucepan. Add seasoning package from stuffing mix. Cover. Reduce heat to low; simmer 15 minutes.

2. Meanwhile, melt butter in large skillet over medium heat. Add onion and bell pepper; cook and stir 3 minutes or until tender. Add squash and basil; cook and stir about 3 minutes or until vegetables are tender.

3. Transfer squash mixture to saucepan with seasoning blend. Add stuffing croutons; mix until all liquid is absorbed. Remove from heat. Cover; let stand 5 minutes. Fluff with fork before serving.

Makes 6 servings

Couscous Provençal

(Pictured on page 44)

2-1/4 cups water
   1 box (10 ounces) couscous
   2 medium tomatoes, seeded and chopped
1-1/3 cups *French's®* French Fried Onions, divided
   1/4 cup chopped pitted kalamata olives
   1/4 cup chopped fresh mint
   1/4 cup fresh lemon juice
   3 tablespoons olive oil
   1 teaspoon ground cumin
   3/4 teaspoon salt
   1/4 teaspoon ground black pepper

1. Bring water to a boil in medium saucepan. Stir in couscous. Cover and remove from heat. Let stand 5 minutes.

2. Stir in remaining ingredients except *2/3 cup* French Fried Onions. Transfer to serving bowl. Sprinkle remaining onions on top.

Makes 6 servings

Oven Roasted Mushrooms and New Potatoes

1-1/2 pounds new potatoes, scrubbed and cut into 1/2-inch chunks (about 4-1/2 cups)
   2 tablespoons vegetable oil
   1 pound fresh white mushrooms, halved or quartered if large (about 5 cups)
   1 red bell pepper, cut into 1/2-inch chunks
   1 teaspoon minced garlic
   1/2 cup sliced green onions
   1 teaspoon salt
   1/2 teaspoon thyme leaves, crushed
   1/4 teaspoon black pepper

Preheat oven to 450°F. Toss potatoes with vegetable oil in 13×9×2-inch baking pan; bake, uncovered, 10 minutes. Stir in mushrooms, bell pepper and garlic; bake, uncovered, about 15 minutes until potatoes are almost tender. Stir in green onions, salt, thyme and black pepper; bake about 10 minutes longer or until vegetables are tender.

Makes 4 servings (about 1-1/2 cups each)

Favorite recipe from **Mushroom Information Center**

Creamy Mac & Cheese Alfredo

   8 ounces elbow macaroni, cooked and drained
   1 jar (1 pound) RAGÚ® Cheesey!® Classic Alfredo Sauce
   3/4 cup chicken broth
   1/4 cup plain dry bread crumbs
   2 tablespoons grated Parmesan cheese (optional)

1. Preheat oven to 350°F. In large bowl, combine hot macaroni, Ragú Alfredo Sauce and broth. Season, if desired, with salt and pepper.

2. In 1-quart baking dish, spoon macaroni mixture; sprinkle with bread crumbs and cheese. Bake uncovered 25 minutes or until heated through.

Makes 4 servings

Herbed Green Bean Casserole

Herbed Green Bean Casserole

(Pictured above and on back cover)

>   1 cup freshly grated Parmesan cheese
>   3/4 cup dried bread crumbs
>   2 teaspoons dried basil
>   2 teaspoons dried parsley
>   1 teaspoon dried oregano
>   1 teaspoon garlic powder
>   1/2 teaspoon salt
>   1/2 teaspoon black pepper
>   1/2 teaspoon dried thyme
>   1/2 cup CRISCO® Oil*
>   2 (14-ounce) cans green beans, drained

*Use your favorite Crisco Oil.

Preheat oven to 350°F.

Combine first 9 ingredients in medium bowl. Add oil to bread crumb mixture; mix well. Reserve 2 tablespoons bread crumb mixture for top of casserole. Combine green beans and remaining bread crumb mixture in ovenproof dish; sprinkle with reserved crumb mixture.

Bake for about 30 minutes or until top is golden and crispy.   *Makes 8 servings*

Substitution: You can replace the canned beans with frozen or blanched and cooled fresh beans. The dried bread crumbs and herbs can be replaced with Italian-style bread crumbs.

Grilled Summer Vegetables Alouette®

>   1 large aluminum foil cooking bag
>   3 cups fresh broccoli florets
>   3 cups sliced summer squash (any type)
>   2 medium red bell peppers, cut in strips
>   1 cup sliced mushrooms
>   1 (6.5-ounce) package or two (4-ounce)
>   packages ALOUETTE® Garlic & Herbs

Preheat grill to medium-high. Open foil bag, layer vegetables evenly inside and spoon Alouette cheese on top. Seal bag by double-folding end. Place on grill and cook 8 to 10 minutes. Using oven mitts, carefully place bag on baking sheet and cut open, allowing steam to escape. If bag sticks to grill rack, cut open and remove vegetables (after grill cools, peel off bag).   *Makes 6 servings*

For oven cooking: Preheat oven to 450°F. Insert ingredients in bag as above. Bake sealed bag on baking sheet 20 to 25 minutes.

Creamy Broccoli and Cheese

>   1 package (8 ounces) cream cheese, softened
>   3/4 cup milk
>   1 packet (1 ounce) HIDDEN VALLEY®
>   The Original Ranch® Salad Dressing &
>   Seasoning Mix
>   1 pound fresh broccoli, cooked and drained
>   1/2 cup (2 ounces) shredded sharp Cheddar cheese

In a food processor fitted with a metal blade, blend cream cheese, milk and salad dressing & seasoning mix until smooth. Pour over broccoli in a 9-inch baking dish; stir well. Top with cheese. Bake at 350°F for 25 minutes or until cheese is melted.

Makes 4 servings

Smoky Kale Chiffonade

(Pictured below)

3/4 pound fresh young kale or mustard greens
3 slices bacon
2 tablespoons crumbled blue cheese

1. Rinse kale well in large bowl of warm water; place in colander. Drain. Discard any discolored leaves and trim away tough stem ends.

2. To prepare chiffonade, roll up leaves jelly-roll fashion. Slice widthwise into 1/2-inch-thick slices; separate into strips.* Set aside.

3. Cook bacon in medium skillet over medium heat until crisp. Remove bacon to paper towel. Remove all but 1 tablespoon drippings.

4. Add reserved kale to drippings in skillet. Cook and stir over medium-high heat 2 to 3 minutes until wilted and tender (older leaves may take slightly longer).**

5. Crumble bacon. Toss bacon and blue cheese with kale. Transfer to warm serving dish. Garnish, if desired. Serve immediately.

Makes 4 side-dish servings

*"Chiffonade" in French literally means "made of rags." In cooking, it means "cut into thin strips."

**If using mustard greens, stir-fry 4 to 6 minutes until wilted and tender.

Savory Beets

2 tablespoons chopped onion
1 tablespoon butter or margarine
3 tablespoons honey
2 tablespoons red or white wine vinegar
  Salt to taste
1/8 teaspoon ground cloves
1 can (16 ounces) sliced beets, drained

Sauté onion in butter in large skillet over medium heat until softened. Add honey, vinegar, salt and cloves; cook and stir until mixture begins to boil. Add beets; cook until thoroughly heated.

Makes 4 servings

Favorite recipe from **National Honey Board**

Smoky Kale Chiffonade

Southern Twice-Baked Sweet Potatoes

(Pictured at right)

4 medium sweet potatoes or yams, baked
1/4 cup HELLMANN'S® or BEST FOODS® Real
    Mayonnaise
1 to 2 tablespoons firmly packed brown sugar
1/2 teaspoon ground cinnamon
1/4 teaspoon ground ginger
1/4 teaspoon salt

Preheat oven to 425°F.

Slice potatoes in half lengthwise. Scoop out pulp, reserving potato skins and pulp.

In medium bowl, combine potato pulp, Hellmann's or Best Foods Real Mayonnaise, brown sugar, cinnamon, ginger and salt. Spoon pulp mixture into potato skins and arrange on baking sheet.

Bake 10 minutes or until heated through. Garnish, if desired, with chopped green onions.

Makes 4 servings

Holiday Wild Rice Pilaf

2 tablespoons butter or margarine
1/2 cup chopped onion
1/2 cup sliced celery
1 can (14-1/2 ounces) chicken broth
1/2 cup water
1 package (6 ounces) original flavor long grain
    and wild rice mix
3/4 cup SUN-MAID® Raisins or Goldens &
    Cherries
1/3 cup coarsely chopped pecans, toasted

MELT butter in medium saucepan or skillet over medium-high heat.

ADD onion and celery; cook 3 minutes, stirring occasionally.

ADD broth, water, rice, contents of seasoning packet and fruit. Bring to a boil. Reduce heat to medium-low. Cover and simmer 25 minutes or until liquid is absorbed.

STIR in pecans.

Makes 4 to 6 servings (about 4-1/2 cups)

Tip: The pilaf makes a wonderful stuffing for turkey or chicken.

Southwest Spaghetti Squash

1 spaghetti squash (about 3 pounds)
1 can (about 14 ounces) Mexican-style diced
    tomatoes, undrained
1 can (about 14 ounces) black beans, rinsed
    and drained
3/4 cup (3 ounces) shredded Monterey Jack
    cheese, divided
1/4 cup finely chopped cilantro
1 teaspoon ground cumin
1/4 teaspoon garlic salt
1/4 teaspoon pepper

Preheat oven to 350°F. Spray baking pan and 1-1/2-quart baking dish with nonstick cooking spray. Cut squash in half lengthwise. Remove and discard seeds. Place squash, cut side down, in prepared pan. Bake 45 minutes to 1 hour or until just tender. Using fork, remove spaghetti-like strands from hot squash and place strands in large bowl. (Use oven mitts to protect hands.)

Add tomatoes with juice, beans, 1/2 cup cheese, cilantro, cumin, garlic salt and pepper; toss well. Spoon mixture into prepared dish. Sprinkle with remaining 1/4 cup cheese.

Bake, uncovered, 30 to 35 minutes or until heated through. Serve immediately.   *Makes 4 servings*

Corn Maque Choux

2 tablespoons butter or margarine
1/2 cup chopped onion
1/2 cup chopped green pepper
4 cups whole kernel corn (canned, fresh or
    frozen, thawed)
1 medium tomato, chopped
1/2 teaspoon TABASCO® brand Pepper Sauce
1/4 teaspoon salt

Melt butter in 3-quart saucepan over medium heat.

Add onion and green pepper; cook 5 minutes or until tender, stirring frequently.

Stir in corn, tomato, TABASCO® Sauce and salt. Reduce heat and simmer 10 to 15 minutes or until corn is tender.   *Makes 3 cups*

Southern Twice-Baked Sweet Potato

Grilled Mesquite Vegetables

(Pictured at right)

2 to 3 tablespoons MRS. DASH® Mesquite
    Grilling Blend
2 tablespoons olive oil, divided
1 eggplant, trimmed and cut into 1/2-inch slices
1 zucchini, quartered lengthwise
1 red onion, peeled and halved
2 red bell peppers, cut into large slices
2 green bell peppers, cut into large slices
1 tablespoon balsamic vinegar

Preheat barbecue grill to medium. In large bowl, combine Mrs. Dash® Mesquite Grilling Blend and 1 tablespoon olive oil. Add vegetables and toss until well coated with olive oil mixture. Place vegetables on grill. Cover and cook, turning vegetables once during cooking, until vegetables are tender and develop grill marks, about 3 to 4 minutes on each side. Remove vegetables from grill as soon as they are cooked. Coarsely chop vegetables into 1/2-inch pieces. Mix remaining olive oil and balsamic vinegar in large bowl. Add cut vegetables and toss to coat. Serve at room temperature. *Makes 6 servings*

Note: Grilling vegetables dehydrates them slightly and intensifies flavors while Mrs. Dash Mesquite adds a third dimension of flavor. This dish makes a colorful accompaniment to any grilled meat.

Glazed Acorn Squash

2 medium acorn squash, halved and seeded
1-1/2 cups water
1/3 cup KARO® Light or Dark Corn Syrup
1 tablespoon margarine or butter, melted
1/2 teaspoon cinnamon
1/4 teaspoon salt

1. Place squash cut-side down in 13×9×2-inch baking dish; add water. Bake in 400°F oven 30 minutes or until squash is nearly fork-tender.

2. Turn squash cut-side up. In small bowl combine corn syrup, margarine, cinnamon and salt. Spoon corn syrup mixture into squash cavities.

3. Bake in 350°F oven 15 minutes or until fork-tender, basting occasionally. *Makes 4 servings*

Cheesy Potato Gratin

3-1/2 pounds baking potatoes, peeled and thinly
    sliced
2 tablespoons HERB-OX® chicken flavored
    bouillon, divided
3 cups shredded Havarti cheese, divided
6 tablespoons all-purpose flour, divided
3 cups heavy whipping cream

Heat oven to 400°F. Spray 13×9-inch baking dish with nonstick cooking spray. Arrange 1/3 of potatoes in dish. Sprinkle with 1 teaspoon bouillon and season to taste with freshly ground pepper. Add 1 cup cheese and 2 tablespoons flour. Continue adding two more layers of potatoes, bouillon, pepper, cheese and flour. In bowl, combine whipping cream and remaining 1 tablespoon chicken bouillon. Pour mixture over potatoes. Bake for 60 minutes or until top is golden brown and potatoes are tender.
Makes 10 to 12 servings

Easy Polenta Marinara

1 can (about 14 ounces) chicken broth
1 cup yellow cornmeal
3 tablespoons grated Parmesan cheese
1-1/2 cups prepared marinara sauce
1/2 cup (2 ounces) shredded mozzarella cheese

1. Preheat oven to 375°F. Grease 9-inch square baking dish; set aside.

2. Combine broth and 1 cup water in medium saucepan. Whisk cornmeal into liquid. Bring to a boil over medium-high heat, stirring to prevent lumps.

3. Reduce heat to medium-low; cook about 7 minutes or until mixture is very thick, stirring constantly. Stir in Parmesan cheese; season with salt and pepper to taste.

4. Pour hot polenta into prepared dish, spreading evenly with spatula. Pour marinara sauce over polenta; sprinkle with mozzarella cheese. Bake 10 minutes or until cheese is melted and sauce is heated through. *Makes 6 servings*

Tip: For a special touch, garnish with fresh basil leaves.

Grilled Sweet Potatoes

(Pictured at right)

4 medium-sized sweet potatoes (2 pounds),
    peeled
1 cup water
1/3 cup *French's®* Honey Dijon Mustard
2 tablespoons olive oil
1 tablespoon minced fresh rosemary *or*
    1 teaspoon dried rosemary
1/2 teaspoon salt
1/4 teaspoon black pepper

1. Cut potatoes diagonally into 1/2-inch-thick slices. Place potatoes and water in shallow microwavable dish. Cover with vented plastic wrap and microwave on HIGH (100%) 6 minutes or until potatoes are crisp-tender, turning once. (Cook potatoes in two batches, if necessary.) Drain well.

2. Combine mustard, oil, rosemary, salt and pepper in small bowl; brush on potato slices. Place potatoes on oiled grid. Grill over medium-high heat 5 to 8 minutes or until potatoes are fork-tender, turning and basting often with mustard mixture.

Makes 4 servings

Tip: The task of selecting sweet potatoes is an easy one. Just look for medium-sized potatoes with thick, dark orange skins that are free from bruises. Sweet potatoes keep best in a dry, dark area at about 55°F. Under these conditions they should last about 3 to 4 weeks.

Sesame Snow Peas

(Pictured on page 44)

1/2 pound snow peas (Chinese pea pods)
2 teaspoons toasted sesame oil
2 teaspoons vegetable oil
2 green onions, cut into 1/4-inch slices
1/2 teaspoon grated fresh gingerroot *or*
    1/4 teaspoon ground ginger
1 medium carrot, cut into matchstick pieces
1 teaspoon soy sauce
1 tablespoon sesame seeds, toasted*

*To toast sesame seeds, heat small skillet over medium heat. Add sesame seeds; cook and stir about 5 minutes or until golden.

1. To de-stem peas, pinch off stem end from each pod and pull strings down pod to remove, if present. (Young tender pods may have no strings.) Make a "V-shaped" cut at opposite end of pod.

2. To stir-fry, place wok or large skillet over medium-high heat. Add sesame and vegetable oils, swirling to coat sides. Heat oils until hot, about 30 seconds. Add peas, onions, ginger and carrot; stir-fry 4 minutes or until peas are bright green and crisp-tender.

3. Stir in soy sauce. Transfer to warm serving dish; sprinkle with sesame seeds. Serve immediately.

Makes 4 side-dish servings

Golden Corn Pudding

2 tablespoons butter or margarine
3 tablespoons all-purpose flour
1 can (14-3/4 ounces) DEL MONTE® Cream Style
    Golden Sweet Corn
1/4 cup yellow cornmeal
2 eggs, separated
1 package (3 ounces) cream cheese, softened
1 can (8-3/4 ounces) DEL MONTE Whole Kernel
    Golden Sweet Corn, drained

1. Preheat oven to 350°F.

2. Melt butter in medium saucepan. Add flour and stir until smooth. Blend in cream style corn and cornmeal. Bring to a boil over medium heat, stirring constantly.

3. Place egg yolks in small bowl; stir in 1/2 cup hot mixture. Pour mixture back into saucepan. Add cream cheese and whole kernel corn.

4. Place egg whites in clean narrow bowl and beat until stiff peaks form. With rubber spatula, gently fold egg whites into corn mixture.

5. Pour mixture into 1-1/2-quart straight-sided baking dish. Bake 30 to 35 minutes or until lightly browned.
Makes 4 to 6 servings

Tip: Pudding can be prepared up to 3 hours ahead of serving time. Cover and refrigerate until about 30 minutes before baking.

Grilled Sweet Potatoes

Fresh Vegetables over Couscous

(Pictured at right)

3 tablespoons BERTOLLI® Olive Oil
2 pounds assorted fresh vegetables*
1 can (15 to 19 ounces) chick-peas or garbanzos,
    rinsed and drained
1/4 cup golden raisins (optional)
1 envelope LIPTON® RECIPE SECRETS®
    Savory Herb with Garlic Soup Mix
1-1/2 cups water
1 to 2 tablespoons lemon juice
1/2 teaspoon ground cumin (optional)
1 box (10 ounces) couscous, prepared according
    to package directions

Use any combination of the following, sliced: zucchini, yellow squash, red onions, carrots, mushrooms or red or green bell peppers.

In 12-inch skillet, heat oil over medium heat and cook vegetables, stirring occasionally, 5 minutes or until tender. Add chick-peas, raisins, savory herb with garlic soup mix blended with water, lemon juice and cumin. Cook, stirring occasionally, 3 minutes. Serve over hot couscous.

Makes about 4 servings

Bar-B-Q Lentils

2-1/2 cups dry USA lentils, rinsed
5 cups water
1 (15-ounce) can tomato sauce
1/2 cup tomato catsup
1/2 cup molasses
2 tablespoons minced onion
2 tablespoons brown sugar
1 tablespoon cider vinegar
1 teaspoon dry mustard
1 teaspoon Worcestershire sauce
1/4 teaspoon liquid smoke flavoring (optional)

Preheat oven to 350°F.

Combine lentils and water in medium saucepan; bring to a boil. Reduce heat and simmer, covered, for 30 minutes or until lentils are tender but still whole. Add remaining ingredients to cooked, undrained lentils.

Transfer mixture to baking dish and bake for 45 minutes. *Makes 6 to 8 servings*

Tip: For an even quicker version of this delicious side dish, add ready-made barbecue sauce to cooked lentils. Season to taste and serve.

Variation: To cooked lentils add 1/2 cup *each* honey and chopped chutney, 2 tablespoons minced onion and 2 teaspoons dry mustard. Season to taste with salt and pepper. Bake as above. Sprinkle with bacon bits and garnish with fresh lime wedges.

Favorite recipe from **USA Dry Pea & Lentil Council**

Herbed Zucchini Ribbons

3 small zucchini (about 3/4 pound total)
2 tablespoons olive oil
1 tablespoon white wine vinegar
2 teaspoons chopped fresh basil leaves *or*
    1/2 teaspoon dried basil leaves, crushed
1/2 teaspoon crushed red pepper flakes
1/4 teaspoon ground coriander
    Salt and black pepper

To make zucchini ribbons, cut tip and stem ends from zucchini with paring knife. Using vegetable peeler, begin at stem end and make continuous ribbons down length of each zucchini.

To steam zucchini ribbons, place steamer basket in large saucepan; add 1 inch of water. (Water should not touch bottom of basket.) Place zucchini ribbons in steamer basket; cover. Bring to a boil over high heat. When pan begins to steam, check zucchini for doneness. (It should be crisp-tender.) Transfer zucchini to warm serving dish with slotted spatula or tongs.

Combine oil, vinegar, basil, red pepper and coriander in small bowl, whisking until oil is thoroughly blended.

Pour dressing mixture over zucchini ribbons; toss gently to coat. Season with salt and pepper to taste. Garnish, if desired. Serve immediately or refrigerate up to 2 days. *Makes 4 side-dish servings*

Fresh Vegetables over Couscous

Bacon and Maple Grits Puff

(Pictured at right)

8 slices bacon
2 cups milk
1-1/4 cups water
1 cup uncooked quick-cooking grits
1/2 teaspoon salt
1/2 cup pure maple syrup
4 eggs
Fresh chives (optional)

Preheat oven to 350°F. Grease 1-1/2-quart round baking or soufflé dish; set aside.

Cook bacon in large skillet over medium-high heat about 7 minutes or until crisp. Remove bacon to paper towel; set aside. Reserve 2 tablespoons bacon drippings.

Combine milk, water, grits and salt in medium saucepan. Bring to a boil over medium heat, stirring frequently. Simmer 2 to 3 minutes or until mixture thickens, stirring constantly. Remove from heat; stir in syrup and reserved 2 tablespoons bacon drippings.

Crumble bacon; reserve 1/4 cup for garnish. Stir remaining crumbled bacon into grits mixture.

Beat eggs in medium bowl. Gradually stir small amount of grits mixture into eggs. Stir egg mixture into remaining grits mixture. Pour into prepared dish.

Bake 1 hour and 20 minutes or until knife inserted into center comes out clean. Top with reserved 1/4 cup bacon. Garnish with fresh chives, if desired. Serve immediately. *Makes 6 to 8 servings*

Note: Puff will fall slightly after being removed from oven.

Fennel with Black Olive Dressing

1-1/4 pounds (about 2 medium-size heads) fennel
1/3 cup lemon juice
1/4 cup olive or salad oil
2/3 cup pitted California ripe olives, coarsely chopped
Salt and pepper

Trim stems and root ends from fennel; core. Reserve feathery wisps of fennel for garnish, if desired. Slice fennel crosswise into 1/4-inch-thick pieces. Bring 3 to 4 quarts water to a boil in large saucepan over high heat. Add fennel and cook, uncovered, just until tender to bite, about 5 minutes. Drain; immerse fennel in ice water until cold. Drain well again. Whisk lemon juice and oil in small bowl; stir in olives and add salt and pepper to taste. To serve, divide fennel among 6 salad plates and spoon dressing over fennel. Garnish with reserved feathery wisps of fennel, if desired. *Makes 6 servings*

Favorite recipe from **California Olive Industry**

Zesty Marinated Peppers with Lemon and Sesame

3 medium (about 1-1/2 pounds) sweet red, yellow and/or orange bell peppers (mix 2 or 3 colors, but not green)
Grated peel of 1/2 SUNKIST® lemon
Juice of 1 SUNKIST® lemon (3 tablespoons)
2 tablespoons vegetable oil
2 teaspoons sesame oil
2 teaspoons honey
1/8 teaspoon salt
2 green onions, thinly sliced diagonally
2 teaspoons toasted sesame seeds

Grill peppers 4 to 6 inches above glowing coals or on HIGH heat of gas barbecue, turning with tongs as each side blackens and blisters. When well-blackened, about 20 to 25 minutes, remove peppers to plastic bag; close or seal and let peppers steam 10 minutes. Let cool enough to handle. Wipe peppers with paper towel to help remove blackened skin. (To avoid loss of flavor, do not rinse with water.) Remove cores; cut in half and remove seeds. Cut into 1/2-inch strips. In bowl, combine lemon peel, juice, oils, honey and salt. Add pepper strips. Marinate, covered, 1 hour* at room temperature. Stir in green onions and sesame seeds. Serve as an accompaniment to grilled fish or beef steaks, or barbecued beef or pork ribs.

Makes about 2 cups

*Pepper mixture can be marinated several hours or overnight in refrigerator. Stir in green onions and sesame seeds just before serving.

Bacon and Maple Grits Puff

Soups

Red Bean Soup with Andouille Sausage

(Pictured at left)

2 tablespoons butter
1 large sweet onion, diced
3 stalks celery, diced
2 large garlic cloves, chopped
8 cups chicken broth
1 ham hock
1-1/2 cups dried red kidney beans, soaked in cold water 1 hour, drained and rinsed
1 bay leaf
2 parsnips, diced
1 sweet potato, diced
1 pound andouille smoked sausage or other pork sausage, cut into 1/2-inch pieces
Salt and pepper

SLOW COOKER DIRECTIONS

1. Melt butter in large saucepan over medium heat. Add onion, celery and garlic. Cook and stir 5 minutes. Place in slow cooker. Add broth, ham hock, kidney beans and bay leaf. Cover; cook on HIGH 2 hours.

2. Remove ham hock; discard. Add parsnips and sweet potato. Cover; cook an additional 2 hours.

3. Add sausage. Cover; cook an additional 30 minutes or until heated through. Remove and discard bay leaf. Season with salt and pepper.   *Makes 6 to 8 servings*

Note: Use a 6-quart slow cooker for this recipe. If using a smaller slow cooker, cut the recipe ingredients in half.

Clockwise from top left: *Swanson® Hearty Chicken Tortilla Soup (p. 88), Cream of Asparagus Soup (p. 68), Southwestern Soup (p. 82) and Red Bean Soup with Andouille Sausage*

Cream of Asparagus Soup

(Pictured on page 66)

  1 pound fresh asparagus
  3-1/2 cups chicken broth, divided
  1/4 cup (1/2 stick) butter or margarine
  1/4 cup all-purpose flour
  1/2 cup half-and-half cream
  1/2 teaspoon salt
  1/8 teaspoon pepper

Trim off coarse ends of asparagus. Cut asparagus into 1-inch pieces. Combine asparagus and 1 cup broth in medium saucepan; cook 12 to 15 minutes or until tender. Remove 1 cup asparagus pieces; set aside. Purée remaining asparagus pieces with broth in blender or food processor.

Melt butter in large saucepan. Remove from heat; stir in flour. Gradually add remaining 2-1/2 cups broth; cook, stirring occasionally, until slightly thickened. Stir in cream, salt, pepper, puréed asparagus mixture and asparagus pieces; heat through. *Makes 6 to 8 servings*

Note: You can substitute 3 chicken bouillon cubes and 3-1/2 cups water for 3-1/2 cups chicken broth.

Potato Soup with Green Chilies & Cheese

(Pictured at right)

  2 tablespoons vegetable oil
  1 medium onion, chopped
  1 garlic clove, minced
  2 cups chopped unpeeled potatoes
  1 tablespoon all-purpose flour
  1-1/2 cups chicken broth
  2 cups milk
  1 can (4 ounces) diced green chilies
  1/2 teaspoon celery salt
  3/4 cup (3 ounces) shredded Monterey Jack cheese
  3/4 cup (3 ounces) shredded Colby or Cheddar cheese
  White pepper
  Chopped celery leaves for garnish

Heat oil in large saucepan over medium heat. Add onion and garlic; cook until onion is tender. Stir in potatoes; cook 1 minute. Stir in flour; continue cooking 1 minute.

Stir in broth; bring to a boil. Cover; reduce heat and simmer 20 minutes or until potatoes are tender.

Stir in milk, chilies and celery salt; heat to simmering. Add cheeses; stir and heat just until cheeses melt. Do not boil. Add pepper to taste. Garnish with celery leaves.

Makes 6 servings

Roasted Tomato Vegetable Soup

  2 pounds grape or cherry tomatoes, stems removed
  1 small onion, peeled, quartered
  1/4 cup extra-virgin olive oil
  1/2 teaspoon kosher salt
  1/4 teaspoon black pepper
  1 jar (12 ounces) roasted red peppers, drained
  2 cans (15 ounces each) VEG•ALL® Original Mixed Vegetables, drained, with liquid reserved
  1 cup water
  5 to 6 leaves fresh basil
  1 bay leaf

Preheat oven to 400°F.

Combine tomatoes, onion, oil, salt and pepper in Dutch oven. Toss to coat. Roast in oven 45 minutes. Remove from oven and let cool for 10 minutes.

Transfer tomato mixture, roasted peppers, Veg•All liquid, water and basil to blender. Blend until smooth. Return soup to Dutch oven.

Add bay leaf and drained Veg•All vegetables. Simmer for 15 to 20 minutes over medium heat. Remove bay leaf. Ladle into bowls and serve.

Makes 8 servings

Serving Suggestion: Top each bowl of soup with croutons and crumbled gorgonzola cheese.

Potato Soup with Green Chilies & Cheese

Hearty 3-Bean & Ham Soup

(Pictured at right)

1 cup chopped onion
1 tablespoon vegetable or olive oil
1 (15-ounce) can each pinto beans, black beans
    and red kidney beans, drained and rinsed
1 cup sliced carrots
3-1/2 cups water
4 cubes HERB-OX® beef bouillon
1 (14-1/2-ounce) can diced tomatoes
1/3 cup chili sauce
3 tablespoons cider vinegar
1 tablespoon firmly packed brown sugar
2 teaspoons Worcestershire sauce
2 teaspoons prepared mustard
1 cup diced ham
2 tablespoons chopped fresh parsley

In large saucepan, sauté onion in oil until golden. Stir in beans and next 9 ingredients. Bring mixture to a boil. Reduce heat, cover and simmer for 25 to 30 minutes or until carrots are tender. Stir in ham and parsley. Ladle into bowls and serve.

Makes 6 to 8 servings

Chicken Soup au Pistou

Nonstick olive oil cooking spray
1/2 pound boneless skinless chicken breasts, cut
    into 1/2-inch pieces
1 large onion, diced
3 cans (14-1/2 ounces each) chicken broth
1 can (15 ounces) whole tomatoes, undrained
1 can (14 ounces) great northern beans, rinsed
    and drained
2 medium carrots, sliced
1 large potato, diced
1/4 teaspoon salt
1/4 teaspoon pepper
1 cup frozen Italian green beans
1/4 cup prepared pesto
    Grated Parmesan cheese (optional)

1. Spray large saucepan with cooking spray; heat over medium-high heat until hot. Add chicken; cook and stir about 5 minutes or until chicken is browned. Add onion; cook and stir 2 minutes.

2. Add chicken broth, tomatoes with juice, great northern beans, carrots, potato, salt and pepper. Bring to a boil, stirring to break up tomatoes. Reduce heat to low. Cover and simmer 15 minutes,

stirring occasionally. Add green beans; cook about 5 minutes more or until vegetables are tender.

3. Ladle soup into bowls. Top each serving with 1-1/2 teaspoons pesto and sprinkle with Parmesan cheese, if desired. *Makes 8 servings*

Calico Minestrone Soup

2 cans (14 ounces each) chicken broth
1/4 cup uncooked small shell pasta
1 can (14-1/2 ounces) DEL MONTE® Stewed
    Tomatoes - Italian Recipe
1 can (8-3/4 ounces) *or* 1 cup kidney beans,
    drained
1/2 cup chopped cooked chicken or beef
1 carrot, cubed
1 stalk celery, sliced
1/2 teaspoon dried basil, crushed

1. Bring broth to boil in large saucepan; stir in pasta and boil 5 minutes.

2. Add remaining ingredients.

3. Reduce heat; cover and simmer 20 minutes. Garnish with grated Parmesan cheese, if desired.
Makes approximately 6 servings (1 cup each)

Cheese Ravioli Soup

4 cans (20 ounces each) chicken broth
1 package (16 ounces) frozen red pepper stir-fry
4 tablespoons MRS. DASH® Classic Italiano
    Blend
1 package (13 ounces) frozen mini cheese ravioli
6 tablespoons grated Parmesan cheese

Combine broth, red pepper stir-fry and Classic Italiano Blend in medium saucepan. Bring to a boil. Add ravioli. Simmer 15 to 20 minutes or until ravioli is done. Serve garnished with grated Parmesan cheese. *Makes 12 servings*

Hearty 3-Bean & Ham Soup

Feelin' Good Vegetable Soup

(Pictured below)

1/2 pound ground turkey or ground beef
1 can (14 ounces) chicken or beef broth
1 can (8 ounces) tomato sauce
1/2 cup uncooked small shell pasta
1 teaspoon chili powder or Cajun seasoning
1/2 teaspoon dried basil
1/8 teaspoon garlic powder
1-1/2 cups frozen mixed vegetables

Cook and stir ground turkey in medium saucepan over medium-high heat until brown; drain off any fat. Stir in broth, tomato sauce, pasta, chili powder, basil and garlic powder. Bring to a boil. Reduce heat; simmer, covered, 5 minutes.

Stir in frozen vegetables. Bring to a boil. Simmer, covered, 5 minutes or until pasta is tender. Serve immediately.   *Makes 4 servings (1 cup each)*

Tip: This soup is perfect for dinner on busy weeknights—it can be prepared in less than 30 minutes! Just add a salad and a loaf of bread and you have a delicious, hearty meal.

Feelin' Good Vegetable Soup

Butch's Black Bean Soup

1/4 cup olive oil
1 medium onion, diced
4 cloves garlic, minced
4 cups water
2 chicken-flavored bouillon cubes
1 large can (2 pounds 8 ounces) black beans, rinsed and drained
1 can (15 ounces) corn, undrained
1 medium potato, peeled and diced
3 ribs celery, diced
2 carrots, diced
1 cup uncooked rice or orzo
1/4 cup fresh cilantro, minced
2 (11-ounce) jars NEWMAN'S OWN® Bandito Salsa (medium or hot) *or* 1 (26-ounce) jar NEWMAN'S OWN® Diavolo Spicy Simmer Sauce

Heat oil in large saucepan; cook and stir onion and garlic over high heat until onion is translucent. Add water and bouillon cubes; bring to a boil. Reduce heat to medium; add beans, corn, potato, celery, carrots, rice and cilantro. Stir in Newman's Own® Bandito Salsa and simmer until rice and vegetables are cooked, about 30 minutes.   *Makes 8 servings*

Chef's Choice Minestrone Soup

2 tablespoons olive oil
1 cup thinly sliced peeled carrots
1/2 cup thinly sliced celery
1/2 cup chopped onion
2 tablespoons MRS. DASH® Tomato Basil Garlic
2 cans (14-1/2 ounces each) beef broth
1 can (14-1/2 ounces) diced tomatoes, undrained
1 cup frozen green beans
1 can (15-1/2 ounces) kidney beans, drained and rinsed
1 cup thinly sliced cabbage
1-1/2 cups cooked medium pasta shells

Heat oil in large stockpot over medium heat. Add carrots, celery and onion. Cook over medium heat until tender. Sprinkle with Mrs. Dash® Tomato Basil Garlic. Add beef broth, tomatoes and green beans; cook over medium heat for 10 minutes. Stir in kidney beans and cabbage; cook another 20 minutes or until heated thoroughly and cabbage is tender. Stir in pasta and heat 1 more minute.

Makes 6 servings

Chicken Corn Chowder with Cheese

Chicken Corn Chowder with Cheese

(Pictured above)

2 tablespoons butter or margarine
1/3 cup chopped celery
1/3 cup chopped red bell pepper
1-1/2 tablespoons all-purpose flour
2 cups milk
1 can (14-3/4 ounces) cream-style corn
1-1/3 cups *French's*® French Fried Onions, divided
1 cup diced cooked chicken
2 tablespoons chopped green chilies
1/2 cup (2 ounces) shredded Cheddar cheese

1. Melt butter in 3-quart saucepan over medium-high heat. Sauté celery and bell pepper 3 minutes or until crisp-tender. Blend in flour; cook 1 minute, stirring constantly. Gradually stir in milk and corn. Bring to a boil. Reduce heat; simmer 4 minutes or until thickened, stirring frequently.

2. Add *2/3 cup* French Fried Onions, chicken and chilies. Cook until heated through. Spoon soup into serving bowls; sprinkle with remaining onions and cheese. Splash on **Frank's RedHot** Sauce to taste, if desired.   *Makes 4 servings*

Variation: For added Cheddar flavor, substitute **French's**® **Cheddar French Fried Onions** for the original flavor.

Helpful Hint

If you don't have cooked chicken on hand for this soup, you can purchase a rotisserie chicken and use the rest for a casserole or sandwiches. Or, look for packages of ready-to-use chicken strips (roasted or grilled) in the supermarket's refrigerated case.

Black-Eyed Pea Soup with Ham & Greens

(Pictured at right)

4 tablespoons CRISCO® Vegetable Oil*
2 medium onions, chopped
1/2 pound cooked ham, diced
1 carrot, peeled and finely chopped
2 cloves garlic, minced
1 pound collard greens, stems and ribs removed,
    finely chopped
1 (14-1/2-ounce) can chicken broth
5 cups water
1 bay leaf
1/2 teaspoon crushed red pepper flakes
2 (16-ounce) cans black-eyed peas
    (about 1-1/2 cups)
    Salt and pepper
2 teaspoons cider vinegar

*Or use your favorite Crisco Oil.

Heat oil in large saucepan over medium heat.
Add onions, ham, carrot and garlic. Cook, stirring
occasionally, until onion is soft. Add collards, broth,
water, bay leaf and crushed red pepper flakes to
saucepan and simmer until greens are tender, about
25 minutes.

Rinse and drain black-eyed peas. Mash 1 can of peas
in medium bowl. Stir mashed and whole peas into
soup and simmer 5 minutes. Season to taste with
salt and pepper; stir in vinegar.

Makes 6 servings

Southwestern Chicken Soup

4 cups chicken broth
1/2 cup long-grain rice, uncooked
1/4 teaspoon ground cumin
1 cup chopped cooked chicken
1/2 cup fresh corn kernels (frozen corn kernels
    may be substituted)
2 tablespoons SONOMA® Dried Tomato Bits
1/4 cup fresh lime juice
1/4 teaspoon cayenne pepper
    Salt to taste

In large saucepan, bring chicken broth to a boil. Stir
in rice and cumin. Cover and cook 15 minutes or
until rice is done. Stir in chicken and corn. Cover
and bring just to a boil; remove from heat. Stir in
tomato bits, lime juice, cayenne and salt.

Makes 4 servings

Turk-A-Leekie Soup

6 cups water
3/4 cup pearl barley
2 teaspoons salt
2 cups chopped cooked turkey
2 large leeks, chopped
1 (14-1/2-ounce) can chicken broth*
1/2 cup chopped dried plums
1/4 cup chopped fresh parsley
2 teaspoons TABASCO® brand Pepper Sauce
    Crusty French bread (optional)

*Or use 2 cups turkey broth. To make broth, simmer leftover turkey
carcass in water to cover, along with herbs and chopped carrot,
onion and celery about 2 to 3 hours or until bones fall apart.

Heat water, barley and salt to boiling in 5-quart
saucepan over high heat. Reduce heat to low;
cover and simmer 1 hour or until barley is tender.
Add turkey, leeks, broth, dried plums, parsley and
TABASCO® Sauce. Over high heat, bring to boil.
Reduce heat to low; cover and simmer 10 minutes,
stirring occasionally. Serve with crusty French
bread, if desired.

Makes 6 servings

Creamy Curry Carrot Soup

2 tablespoons butter
2 to 3 teaspoons curry powder
1 teaspoon salt
1 medium onion, finely chopped
4 medium carrots, shredded
3 (14-1/2-ounce) cans chicken broth, divided
3 cups cooked long grain rice
1 cup whipping cream

Melt butter in large saucepan over medium-high
heat. Blend in curry powder and salt, stirring
constantly for 30 seconds. Add onion and carrots;
sauté 7 to 9 minutes, stirring frequently.

Carefully spoon mixture into blender or food
processor. Add 1 can broth; blend but don't purée.

Return mixture to saucepan; add remaining 2 cans
broth and rice. Heat over medium-high heat until
hot, about 5 minutes. Remove from heat and stir
in whipping cream. *Makes 8 servings*

Favorite recipe from **USA Rice**

*Black-Eyed Pea Soup with
Ham & Greens*

Hoppin' John Soup

(Pictured at right)

    1 bag SUCCESS® Brown Rice
1/4 pound spicy turkey sausage
1/2 cup chopped onion
1/2 pound turnips, peeled and chopped
    2 carrots, peeled and chopped
1/2 teaspoon salt
1/2 teaspoon pepper
    3 cups chicken broth
    1 package (8 ounces) frozen black-eyed peas,
        thawed and drained
    1 package (8 ounces) frozen chopped mustard
        greens, thawed and drained
1/2 teaspoon red pepper flakes

Prepare rice according to package directions.

Brown sausage in large saucepan or Dutch oven over medium-high heat; drain. Add onion, turnips, carrots, salt and pepper. Reduce heat to low; simmer 7 minutes. Add broth; simmer 5 minutes. Add rice, peas and greens; simmer 10 minutes, stirring occasionally. Sprinkle with red pepper flakes.   *Makes 6 servings*

Pineapple Gazpacho

    3 cups DOLE® Fresh Pineapple Chunks,
        cut into smaller chunks, divided
    2 medium cucumbers, peeled, seeded and
        chopped, divided
    1 cup chopped yellow bell pepper, divided
1/2 cup chopped onion, divided
    1 cup DOLE® Pineapple Juice
    1 tablespoon white vinegar
    1 teaspoon chopped jalapeño
    2 tablespoons sugar

• Combine half of pineapple chunks, cucumbers, bell pepper and onion in medium bowl; set aside.

• Combine remaining pineapple chunks, cucumbers, bell pepper, onion, pineapple juice, vinegar and jalapeño in blender or food processor container. Cover; blend until smooth. Stir into reserved pineapple mixture.

• Stir in sugar. Cover; refrigerate 2 hours or until chilled. Garnish with jalapeño slices, if desired.
                    Makes 6 servings

Ranch Clam Chowder

    3 cans (6-1/2 ounces each) chopped clams
    6 slices bacon, chopped*
1/4 cup finely chopped onion
1/4 cup all-purpose flour
2-1/2 cups milk
    1 packet (1 ounce) HIDDEN VALLEY®
        The Original Ranch® Salad Dressing &
        Seasoning Mix
    2 cups frozen cubed O'Brien potatoes
    2 cups frozen corn kernels
1/8 teaspoon dried thyme (optional)

Bacon pieces can be used.

Drain clams, reserving juice (about 1-1/3 cups); set aside. Cook bacon until crisp in a large pot or Dutch oven; remove with slotted spoon, reserving 1/4 cup drippings.** Set aside bacon pieces. Heat bacon drippings over medium heat in same pot. Add onion; sauté 3 minutes. Sprinkle with flour; cook and stir 1 minute longer. Gradually whisk in reserved clam juice and milk, stirring until smooth. Whisk in salad dressing & seasoning mix until blended. Stir in potatoes, corn and thyme, if desired. Bring mixture just to a boil; reduce heat and simmer 10 minutes, stirring occasionally. Stir in clams; heat through. Sprinkle bacon over each serving.   *Makes 4 to 6 servings*

**You may substitute 1/4 cup butter for the bacon drippings.*

Tortellini Vegetable Soup

    1 (14-ounce) package turkey or pork breakfast
        sausage, crumbled
    2 quarts water
    6 cubes HERB-OX® beef flavored bouillon
1/2 teaspoon garlic powder
    1 (9-ounce) package fresh cheese tortellini pasta
    1 (16-ounce) package frozen vegetable
        combination (broccoli, cauliflower, red
        pepper), thawed

In Dutch oven over medium-high heat, cook sausage until browned; drain. Add water, bouillon and garlic powder; bring to a boil. Add pasta; boil 5 minutes. Stir in vegetables. Simmer, uncovered, 10 minutes or until vegetables and pasta are tender.   *Makes 8 servings*

Gazpacho

(Pictured at right)

3 cups tomato juice
4 tomatoes, chopped
1 green bell pepper, chopped
1 cucumber, chopped
1 cup chopped celery
1 cup chopped green onions
3 tablespoons red wine vinegar
2 tablespoons FILIPPO BERIO® Olive Oil
1 tablespoon chopped fresh parsley
1 to 2 teaspoons salt
1 clove garlic, finely minced
  Freshly ground black pepper or hot pepper
    sauce

In large bowl, combine tomato juice, tomatoes, bell pepper, cucumber, celery, green onions, vinegar, olive oil, parsley, salt and garlic. Cover; refrigerate several hours or overnight before serving. Season to taste with black pepper or hot pepper sauce. Serve cold.   *Makes 10 to 12 servings*

Zucchini-Tomato-Noodle Soup

10 cups cubed zucchini
3/4 cup water
4 cups chopped onion
1/2 cup (1 stick) butter
8 cups quartered tomatoes
4 chicken bouillon cubes
3 cloves garlic, chopped
1 teaspoon Beau Monde seasoning*
1 teaspoon salt
1 teaspoon black pepper
4 cups uncooked 100% durum noodles, hot,
  cooked and drained
Garlic bread (optional)

A seasoning salt available in most supermarkets. Celery salt can be substituted.

Combine zucchini and water in Dutch oven. Cook over medium heat until crisp-tender. Cook and stir onion in hot butter in medium skillet over medium heat until tender. Add onion mixture, tomatoes, bouillon cubes, garlic, seasoning, salt and pepper to zucchini mixture. Simmer until tender. Add noodles; heat through. Serve with garlic bread, if desired.
          Makes 8 servings

Favorite recipe from **North Dakota Wheat Commission**

Chicken Rotini Soup

1/2 pound boneless skinless chicken breasts,
    cut into 1/2-inch pieces
1 cup water
2 tablespoons butter or margarine
4 ounces fresh mushrooms, sliced
1/2 medium onion, chopped
4 cups chicken broth
1 teaspoon Worcestershire sauce
1/4 teaspoon dried tarragon leaves, crushed
3/4 cup uncooked rotini
1 small zucchini
  Fresh basil for garnish

Combine chicken and water in medium saucepan. Bring to a boil over high heat. Reduce heat to medium-low; simmer 2 minutes. Drain water and rinse chicken. Melt butter in 5-quart Dutch oven or large saucepan over medium heat. Add mushrooms and onion; cook and stir until onion is tender. Stir in chicken, chicken broth, Worcestershire and tarragon. Bring to a boil over high heat. Stir in uncooked pasta. Reduce heat to medium-low; simmer, uncovered, 5 minutes. Cut zucchini into 1/8-inch slices; halve any large slices. Add to soup; simmer, uncovered, about 5 minutes or until pasta is tender. Garnish, if desired.   *Makes 4 servings*

Taco Twist Soup

1 pound ground beef
2 teaspoons chili powder
1 teaspoon ground cumin
1 can (14 ounces) SWANSON® Beef Broth
1 cup PACE® Picante Sauce
1 can (14-1/2 ounces) diced tomatoes in juice
1 cup uncooked corkscrew pasta
  Sour cream

1. **COOK** beef, chili powder and cumin in skillet until browned. Pour off fat.

2. **ADD** broth, picante sauce and tomatoes. Heat to a boil. Stir in pasta. Cook over medium heat 15 minutes or until done, stirring occasionally. Garnish with sour cream.

Tortellini Soup

(Pictured at right)

3 cloves garlic, minced
1 tablespoon butter or margarine
1 can (48 ounces) COLLEGE INN® Chicken or
    Beef Broth
1 package (about 19 ounces) frozen cheese
    tortellini
1 package (10 ounces) frozen chopped spinach,
    thawed
2 cans (14-1/2 ounces each) stewed tomatoes,
    undrained, cut into pieces
    Grated Parmesan cheese

In large saucepan over medium-high heat, cook
garlic in butter for 1 to 2 minutes. Add broth and
tortellini. Heat to a boil; reduce heat and simmer
10 minutes. Add spinach and tomatoes; simmer
5 minutes longer. Sprinkle each serving with cheese.
Makes 8 to 10 servings (about 11 cups)

Tomato-Lentil Soup

2 tablespoons olive oil
2 cups chopped onion
1 cup sliced celery
1 carrot, peeled, sliced
6 cups water
1 cup dry lentils
1 can (6 ounces) CONTADINA® Tomato Paste
1/2 cup dry red wine or chicken broth
1/4 cup chopped fresh parsley *or* 1 tablespoon
    dried parsley flakes
3 small chicken bouillon cubes
1 teaspoon salt
1/2 teaspoon Worcestershire sauce
1/4 teaspoon black pepper
    Shredded or grated Parmesan cheese (optional)

1. Heat oil in large saucepan over medium-high heat.
Add onion, celery and carrot; sauté until vegetables
are tender.

2. Stir in water, lentils, tomato paste, wine, parsley,
bouillon cubes, salt, Worcestershire sauce and
pepper. Bring to a boil.

3. Reduce heat to low; simmer, uncovered, 45 to
50 minutes or until lentils are tender. Sprinkle
with Parmesan cheese, if desired.   *Makes 9 cups*

Hearty White Bean Soup

1 tablespoon BERTOLLI® Olive Oil
1 medium onion, chopped
2 medium carrots, sliced
2 ribs celery, sliced
1 clove garlic
2 cans (19 ounces each) cannellini or white
    kidney beans, rinsed and drained
1 envelope LIPTON® RECIPE SECRETS® Savory
    Herb with Garlic Soup Mix
2 cups water
3 cups coarsely chopped escarole or spinach
1 medium tomato, diced
1/4 cup crumbled feta cheese (optional)

In 3-quart saucepan, heat oil over medium heat.
Add onion, carrots, celery and garlic; cook, stirring
occasionally, 5 minutes or until tender. Stir in beans
and soup mix blended with water. Bring to a boil
over high heat. Reduce heat to low and simmer
uncovered 15 minutes or until vegetables are tender.
Stir in escarole and tomato and cook 2 minutes or
until heated through. Top with cheese.
Makes about 6 cups

Vegetable Medley Soup

1 package KNORR® Recipe Classics™ Vegetable
    Soup, Dip and Recipe Mix
5 cups water
1 medium onion, sliced into thin wedges
1 cup sliced mushrooms
1 tablespoon barbecue sauce or 1 teaspoon
    Worcestershire sauce
1/8 to 1/4 teaspoon ground black pepper
2 cups diagonally sliced fresh asparagus or
    1 package (10 ounces) frozen cut asparagus

• In 4-quart Dutch oven or saucepan, combine
recipe mix, water, onion, mushrooms, barbecue
sauce and pepper.

• Bring to a boil over medium-high heat, stirring
occasionally. Reduce heat to low and simmer
covered 10 minutes, stirring occasionally.

• Add asparagus and simmer 5 minutes or until
vegetables are tender.   *Makes 6 (1-cup) servings*

Potato & Cheddar Soup

Potato & Cheddar Soup

(Pictured above)

2 cups water
2 cups cubed peeled red potatoes
3 tablespoons butter or margarine
1 small onion, finely chopped
3 tablespoons all-purpose flour
    Cayenne and black pepper to taste
3 cups milk
1/2 teaspoon sugar
1 cup shredded Cheddar cheese
1 cup cubed cooked ham

1. Bring water to a boil in large saucepan. Add potatoes and cook until tender. Drain, reserving liquid. Measure 1 cup, adding water if necessary.

2. Melt butter in saucepan over medium heat. Add onion; cook and stir until tender but not brown. Add flour; season with cayenne and black pepper. Cook 3 to 4 minutes. Gradually add potatoes, reserved liquid, milk and sugar to onion mixture; stir well. Add cheese and ham. Simmer over low heat 30 minutes, stirring frequently.

Makes 12 servings

Tip: Turn simple soup into a filling supper by serving it in individual bread bowls. Buy or bake small, round loaves of a hearty bread, such as Italian or sourdough. Slice a small piece from the top and then remove the inside of the loaf, leaving a 1-1/2 inch shell. Fill with soup and serve.

Southern Italian Clam Chowder

2 slices bacon, diced
1 cup chopped onion
1/2 cup chopped peeled carrots
1/2 cup chopped celery
2 cans (14.5 ounces each) CONTADINA®
    Recipe Ready Diced Tomatoes, undrained
1 can (8 ounces) CONTADINA Tomato Sauce
1 bottle (8 ounces) clam juice
1/2 teaspoon chopped fresh rosemary *or*
    1/4 teaspoon dried rosemary leaves, crushed
1/8 teaspoon ground black pepper
2 cans (6-1/2 ounces each) chopped clams,
    undrained

1. Sauté bacon in large saucepan until crisp. Add onion, carrots and celery; sauté for 2 to 3 minutes or until vegetables are tender.

2. Stir in undrained tomatoes, tomato sauce, clam juice, rosemary and pepper. Bring to a boil.

3. Reduce heat to low; simmer, uncovered, for 15 minutes. Stir in clams and juice. Simmer for 5 minutes or until heated through.

Makes 8 cups

Southwestern Soup

(Pictured on page 66)

1 bag (16 ounces) BIRDS EYE® frozen Corn
2 cans (15 ounces each) chili
1 cup hot water
1/2 cup chopped green bell pepper

• Combine all ingredients in saucepan.

• Cook over medium heat 10 to 12 minutes.

Makes 4 to 6 servings

Swanson® Hearty Beef Barley Soup

(Pictured below)

1 pound boneless beef sirloin *or* top round steak,
    cut into 1-inch cubes
2 cups sliced mushrooms
1/4 teaspoon garlic powder
2 cans (14 ounces each) SWANSON® Beef Broth
    (3-1/2 cups)
2 medium carrots, sliced
1/4 teaspoon dried thyme leaves, crushed
    Generous dash pepper
1/2 cup quick-cooking barley

COOK beef in nonstick saucepan until browned and juices evaporate, stirring often.

ADD mushrooms and garlic powder and cook until tender.

ADD broth, carrots, thyme and pepper. Heat to a boil. Stir in barley. Cover and cook over low heat 20 minutes or until barley is done.

Makes 4 servings

Hearty Buffalo-Style Vegetable Soup

2 cans (10-1/2 ounces *each*) condensed chicken
    or beef broth
2-1/2 cups water
3 tablespoons *Frank's® RedHot®* Original
    Cayenne Pepper Sauce
1 bag (16 ounces) frozen vegetables
1-1/2 cups diced cooked chicken or Polish sausage
6 thick slices French bread
3 tablespoons blue cheese, crumbled

1. Combine broth, water and **Frank's RedHot** Sauce in large saucepan. Heat to boiling. Add vegetables and chicken. Reduce heat to medium-low. Cook, covered, 7 minutes or until vegetables are tender.

2. Preheat oven broiler. Toast bread slightly on both sides. Top one side with blue cheese. Place under broiler until cheese is melted and bread is crisp.

3. Ladle soup into warm bowls. Top each bowl with one blue cheese toast. *Makes 6 servings*

Swanson® Hearty Beef Barley Soup

West Coast Bouillabaisse

(Pictured at right)

1 cup sliced onion
2 stalks celery, cut diagonally into slices
2 cloves garlic, minced
1 tablespoon vegetable oil
4 cups chicken broth
1 can (28 ounces) tomatoes with juice, cut up
1 can (6-1/2 ounces) minced clams with juice
1/2 cup dry white wine
1 teaspoon Worcestershire sauce
1/2 teaspoon dried thyme, crushed
1/4 teaspoon bottled hot pepper sauce
1 bay leaf
1 cup frozen cooked bay shrimp, thawed
1 (7-ounce) STARKIST Flavor Fresh Pouch®
Tuna (Albacore or Chunk Light)
Salt and pepper to taste
6 slices lemon
6 slices French bread

In Dutch oven sauté onion, celery and garlic in oil for 3 minutes. Stir in broth, tomatoes with juice, clams with juice, wine, Worcestershire, thyme, hot pepper sauce and bay leaf. Bring to a boil; reduce heat. Simmer for 15 minutes. Stir in shrimp and tuna; cook for 2 minutes to heat. Remove bay leaf. Season with salt and pepper. Garnish with lemon slices and serve with bread.   *Makes 6 servings*

Fiesta Pork Soup

1 pound lean ground pork
1 (14-1/2-ounce) can chicken broth
1 (8-ounce) jar picante sauce
1/8 teaspoon ground cumin
1/8 teaspoon ground pepper
1 (11-ounce) can condensed fiesta nacho cheese
soup
1 cup small round tortilla chips
1/4 cup sour cream

In medium saucepan, cook and stir pork until browned. Drain. Add chicken broth, picante sauce, cumin and pepper; bring to a boil. Reduce heat; cover and simmer 15 minutes, stirring occasionally. Stir in cheese soup; simmer until heated through. Do not boil. Pour into serving bowls; garnish with tortillas chips and sour cream.   *Makes 5 servings*

Favorite recipe from **National Pork Board**

Creamy Potato Soup

1 medium onion, finely chopped
1 tablespoon butter or margarine
1-1/4 pounds DOLE® Yukon Gold or White Potatoes,
peeled and diced
3 cups chicken broth
2 cups water
1/2 teaspoon dried thyme leaves, crushed
1/2 teaspoon salt
1/8 teaspoon white pepper
Pinch ground nutmeg
1/2 cup half and half or whipping cream

• Cook onion in melted butter in large saucepan until tender. Stir in potatoes, chicken broth, water, thyme, salt and pepper. Heat to boiling. Reduce heat to low; cook 10 to 15 minutes or until potatoes are tender. Cool slightly.

• Pour potato mixture into blender or food processor container. Cover; blend until smooth. Stir in nutmeg and half and half. Pour soup into saucepan. Heat until warm (do not boil).
Makes 5 servings

Hot 'n' Chilly Mango Melon Soup

1 medium cantaloupe, seeded and cut into
2-inch pieces (4 cups)
2 mangos, seeded and cut into 2-inch pieces
(2 cups)
1 cup plain yogurt
1/4 cup honey
2 to 3 tablespoons *Frank's*® *RedHot*® Original
Cayenne Pepper Sauce
1 tablespoon grated peeled fresh ginger
1 can (12 ounces) cold ginger ale

Combine cantaloupe and mango in blender or food processor. Cover; blend until very smooth. (Blend in batches if necessary.) Transfer to large bowl. Stir in yogurt, honey, **Frank's RedHot** Sauce and ginger. Cover; refrigerate at least 3 hours or overnight.

Stir in ginger ale just before serving. Garnish with mint, if desired.   *Makes 6 cups*

West Coast Bouillabaisse

Sausage & Rice Soup

(Pictured at right)

2 tablespoons butter or margarine
1 large or 2 medium leeks, white and light green
    parts sliced
2 carrots, thinly sliced
1 package (16 ounces) JENNIE-O TURKEY
    STORE® Extra Lean Smoked Sausage
2 cups diced mixed bell peppers (red and yellow)
2 cans (14-1/2 ounces each) chicken broth
1 cup water
3/4 cup quick-cooking brown rice, uncooked
1/2 teaspoon dried sage
1/4 teaspoon freshly ground black pepper
    Chopped fresh chives (optional)

Melt butter in large saucepan over medium heat.
Add leeks and carrots; cook 5 minutes, stirring
occasionally. Meanwhile, cut sausage into 1/2-inch
slices. Add sausage to saucepan; cook 5 minutes,
stirring occasionally. Add bell peppers, broth, water,
rice, sage and pepper; bring to a boil over high heat.
Reduce heat; simmer uncovered 15 minutes or until
rice is tender. Ladle into bowls; top with chives, if
desired. *Makes 6 servings*

Santa Fe Tomato Chowder

1 tablespoon butter or margarine
2 teaspoons minced garlic
4 ripe tomatoes, chopped
1 can (15 ounces) tomato sauce
1 cup water
1 cup frozen corn kernels
1/4 cup chopped fresh cilantro
1 tablespoon *Frank's® RedHot®* Original Cayenne
    Pepper Sauce
1/2 teaspoon chili powder
1 ripe avocado, peeled and chopped
1 cup (4 ounces) shredded Monterey Jack cheese
1-1/3 cups *French's®* French Fried Onions

1. Melt butter in large saucepan. Add garlic; cook and
stir 1 minute. Add tomatoes; cook 5 minutes. Stir in
tomato sauce, water, corn, cilantro, **Frank's RedHot**
Sauce and chili powder.

2. Bring to a boil over high heat. Reduce heat; simmer
10 minutes. Spoon soup into serving bowls; sprinkle
with avocado, cheese and French Fried Onions.
Makes 4 servings

Variation: For added Cheddar flavor, substitute
French's® **Cheddar French Fried Onions** for
the original flavor.

Velvety Leek & Wild Rice Soup

1/2 pound zucchini, peeled and coarsely chopped
1/2 pound fennel, coarsely chopped
2 large leeks, chopped (white part only)
2 tablespoons butter
4 cups chicken broth
4 tablespoons chopped fresh dill, divided
    Salt and white pepper to taste
1 cup heavy cream
3 cups cooked wild rice

In large saucepan, cook zucchini, fennel and leeks
in butter over medium heat 10 to 15 minutes. Add
broth, 3 tablespoons dill, salt and pepper. Simmer,
uncovered, 20 minutes. Remove from heat; purée in
food processor or blender (in batches if necessary).
When ready to serve, return to saucepan over low
heat. Add cream, adjust seasonings and heat through.
Do not boil. In bottom of each shallow soup bowl,
mound 1/2 cup wild rice in center. Ladle soup
around rice and garnish with remaining 1 tablespoon
dill. *Makes 6 servings*

Favorite recipe from **Minnesota Cultivated Wild
Rice Council**

Helpful Hint

*Leeks are notorious for collecting
soil and grit between the leaf layers;
they must be cleaned well before
using. Make a deep cut into each
leek lengthwise to within an inch
of the root end. (If the leek is cut
into halves it will fall apart.)
Rinse the leeks thoroughly
under cold running water to
remove embedded soil.*

Swanson® Hearty Chicken Tortilla Soup

(Pictured on page 66)

1 pound boneless chicken breasts, cut up
2 cans (14 ounces each) SWANSON® Chicken
    Broth (3-1/2 cups)
1/2 cup uncooked regular long-grain white rice
1 teaspoon cumin
1 can (11 ounces) Mexican-style corn
1 cup PACE® Chunky Salsa
2 tablespoons lime juice
1 tablespoon chopped fresh cilantro
    Crisp Tortilla Strips (recipe follows)

SPRAY saucepan with vegetable cooking spray and heat 1 minute. Add chicken and cook until browned, stirring often.

ADD broth, rice and cumin. Heat to a boil. Cover and cook over low heat 20 minutes.

STIR in corn, salsa, lime juice and cilantro and heat through. Top with *Crisp Tortilla Strips*.

Makes 6 servings

Crisp Tortilla Strips: Preheat oven to 425°F. Cut 4 corn tortillas into thin strips and place on baking sheet. Spray with vegetable cooking spray. Bake 10 minutes or until golden.

Italian Vegetable Soup

1 package KNORR® Recipe Classics™ Tomato
    Basil Soup, Dip and Recipe Mix
4 cups water
2 cups sliced fennel or broccoli florets
1 large zucchini, diced (about 2 cups)
1 teaspoon dried oregano
    Grated Parmesan cheese (optional)

In 4-quart Dutch oven, combine recipe mix, water, fennel, zucchini and oregano. Bring to a boil over medium-high heat, stirring occasionally.

Reduce heat, cover and simmer 15 minutes or until vegetables are tender, stirring occasionally.

Sprinkle lightly with Parmesan cheese, if desired.

Makes 6 (1-cup) servings

Hearty Pasta and Chick-Pea Chowder

(Pictured at right)

6 ounces uncooked rotini pasta
2 tablespoons olive oil
3/4 cup chopped onion
1/2 cup thinly sliced carrot
1/2 cup chopped celery
2 garlic cloves, minced
1/4 cup all-purpose flour
1-1/2 teaspoons dried Italian seasoning
1/8 teaspoon crushed red pepper flakes
1/8 teaspoon black pepper
2 cans (14-1/2 ounces each) chicken broth
1 can (15 ounces) chick-peas, rinsed and drained
1 can (14-1/2 ounces) Italian-style stewed
    tomatoes
6 slices bacon
    Grated Parmesan cheese

Cook rotini according to package directions. Rinse, drain and set aside.

Meanwhile, heat oil in 4-quart Dutch oven over medium-high heat until hot. Add onion, carrot, celery and garlic. Cook and stir over medium heat 5 to 6 minutes or until vegetables are crisp-tender.

Remove from heat. Stir in flour, Italian seasoning, red pepper flakes and black pepper until well blended. Gradually stir in broth. Return to heat and bring to a boil, stirring frequently. Boil, stirring constantly, 1 minute. Reduce heat to medium. Stir in cooked pasta, chick-peas and tomatoes. Cook 5 minutes or until heated through.

Meanwhile, place bacon between double layer of paper towels on paper plate. Microwave at HIGH 5 to 6 minutes or until bacon is crisp. Drain and crumble.

Sprinkle each serving with bacon and grated cheese. Serve immediately.

Makes 6 servings (about 7 cups)

Serving Suggestion: Serve with crusty bread, salad greens tossed with Italian dressing, and fruit cobbler.

Hearty Pasta and Chick-Pea Chowder

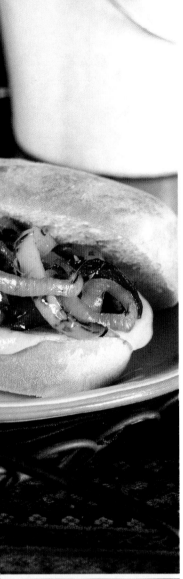

Sandwiches

Over the Top Grilled Cheese

(Pictured at left)

> 1/2 cup Squeeze PARKAY®, divided
> 1-1/2 cups chopped pecans
> 3 tablespoons honey
> 1/4 teaspoon ground cinnamon
> 1/8 teaspoon nutmeg
> 8 slices bread
> 12 (1-ounce) slices COUNTY LINE® Cheddar Cheese
> 1 large Granny Smith apple, sliced 1/4 inch thick

1. Melt 1/3 cup Parkay over low heat; stir in pecans until well coated. Stir in honey, cinnamon and nutmeg until well blended.

2. Using pastry brush, spread remaining Parkay over entire surface of one side of each slice of bread.

3. Place 4 slices bread, Parkay side down, in large nonstick skillet. Top with 2 slices Cheddar cheese to cover. Spread about 1/3 cup pecan mixture on top of cheese. Place 3 apple slices on each sandwich; top with one slice cheese. Top with remaining bread slices, Parkay side up. Cover pan with lid and cook over medium-low heat for 5 minutes.

4. Lift sandwiches with spatula to check color (sandwiches should be deep golden brown before turning). Using two spatulas, carefully flip sandwiches to cook other side. Cover and cook 5 minutes or until golden brown on both sides.

Makes 4 servings

Helpful Hint

Granny Smith apples provide a tart flavor that balances the sweet honey in this sandwich. McIntosh apples can also be used.

Clockwise from top left: *Ham, Apple and Cheese Turnovers (p. 104), BelGioioso® Asiago and Sweet Pepper Sandwiches (p. 105), Over the Top Grilled Cheese and Hot Beef Sandwich (p. 94)*

Easy Barbecue Sloppy Joes

1 pound lean ground beef or turkey
1 small onion, chopped
1 green bell pepper, chopped
1 can (10-3/4 ounces) condensed cream of
    tomato soup or tomato bisque, undiluted
1/4 cup prepared barbecue sauce
1/2 teaspoon salt
1/2 teaspoon hot pepper sauce (optional)
4 BAYS® English Muffins, split, lightly toasted
4 slices American or Cheddar cheese, cut in half
    diagonally

Crumble meat into large deep skillet; add onion and bell pepper. Cook over medium heat until meat is no longer pink, stirring occasionally. Pour off drippings. Add soup, barbecue sauce, salt and hot pepper sauce; simmer, uncovered, 8 minutes, stirring occasionally. Serve over split muffins topped with cheese.

Makes 4 servings

Grilled Ratatouille Sandwich

(Pictured at right)

1/3 cup olive oil
1/3 cup *French's®* Bold n' Spicy Brown Mustard
1 tablespoon chopped fresh rosemary *or*
    1 teaspoon dried rosemary
3 cloves garlic, minced
1/2 cup kalamata olives, pitted and chopped
1/2 small eggplant (about 3/4 pound)
1 medium zucchini
1 large red onion
2 large ripe plum tomatoes
1 large red bell pepper
1 (12-inch) sourdough baguette, cut lengthwise
    in half (about 12 ounces)

1. Combine oil, mustard, rosemary and garlic in bowl. Place olives in food processor; add 2 tablespoons mustard mixture. Cover and process until smooth; set aside. Reserve remaining mustard mixture.

2. Cut eggplant and zucchini lengthwise into 1/4-inch-thick slices. Cut onion and tomatoes crosswise into 1/2-inch-thick slices. Cut red bell pepper lengthwise into 2-inch-wide pieces; discard seeds. Place vegetables on platter. Baste with reserved mustard mixture.

3. Place vegetables on oiled grid or vegetable basket. Grill over medium-high heat 3 to 5 minutes or until vegetables are tender, basting and turning once.

4. To serve, remove and discard excess bread from bread halves. Spread olive mixture on cut surfaces of bread. Layer vegetables on bottom half of bread; cover with top half. Cut crosswise into 4 portions.

Makes 4 servings

Mediterranean Pork Sandwiches

3/4 cup LAWRY'S® Lemon Pepper Marinade
    With Lemon Juice, divided
6 boneless pork loin chops, thinly sliced
2 teaspoons BERTOLLI® Olive Oil
1 onion, halved and sliced
1 loaf French bread, halved lengthwise and cut
    into 6 sections
1/4 cup shredded Parmesan cheese
1 teaspoon crumbled dried rosemary
6 strips roasted red bell pepper

In large resealable plastic bag, place 1/2 cup Lemon Pepper Marinade and pork; seal bag. Marinate in refrigerator for 30 minutes. Meanwhile, in large skillet, heat oil over medium-high heat. Add onion and cook until golden brown and tender, about 10 minutes. Spoon onion into small bowl and set aside. Remove pork from bag, discarding used marinade. Add pork to same skillet and brown for about 1 to 2 minutes per side until thoroughly cooked. Brush cut tops of bread with remaining Marinade. Sprinkle evenly with cheese and rosemary. Broil bread until lightly browned around edges, about 2 minutes. Top each bread "bottom" with pork, roasted pepper, onion and bread top.

Makes 6 servings

Variation: For a flavor variation, try LAWRY'S® Herb & Garlic Marinade With Lemon Juice instead of Lemon Pepper Marinade.

Grilled Ratatouille Sandwich

Buffalo-Style Wraps

(Pictured at right)

2/3 cup *Frank's® RedHot®* Original Cayenne
    Pepper Sauce, divided
1 tablespoon oil
4 boneless skinless chicken breast halves
1/4 cup blue cheese salad dressing
1 cup shredded lettuce
1 cup (4 ounces) shredded Monterey Jack cheese
4 (10-inch) flour tortillas, heated

1. Combine *1/3 cup **Frank's RedHot** Sauce* and oil in resealable plastic food storage bag. Add chicken. Seal bag; toss to coat evenly. Marinate in refrigerator 30 minutes or overnight.

2. Broil or grill chicken 10 to 15 minutes or until no longer pink in center. Slice chicken into long thin strips. In bowl, toss chicken with remaining *1/3 cup **Frank's RedHot** Sauce* and dressing.

3. Arrange chicken, lettuce and cheese down center of tortillas, dividing evenly. Fold bottom third of each tortilla over filling; fold sides towards center. Tightly roll up to secure filling. Cut in half to serve.

Makes 4 servings

Grilled Reuben Sandwiches

1/4 cup light or regular mayonnaise
2 tablespoons chili sauce or ketchup
1 teaspoon prepared horseradish
8 slices rye or pumpernickel bread
2 tablespoons butter or margarine, softened
8 slices SARGENTO® Deli Style Sliced Swiss
    Cheese
1 pound thinly sliced deli corned beef or turkey
    pastrami
3/4 cup well drained sauerkraut

1. In small bowl, combine mayonnaise, chili sauce and horseradish; mix well.

2. Spread one side of each slice of bread with butter. Place cheese over other side of bread. Arrange corned beef over half of bread, top with mayonnaise mixture and sauerkraut. Close sandwiches with remaining half of bread, cheese side down and butter side up.

3. Cook on preheated large griddle (or cook two sandwiches at a time in large skillet) over medium-low heat 4 to 5 minutes per side or until bread is toasted and cheese is melted.
Makes 4 servings

Hot Beef Sandwiches

(Pictured on page 90)

1 beef chuck roast (3 to 4 pounds), cut into
    chunks
1 jar (6 ounces) sliced dill pickles, undrained
1 can (14 ounces) crushed tomatoes with
    Italian seasoning
1 medium onion, diced
4 garlic cloves, minced
1 teaspoon mustard seeds
    Hamburger buns

SLOW COOKER DIRECTIONS

1. Place beef in slow cooker. Pour pickles with juice over top of beef. Add tomatoes, onion, garlic and mustard seeds.

2. Cover; cook on LOW 8 to 10 hours.

3. Remove beef from slow cooker. Shred beef with two forks. Return beef to tomato mixture; mix well. Serve beef mixture on buns.

Makes 6 to 8 servings

Serving Suggestion: Garnish sandwiches with lettuce, sliced tomatoes, Bermuda red onion, shredded slaw or other fixings to taste.

Philly-Style Cheese Steaks

1 pound minute or cubed steaks
1 envelope LIPTON® RECIPE SECRETS®
    Onion Soup Mix
1/2 cup water
4 hoagie or Italian rolls, split
1 cup shredded Cheddar cheese (about
    4 ounces)

1. In 10-inch skillet, cook steaks over medium-high heat 2 minutes or until desired doneness, turning once. Remove steaks and keep warm.

2. In same skillet, add soup mix blended with water; cook 2 minutes. Return steaks to skillet and cook 1 minute or until heated through. To serve, arrange steaks on rolls; top with sauce and Cheddar cheese.
Makes 4 servings

Buffalo-Style Wraps

Add vegetables and stir-fry 2 minutes until just tender. Pour sauce mixture over stir-fry and cook 1 minute.

3. Arrange cabbage on rolls and top with equal portions of stir-fry. Close rolls. Serve warm.

Makes 4 servings

Tip: If desired, substitute 1 pound sliced boneless pork or steak for the chicken.

Italian-Style Shredded Beef

1 (2-1/2-pound) boneless eye of round beef roast
1 medium onion, thinly sliced
1 (6-ounce) can Italian flavored tomato paste
6 teaspoons HERB-OX® beef flavored bouillon
1/2 cup water
12 kaiser rolls
12 (1-ounce) slices Provolone cheese

SLOW COOKER DIRECTIONS

Place roast in 3-1/2-quart slow cooker. Add onion and remaining ingredients. Cover and cook on HIGH for 5 to 6 hours or until meat is tender. Remove roast from cooker. Using two forks, shred meat. Return meat to cooker; stirring to coat with sauce. Evenly divide meat among Kaiser rolls. Top with cheese and serve. *Makes 12 servings*

Glazed Teriyaki Chicken Stir-Fry Sub

Glazed Teriyaki Chicken Stir-Fry Sub

(Pictured above)

1/4 cup *French's*® Honey Dijon Mustard
2 tablespoons teriyaki sauce
1 tablespoon sugar
1 tablespoon grated, peeled fresh gingerroot
1 tablespoon cider or red wine vinegar
1 tablespoon vegetable oil
1 pound boneless skinless chicken, cut into thin strips
1 cup coarsely chopped red or yellow bell peppers
1/2 cup each coarsely chopped red onion and plum tomatoes
4 Italian hero rolls, split (about 8 inches each)
2 cups shredded Napa cabbage or romaine lettuce

1. Combine mustard, teriyaki sauce, sugar, ginger and vinegar in small bowl; set aside.

2. Heat oil in large skillet or wok over high heat. Stir-fry chicken 5 minutes until no longer pink.

Helpful Hint

When using a slow cooker, keep the lid on! The slow cooker can take as long as 30 minutes to regain heat lost when the cover is removed. Remove the cover only when instructed to do so by the recipe. Spinning the cover until the condensation falls off will allow you to see inside the slow cooker without removing the lid.

Apple-Cheddar Panini

(Pictured below)

1 tablespoon butter
2 cups thinly sliced apples*
1/4 teaspoon ground cinnamon
8 teaspoons apple jelly
8 slices egg bread
4 (1-ounce) slices mild Cheddar cheese

Use sweet apples such as Fuji or Gala.

Melt butter in large nonstick skillet. Add apple slices and sprinkle with cinnamon. Cook over medium heat 5 minutes, stirring frequently, or until golden and tender. Remove from skillet; wipe out skillet with paper towel.

Spread 2 teaspoons apple jelly on each of 4 bread slices; top with 1 cheese slice. Arrange 1/4 of apple slices over each cheese slice. Top with remaining 4 bread slices.

Heat same skillet over medium-high heat. Place each sandwich in skillet. Do not crowd. Press lightly with spatula. Cook sandwiches over medium-low heat 3 to 4 minutes per side or until bread is browned and cheese melts. Cut each sandwich diagonally into halves.   *Makes 4 servings*

Shrimp Remoulade Subs

1 pound small or medium shrimp, peeled and
   deveined
1/4 cup finely chopped celery
1/4 cup finely chopped green onions
1/4 cup country-style mustard
1 tablespoon chopped fresh parsley
1 tablespoon olive oil
1 tablespoon cider vinegar
2 teaspoons TABASCO® brand Pepper Sauce
4 (6-inch) French rolls
   Red leaf lettuce
1 ounce Brie cheese, thinly sliced

Place shrimp in 2-quart saucepan with enough water to cover. Heat to boiling over high heat; boil 2 minutes or until shrimp turn pink. Drain well; set aside to cool. Combine celery, green onions, mustard, parsley, oil, vinegar and TABASCO® Sauce in medium bowl. Add shrimp; mix well.

To serve, cut rolls crosswise in half. Arrange lettuce on bottom halves of rolls; top with shrimp remoulade mixture, Brie slices and remaining roll halves.   *Makes 4 servings*

Apple-Cheddar Panini

Sausage, Pepper & Onion Heroes

(Pictured at right)

1 green bell pepper
1 yellow or red bell pepper
2 tablespoons olive oil, divided
4 slices (1/4 inch) red or yellow onion, separated into rings
1 package JENNIE-O TURKEY STORE®
    Sweet Lean Italian Sausage
5 hoagie or submarine sandwich rolls, split, toasted if desired
3/4 cup prepared pizza or spaghetti sauce, heated

Prepare grill or preheat broiler. Cut bell peppers lengthwise into 1/4-inch strips. Heat 1 tablespoon oil in large skillet over medium heat. Add pepper strips and onion rings; cook about 15 minutes or until vegetables are tender, stirring frequently. Sprinkle lightly with salt, if desired. Meanwhile, brush remaining 1 tablespoon oil over sausages. Grill or broil about 5 inches from heat source 14 to 16 minutes or until lightly browned and no longer pink in center, turning occasionally. Serve sausages in rolls topped with pizza sauce and vegetables.

Makes 5 servings

Rice and Chicken Wraps

8 boneless, skinless chicken tenderloins
2 cups water
1 box UNCLE BEN'S® Fast Cook Recipe Long Grain & Wild Rice
1/2 cup ranch salad dressing
1 cup shredded lettuce
8 (10-inch) flour tortillas

Spray large skillet with nonstick cooking spray. Add chicken; cook over medium-high heat 10 to 12 minutes or until lightly browned on both sides. Add water, rice and contents of seasoning packet. Bring to a boil. Cover; reduce heat and simmer 10 minutes or until chicken is no longer pink in center and liquid is absorbed. Stir in salad dressing.

Spoon rice mixture evenly down center of each tortilla; top with lettuce. Fold in both sides of tortillas; roll up tortilla tightly from bottom, keeping filling firmly packed. Slice each wrap diagonally into 2 pieces. *Makes 4 servings*

Tuna Supper Sandwiches

2 cups shredded Cheddar cheese
1/3 cup chopped green onions, including tops
1/3 cup chopped red bell pepper
1 can (2-1/4 ounces) sliced ripe olives, drained
2 tablespoons minced fresh parsley
1 teaspoon curry powder
    Seasoned salt to taste
1 (7-ounce) STARKIST Flavor Fresh Pouch® Tuna
    (Albacore or Chunk Light)
1/2 cup mayonnaise
6 soft French rolls (7 inches *each*), halved lengthwise

In medium bowl, place cheese, onions, red pepper, olives, parsley, curry powder and salt; mix lightly. Add tuna and mayonnaise; toss lightly with fork. Cover baking sheet with foil; place rolls on foil. Spread about 1/3 cup mixture on each half. Bake in 450°F oven 10 to 12 minutes or until tops are bubbling and beginning to brown. Cool slightly before serving. *Makes 12 servings*

Summer Ham Sandwiches

1/2 cup vanilla yogurt
2 teaspoons orange juice
1 teaspoon HOUSE OF TSANG® Light Soy Sauce
1/2 teaspoon grated orange peel
1/4 teaspoon ground ginger
1 cup (6 ounces) diced CURE 81® ham
1/3 cup chopped water chestnuts
4 romaine lettuce leaves
1 avocado, peeled and thinly sliced
1 grapefruit, peeled and sliced
1 orange, peeled and sliced
4 slices rye bread

In bowl, combine yogurt, orange juice, soy sauce, orange peel and ginger. In bowl, combine ham, water chestnuts and 2 tablespoons yogurt mixture. Arrange lettuce, avocado slices, grapefruit and orange sections on bread slices. Spoon ham mixture over each. Serve with remaining yogurt mixture. *Makes 4 servings*

Sausage, Pepper & Onion Heroes

Quick & Tangy Roast Beef Sandwiches

(Pictured at right)

1 can (10-3/4 ounces) CAMPBELL'S®
    Tomato Soup
2 tablespoons vinegar
1 tablespoon packed brown sugar
1 tablespoon Worcestershire sauce
12 ounces deli sliced cooked roast beef
4 hamburger rolls

1. **MIX** soup, vinegar, sugar and Worcestershire in skillet. Heat to a boil.

2. **ADD** beef and heat through.

3. **SERVE** on rolls.   *Makes 4 sandwiches*

Vegetable Calzones

1 loaf (1 pound) frozen bread dough
1 package (10 ounces) frozen chopped broccoli,
    thawed and well drained
1 cup (8 ounces) BELGIOIOSO® Ricotta Cheese
1 cup (8 ounces) shredded BELGIOIOSO® Sharp
    Provolone Cheese
1 clove garlic, minced
1/4 teaspoon black pepper
1 egg
1 tablespoon water
4 cups marinara sauce
    Grated BELGIOIOSO® Parmesan Cheese

Thaw bread dough; let rise according to package directions. Combine broccoli, BelGioioso® Ricotta, BelGioioso Provolone Cheese, garlic and pepper. Punch down bread dough; turn out onto lightly floured surface. Divide into 4 equal pieces. Roll out each piece into 8-inch circle. Place about 1/4 cup cheese mixture on half of circle, leaving 1-inch border. Fold dough over to cover filling, forming semi-circle; press edges with fork tines to seal.

Beat egg and water in small bowl. Brush with egg mixture. Place on greased baking sheet. Bake at 350°F 30 minutes or until brown and puffed. Transfer to rack; cool 10 minutes. Heat marinara sauce until hot and pour over calzones. Top with BelGioioso Parmesan Cheese.   *Makes 4 servings*

Little Italy Sausage Sandwiches

1 pound Italian sausage links, casings removed
1 large onion, sliced (about 1 cup)
1 can (6 ounces) HUNT'S® Tomato Paste
1 cup water
2 cups mixed salad greens
    Bottled balsamic salad dressing
4 French rolls (about 6 inches long), split
    lengthwise

COOK sausage and onion over medium-high heat in a nonstick skillet until sausage is crumbly and no longer pink and onion slices are soft. Blend in paste and water.

BRING to a boil; reduce heat to low and cook for 10 minutes. Season sauce to taste.

TOSS salad greens with dressing. Fill each roll with equal amounts of greens and sausage with sauce. Serve immediately.   *Makes 4 servings*

Hot Smoked Turkey Submarine Sandwich

1 tablespoon olive oil
1 teaspoon dried basil leaves
1/8 teaspoon garlic powder
4 submarine sandwich rolls or French bread
    rolls, cut lengthwise into halves
6 ounces sliced mozzarella cheese
1 package (6 ounces) HILLSHIRE FARM®
    Deli Select Smoked Turkey Breast
2 tablespoons sliced pitted black olives
2 tomatoes, thinly sliced
1/8 teaspoon coarsely ground black pepper

Preheat oven to 375°F.

Combine oil, basil and garlic powder in small bowl. Brush cut sides of rolls with oil mixture. On bottom half of rolls, evenly layer 1/2 of cheese, Smoked Turkey, olives, remaining cheese and tomatoes. Sprinkle with pepper; top with roll top. Wrap each sandwich in heavy duty aluminum foil. Bake 10 minutes or until heated through.

Makes 4 servings

Quick & Tangy Roast Beef Sandwich

Chick-Pea Burgers

(Pictured at right)

1 can (15 ounces) chick-peas, rinsed and drained
1/3 cup chopped carrots
1/3 cup herbed croutons
1/4 cup chopped fresh parsley
1/4 cup chopped onion
1 egg white
1 teaspoon minced garlic
1 teaspoon lemon peel
1/2 teaspoon pepper
1/8 teaspoon salt (optional)
4 whole-grain hamburger buns
 Tomato slices, lettuce leaves and salsa
 (optional)

1. Place chick-peas, carrots, croutons, parsley, onion, egg white, garlic, lemon peel, pepper and salt, if desired, in food processor fitted with metal blade; cover and process until combined. Shape mixture into 4 patties.

2. Spray 12-inch nonstick skillet with cooking spray; heat over medium heat. Add patties to skillet; cook 4 to 5 minutes or until browned. Spray tops of patties with cooking spray; turn and cook 4 to 5 minutes or until browned.

3. Serve patties on buns with tomato, lettuce and salsa, if desired.   *Makes 4 servings*

Calzone Italiano

Pizza dough for one 14-inch pizza
1 can (15 ounces) CONTADINA® Pizza Sauce, divided
3 ounces sliced pepperoni *or* 1/2 pound crumbled Italian sausage, cooked, drained
2 tablespoons chopped green bell pepper
1 cup (4 ounces) shredded mozzarella cheese
1 cup (8 ounces) ricotta cheese

1. Divide dough into 4 equal portions. Place on lightly floured, large, rimless cookie sheet. Press or roll out dough to 7-inch circles.

2. Spread 2 tablespoons pizza sauce onto half of each circle to within 1/2 inch of edge; top with 1/4 each pepperoni, bell pepper and mozzarella cheese.

3. Spoon 1/4 cup ricotta cheese onto remaining half of each circle; fold dough over. Press edges together tightly to seal. Cut slits into top of dough to allow steam to escape.

4. Bake in preheated 350°F oven for 20 to 25 minutes or until crusts are golden brown. Meanwhile, heat remaining pizza sauce; serve over calzones.
Makes 4 servings

Note: If desired, 1 large calzone may be made instead of 4 individual calzones. To prepare, shape dough into 1 (13-inch) circle. Spread 1/2 cup pizza sauce onto half of dough; proceed as above. Bake for 25 minutes.

Southwest Turkey & Rice Wraps

2-1/2 cups shredded cooked turkey
3/4 cup long grain white rice
1 package (1 ounce) LAWRY'S® Taco Spices & Seasonings
1-3/4 cups water
1 can (8 ounces) tomato sauce
1 large tomato, chopped
1/3 cup chopped green onion
8 large (burrito size) flour tortillas, warmed to soften
 Shredded cheddar cheese, salsa and guacamole (optional garnish)

In large deep skillet, add turkey, rice, Taco Spices & Seasonings, water and tomato sauce. Bring to a boil; cover, reduce heat to low and cook for 20 minutes. Stir in tomato and onion. Scoop 1/2 cup filling on each tortilla. Fold in sides and roll up to enclose filling. Top each wrap with cheese, if desired, and heat in 350°F oven until cheese melts, about 5 minutes. Garnish each wrap with salsa and guacamole, if desired.   *Makes 8 servings*

Variations: Use one pound browned and drained ground beef or chicken instead of turkey. For a flavor twist, try 1 package Lawry's® Burrito Spices & Seasonings or Lawry's® Hot Taco Spices & Seasonings in place of Taco Spices & Seasonings.

Chick-Pea Burger

Tuscan-Style Sausage Sandwich

Ham, Apple and Cheese Turnovers

(Pictured on page 90)

  1-1/4 cups chopped cooked ham
    3/4 cup finely chopped red apple
    3/4 cup (3 ounces) shredded Cheddar cheese
      1 tablespoon brown mustard (optional)
      1 package (about 14 ounces) refrigerated pizza dough

1. Preheat oven to 400°F. Spray 15×10×1-inch jelly-roll pan with nonstick cooking spray. Combine ham, apple, cheese and mustard, if desired, in medium bowl.

2. Roll pizza dough into 15×10-inch rectangle on lightly floured surface. Cut into six (5-inch) squares. Top each square with 1/6 of ham mixture. Moisten edges with water. Fold dough over filling. Press edges to seal. Place on prepared baking sheet.

3. Prick tops of each turnover with tines of fork. Bake about 15 minutes or until golden brown. Serve warm or allow to cool on wire rack 1 hour.

Makes 6 servings

Tuscan-Style Sausage Sandwiches

(Pictured above)

  1 pound hot or sweet Italian sausage links, sliced
  1 box (10 ounces) frozen chopped spinach, thawed and squeezed dry
  1 small onion, sliced
1/2 cup fresh or drained canned sliced mushrooms
  1 jar (1 pound 10 ounces) RAGÚ® Robusto!® Pasta Sauce
  1 loaf Italian or French bread (about 16 inches long), cut into 4 rolls

In 12-inch skillet, brown sausage over medium-high heat. Stir in spinach, onion and mushrooms. Cook, stirring occasionally, 5 minutes or until sausage is cooked through. Stir in Ragú Pasta Sauce; heat through.

For each sandwich, split open each roll and evenly spoon in sausage mixture. Sprinkle with crushed red pepper flakes, if desired. *Makes 4 servings*

Provençal Chicken Sandwich

1/2 pound sliced deli chicken breast, cut into 1/2-inch-wide strips
1/2 cup sliced roasted red peppers
1/2 cup sliced red onion
1/4 cup sliced pitted ripe olives
  1 tablespoon extra-virgin olive oil
  1 tablespoon red wine vinegar
1/2 teaspoon salt
1/4 teaspoon pepper
  2 tablespoons chopped fresh parsley
  4 submarine or hoagie sandwich rolls

1. Combine chicken, roasted peppers, onion and olives in medium bowl.

2. Whisk together oil, vinegar, salt and pepper in small bowl. Pour over chicken mixture; toss until coated. Cover and refrigerate at least 30 minutes or up to 24 hours.

3. Stir parsley into chicken mixture. Cut rolls in half; fill with chicken mixture. Serve immediately.

Makes 4 servings

Morning Meltdown

(Pictured below)

8 eggs, beaten
1/4 cup *French's® Classic Yellow®* Mustard or
    French's® Sweet 'n Zesty Mustard
4 soft onion rolls, split
8 slices sandwich-style dill pickles
8 slices deli ham (6 ounces)
4 slices Swiss cheese
    Frank's® RedHot® Cayenne Pepper Sauce
    (optional)

1. Coat nonstick skillet with vegetable cooking spray. Heat over medium-high heat. Add eggs and scramble just until eggs are set.

2. Spread mustard on bottom half of rolls. Top with pickles, ham and cheese, dividing evenly. Spoon eggs on top of cheese layer and cover with top half of rolls.

3. Wrap sandwiches in foil. Bake 10 minutes at 400°F until hot and cheese melts slightly. If desired, splash on *Frank's® RedHot®* Sauce. *Makes 4 servings*

BelGioioso® Asiago and Sweet Pepper Sandwiches

(Pictured on page 90)

2 tablespoons olive oil
1 red bell pepper, sliced into strips
1 yellow bell pepper, sliced into strips
1 medium onion, thinly sliced
1 teaspoon dried thyme
    Hot pepper sauce to taste
    Salt and pepper to taste
4 ounces BELGIOIOSO® Asiago Cheese,
    thinly sliced
4 Italian sandwich rolls, sliced open lengthwise

Heat olive oil in large skillet. Add red and yellow bell peppers and cook over medium heat about 6 minutes. Add onion and cook until vegetables are softened. Stir in thyme, hot pepper sauce, salt and pepper to taste.

Layer BelGioioso® Asiago Cheese on bottom half of bread and top with vegetable mixture. Serve immediately. *Makes 4 servings*

Morning Meltdown

Turkey and Slaw Sandwiches

1 cup thinly sliced cabbage
1/2 cup thinly sliced red bell pepper
1 tablespoon mayonnaise or salad dressing
1 teaspoon prepared mustard
8 slices rye bread
12 ounces JENNIE-O TURKEY STORE® Turkey, cooked, sliced

In bowl, combine cabbage, bell pepper, mayonnaise and mustard. Let stand 15 minutes. Spread cabbage mixture on 4 bread slices. Top with turkey slices. Cover with remaining bread slices.

Makes 4 servings

Grilled Steak & Blue Cheese Sandwiches

(Pictured at right)

6 to 8 cloves Grilled Garlic (recipe follows), mashed
4 boneless lean, tender beef steaks, such as beef tenderloin or top loin steaks (4 to 6 ounces each), 1 inch thick
Freshly ground or cracked black pepper
2 medium yellow onions
Olive oil
4 French rolls
1/2 cup crumbled blue cheese
2 small tomatoes, sliced
Mixed greens

Prepare Grilled Garlic. Spread garlic onto both sides of steaks; season generously with pepper. Slice onions into 1/2-inch-thick slices; brush lightly with oil. Insert wooden picks into onion slices from edges to prevent separating into rings. (Soak wooden picks in hot water 15 minutes to prevent burning.) Lightly oil grid to prevent sticking. Place steaks in center of covered grill over medium-hot KINGSFORD® Briquets; place onion slices around steaks. Grill steaks and onion slices 12 to 15 minutes or until steaks are medium-rare or to desired doneness, turning once. Remove steaks from grill; keep warm. Move onions to center of grill and continue grilling 10 to 15 minutes longer until tender and golden brown. Grill rolls, cut sides down, until toasted. Slice steaks into thin strips. Arrange beef over grilled rolls; top with blue cheese, onions, tomatoes and greens. *Makes 4 sandwiches*

Grilled Garlic

1 or 2 heads garlic
Olive oil

Peel outermost papery skin from garlic heads. Brush heads with oil. Grill heads at edge of grid on covered grill over medium-hot KINGSFORD® Briquets 30 to 45 minutes or until cloves are soft and buttery. Remove from grill; cool slightly. Gently squeeze softened garlic head from root end so that cloves slip out of skins into small bowl. Use immediately or cover and refrigerate up to 1 week.

Apple-Kissed Turkey Burgers

CRISCO® No-Stick Butter Flavor Spray
3/4 pound ground turkey
1/2 cup shredded, peeled red apple
2 green onions, thinly sliced
3/4 teaspoon lemon pepper
1/4 teaspoon salt
1/8 teaspoon apple pie spice*
1/2 cup bottled chili sauce
1/2 cup SMUCKER'S® Apple Jelly
4 plain or whole wheat hamburger buns, split (toasted, if desired)
Lettuce (optional)

Substitute a pinch of cinnamon and a pinch of allspice for apple pie spice, if desired.

1. Preheat broiler. Spray broiler pan with cooking spray.

2. Combine turkey, apple, green onions, lemon pepper, salt and apple pie spice in large bowl. Shape mixture into 4 patties about 3/4 inch thick. Combine chili sauce and apple jelly in small saucepan.

3. Broil patties about 6 inches from heat for 6 minutes. Turn with slotted spatula; broil 6 minutes more or until no longer pink in center.

4. Meanwhile, place sauce over medium heat; cook for 10 minutes, stirring occasionally. Cool slightly.

5. Place lettuce, if desired, and burgers on bottom halves of buns. Top each with 2 tablespoons sauce. Cover with bun tops. Serve immediately.

Makes 4 servings

Grilled Steak & Blue Cheese Sandwiches

Breads

Lots o' Chocolate Bread

(Pictured at left)

2 cups mini semisweet chocolate chips, divided
2/3 cup packed light brown sugar
1/2 cup (1 stick) butter, softened
2 eggs
2-1/2 cups all-purpose flour
1-1/2 cups applesauce
1-1/2 teaspoons vanilla
1 teaspoon baking soda
1 teaspoon baking powder
1/2 teaspoon salt
1 tablespoon shortening (do not use butter, margarine, spread or oil)

1. Preheat oven to 350°F. Grease 5 (5-1/2×3-inch) mini loaf pans. Place 1 cup chocolate chips in small microwavable bowl. Microwave at HIGH 1 minute; stir. Microwave at 30-second intervals, stirring after each interval, until chocolate is melted and smooth; set aside.

2. Beat brown sugar and butter in large bowl until creamy. Add melted chocolate and eggs; beat until well blended. Add flour, applesauce, vanilla, baking soda, baking powder and salt; beat until well blended. Stir in 1/2 cup chocolate chips. Spoon batter evenly into prepared pans.

3. Bake 35 to 40 minutes or until centers crack and are dry to the touch. Cool in pans on wire rack 10 minutes. Remove from pans to wire racks; cool completely.

4. Place remaining 1/2 cup chocolate chips and shortening in small microwavable bowl. Microwave at HIGH 1 minute; stir. Microwave at 30-second intervals, stirring after each interval, until chocolate is melted and mixture is smooth. Drizzle loaves with glaze; let stand until set.   *Makes 5 mini loaves*

Gift Idea: Wrap each loaf in plastic wrap or cellophane and place in a colorful gift bag. With each loaf include a sampling of single serving packets of gourmet coffee or tea.

Clockwise from top left: *Sugar-and-Spice Twist (p. 113), Lots o' Chocolate Bread, Baby Bran Muffins with Citrus Spread (p. 122) and Toll House® Crumbcake (p. 118)*

Breakfast Blossoms

(Pictured at right)

**1 (12-ounce) can buttermilk biscuits
(10 biscuits)
3/4 cup SMUCKER'S® Strawberry Preserves
1/4 teaspoon ground cinnamon
1/4 teaspoon ground nutmeg**

1. Preheat oven to 375°F. Grease ten 2-1/2- or 3-inch muffin pan cups. Separate dough into 10 biscuits. Separate each biscuit into 3 equal sections or leaves. Stand 3 sections evenly around side and bottom of cup, overlapping slightly. Press dough edges firmly together.

2. Combine preserves, cinnamon and nutmeg in small bowl; stir until well blended. Place 1 tablespoon preserves mixture in center of each cup.

3. Bake at 375°F for 10 to 12 minutes or until lightly browned. Cool slightly before removing from pan. Serve warm. *Makes 10 rolls*

Oat Raisin Bread

**1-1/2 cups all-purpose flour
1 cup whole wheat flour
1 cup uncooked quick or old-fashioned oats
2 teaspoons baking soda
1/2 teaspoon salt
1-1/2 cups buttermilk
1/2 cup KARO® Light or Dark Corn Syrup
1/2 cup packed brown sugar
2 eggs
1/4 cup MAZOLA® Oil
1 cup raisins**

1. Preheat oven to 350°F. Grease and flour two 9×5×3-inch loaf pans.

2. In large bowl combine flours, oats, baking soda and salt.

3. In small bowl combine buttermilk, corn syrup, brown sugar, eggs and oil until blended. Stir into flour mixture just until moistened. Stir in raisins. Pour batter into prepared pans.

4. Bake 45 to 50 minutes or until toothpick inserted into center comes out clean. Cool in pans 10 minutes. Remove from pans; cool on wire rack. *Makes 2 loaves*

Blueberry Breakfast Braid

**5 to 5-1/3 cups all-purpose flour
1/2 cup sugar
2 envelopes FLEISCHMANN'S® RapidRise™ Yeast
1 teaspoon salt
1 tablespoon finely shredded orange peel
1/2 teaspoon ground cinnamon
1 cup milk
1/2 cup orange juice
1/2 cup (1 stick) butter or margarine
2 large eggs
Blueberry Filling (recipe follows)
1 egg yolk plus 1 tablespoon milk
(egg mixture)**

In large bowl, combine 2 cups flour, sugar, undissolved yeast, salt, orange peel and cinnamon. Heat milk, orange juice and butter until very warm (120° to 130°F). Stir into dry ingredients. Beat 2 minutes at medium speed of electric mixer, scraping bowl occasionally. Add eggs and 1 cup flour; beat 2 minutes at high speed. Stir in enough remaining flour to make a soft dough. Knead on lightly floured surface until smooth and elastic, about 8 to 10 minutes. Cover; let rest 10 minutes.

Divide dough in half; divide each half into 3 equal portions. Roll each to 20×6-inch rectangle. Spread Blueberry Filling evenly. Beginning at long end, roll each up tightly as for jelly roll. Pinch seams to seal to form ropes. Braid ropes; place on greased baking sheets. Cover; let rise in warm, draft-free place until doubled in size, about 1 hour. Brush with egg mixture.

Bake at 350°F for 30 to 35 minutes or until done. Remove from sheets; cool on wire rack.
Makes 2 loaves

Blueberry Filling: Combine 1 cup fresh or frozen blueberries, 1 cup sugar and 1/4 cup water in medium saucepan; bring to a boil over medium heat. Cook 20 minutes, stirring occasionally, until very thick. Stir in 3 tablespoons cornstarch dissolved in 3 tablespoons water; cook 5 minutes, stirring constantly. Let cool.

Breakfast Blossoms

Caramel-Nut Sticky Biscuits

(Pictured below)

TOPPING

- 2/3 cup firmly packed brown sugar
- 1/4 cup light corn syrup
- 1/4 cup (1/2 stick) margarine, melted
- 1/2 teaspoon ground cinnamon
- 1 cup pecan halves

BISCUITS

- 2 cups all-purpose flour
- 1 cup QUAKER® Oats (quick or old fashioned, uncooked)
- 1/4 cup granulated sugar
- 1 tablespoon baking powder
- 3/4 teaspoon baking soda
- 1/2 teaspoon salt (optional)
- 1/2 teaspoon ground cinnamon
- 1/3 cup (5-1/3 tablespoons) margarine
- 1 cup buttermilk*

Sour milk can be substituted for buttermilk. For 1 cup sour milk, combine 1 tablespoon vinegar or lemon juice and enough milk to make 1 cup; let stand 5 minutes.

Caramel-Nut Sticky Biscuits

Heat oven to 425°F. For topping, combine first four ingredients; mix well. Spread onto bottom of 9-inch square baking pan. Sprinkle with pecans; set aside. For biscuits, combine dry ingredients; mix well. Cut in margarine with pastry blender or two knives until crumbly. Stir in buttermilk, mixing just until moistened. Knead gently on lightly floured surface 5 to 7 times; pat into 8-inch square. Cut with knife into sixteen 2-inch square biscuits; place over topping in pan. Bake 25 to 28 minutes or until golden brown. Let stand 3 minutes; invert onto large platter. Serve warm.   *Makes 16 servings*

Cinnamon Coffee-Crumb Muffins

- 3 cups all-purpose flour
- 1 tablespoon baking powder
- 1 teaspoon ground cinnamon
- 1/4 teaspoon salt
- 1-1/4 cups sugar
- 1/2 cup (1 stick) SHEDD'S® Spread Country Crock® Spread
- 2 eggs
- 1 tablespoon instant coffee crystals or instant espresso
- 1 teaspoon vanilla extract
- 1 cup milk
- Crumb Topping (recipe follows)

Preheat oven to 400°F. Grease 12-cup muffin pan or line with paper cupcake liners; set aside.

In large bowl, combine flour, baking powder, cinnamon and salt; set aside.

In large bowl, with electric mixer, beat sugar and SHEDD'S® Spread Country Crock Spread on medium-high speed until light and fluffy, about 5 minutes. Beat in eggs, coffee and vanilla, scraping side occasionally. Alternately beat in flour mixture and milk until blended. Evenly spoon batter into prepared pan; sprinkle with Crumb Topping.

Bake 23 minutes or until toothpick inserted in centers comes out clean. On wire rack, cool 10 minutes; remove from pan and cool completely.

Makes 12 muffins

Crumb Topping: In small bowl, combine 1/4 cup all-purpose flour, 2 tablespoons sugar and 1/4 teaspoon ground cinnamon. With pastry blender or 2 knives, cut in 2 tablespoons Shedd's® Spread Country Crock Spread until mixture is size of coarse crumbs.

Zucchini-Orange Bread

Zucchini-Orange Bread

(Pictured above)

> 1 package (about 17 ounces) cranberry-orange
>   muffin mix
> 1-1/2 cups shredded zucchini (about 6 ounces)
>   1 cup water
>   1 teaspoon ground cinnamon
>   1 teaspoon grated orange peel (optional)
>   Cream cheese (optional)

1. Preheat oven 350°F. Grease 8×4×3-inch loaf pan; set aside.

2. Combine muffin mix, zucchini, water, cinnamon and orange peel, if desired, in medium bowl; stir until just moistened. Spoon batter into prepared loaf pan; bake 40 minutes or until toothpick inserted into center comes out almost clean.

3. Cool in pan on wire rack 5 minutes. Remove bread from pan to wire rack; cool completely. Serve plain or with cream cheese, if desired.

Makes about 16 slices

Sugar-and-Spice Twists

(Pictured on page 108)

> 1 tablespoon granulated sugar
> 1/4 teaspoon ground cinnamon
>   1 package (6-count) refrigerated breadsticks

1. Preheat oven to 350°F. Spray baking sheet with nonstick cooking spray; set aside.

2. Combine sugar and cinnamon in shallow dish or plate.

3. Divide breadstick dough into 6 pieces. Roll each piece into 12-inch rope. Roll in sugar-cinnamon mixture. Twist into pretzel shape. Place on prepared baking sheet. Bake 15 to 18 minutes or until lightly browned. Remove from baking sheet. Cool 5 minutes. Serve warm. *Makes 6 servings*

Hint: Use colored sugar sprinkles in place of the granulated sugar in this recipe for a fun "twist" of color that's perfect for holidays, birthdays or simple everyday celebrations.

Easy Cheesy Artichoke & Spinach Bread

(Pictured at right)

1 can (14 ounces) artichoke hearts, drained and chopped
1 package (10 ounces) frozen chopped spinach or chopped broccoli, thawed and squeezed dry
1 cup HELLMANN'S® or BEST FOODS® Real Mayonnaise
1 cup grated Parmesan cheese
1 clove garlic, finely chopped or 1/4 teaspoon LAWRY'S® Garlic Powder With Parsley (optional)
1 loaf French or Italian bread (about 16 inches long), halved lengthwise

1. Preheat oven to 350°F.

2. In small bowl, combine all ingredients except bread; evenly spread on bread. Bake 12 minutes or until golden and heated through.

Makes 8 servings

Banana Blueberry Muffins

2 ripe, medium DOLE® Bananas
6 tablespoons margarine
6 tablespoons brown sugar
1 egg
1-1/2 cups all-purpose flour
1/2 teaspoon baking powder
1/2 teaspoon baking soda
1/2 teaspoon salt
1/2 teaspoon grated lemon peel
1 cup DOLE® Fresh Frozen Blueberries

• Purée bananas in blender (1 cup).

• Beat margarine and sugar in large bowl until light and fluffy. Mix in bananas and egg.

• Combine flour, baking powder, baking soda, salt and lemon peel in medium bowl. Blend into margarine mixture just until moistened. Fold in blueberries.

• Line 6 large muffin cups with paper liners; spray lightly with vegetable cooking spray. Spoon batter evenly into cups.

• Bake at 375°F 20 to 25 minutes.

Makes 6 muffins

Easy Herb Bread

1 loaf Italian or French bread
1/4 cup CRISCO® Oil*
2 tablespoons minced parsley
2 teaspoons Italian seasoning
1/2 teaspoon salt
1/4 teaspoon freshly ground black pepper
1/4 cup freshly grated Parmesan cheese

Use your favorite Crisco Oil.

1. Heat oven to 425°F. Cover baking sheet with heavy-duty aluminum foil.

2. Slice bread in half lengthwise. Combine oil, parsley, Italian seasoning, salt and pepper in small bowl. Spread mixture onto both bread halves. Sprinkle cheese on bread.

3. Place bread halves on baking sheet. Bake at 425°F for 5 to 7 minutes or until heated through and lightly brown. Slice and serve.

Makes 4 to 6 servings

Holiday Coffeecake

2 cups biscuit mix
1 (14-ounce) can EAGLE BRAND® Sweetened Condensed Milk (NOT evaporated milk)
3/4 cup sour cream
1/4 cup (1/2 stick) butter or margarine, melted
2 eggs
1-1/2 teaspoons ground cinnamon, divided
1/2 cup chopped pecans
2 tablespoons firmly packed light brown sugar
1 tablespoon butter or margarine, melted

1. Preheat oven to 350°F. In large mixing bowl, beat biscuit mix, EAGLE BRAND®, sour cream, 1/4 cup butter, eggs and 1/2 teaspoon cinnamon until smooth. Pour batter into lightly greased 11×7-inch baking dish.

2. In small mixing bowl, combine pecans, brown sugar, 1 tablespoon butter and remaining 1 teaspoon cinnamon. Sprinkle mixture evenly over batter. Bake 40 to 45 minutes or until wooden pick inserted in center comes out clean. Cool in dish on wire rack 10 minutes. *Makes 8 servings*

Easy Cheesy Artichoke & Spinach Bread

Reese's® Peanut Butter and Milk Chocolate Chip Crescents

    1/2 cup REESE'S® Peanut Butter and Milk
        Chocolate Chips
    2 tablespoons finely chopped nuts
    1 can (8 ounces) refrigerated quick crescent
        dinner rolls
        Peanut Butter Chocolate Drizzle (recipe
        follows) or powdered sugar (optional)

1. Heat oven to 375°F.

2. Stir together chips and nuts in small bowl. Unroll dough to form 8 triangles. Lightly sprinkle 1 heaping tablespoon chip mixture on top of each; gently press into dough. Starting at shortest side of triangle, roll dough to opposite point. Place rolls, point side down, on ungreased cookie sheet; curve into crescent shape.

3. Bake 10 to 12 minutes or until golden brown. Prepare Peanut Butter Chocolate Drizzle; drizzle over crescents or sprinkle with powdered sugar, if desired. Serve warm.   *Makes 8 crescents*

Peanut Butter Chocolate Drizzle: Place 1/4 cup REESE'S® Peanut Butter and Milk Chocolate Chips and 1 teaspoon shortening (do *not* use butter, margarine or oil) in small microwave-safe bowl. Microwave at HIGH (100%) 30 seconds; stir. If necessary, microwave at HIGH an additional 15 seconds at a time, stirring after each heating, just until chips are melted when stirred.

Cinnamon-Pecan Pull-Apart Bread

(Pictured at right)

    1-1/2 cups water
        3/4 cup (1-1/2 sticks) butter, divided
        1 teaspoon salt
    3-3/4 cups all-purpose flour
    1-1/4 cups sugar, divided
        2 teaspoons active dry yeast
        3/4 cup finely chopped pecans
    1-1/2 teaspoons ground cinnamon
        1/2 cup raisins

1. Measuring carefully, place water, 1/4 cup butter, salt, flour, 1/4 cup sugar and yeast in bread machine pan in order specified by owner's manual. Program dough cycle setting; press start.

2. Melt remaining 1/2 cup butter. Combine remaining 1 cup sugar, pecans and cinnamon in small bowl. Divide dough in half; shape each half into twenty balls. Dip balls first in butter, then in sugar mixture. Arrange 20 balls in bottom of greased 12-cup fluted tube pan; sprinkle with raisins. Top with remaining 20 balls. Cover; let rise in warm place 45 minutes or until doubled.

3. Preheat oven to 350°F. Bake 35 to 40 minutes or until evenly browned. Invert onto heatproof serving plate; let stand 1 minute before removing pan. Serve warm.   *Makes 8 to 12 servings*

Lemon Blueberry Loaf

BREAD
    1 package DUNCAN HINES® Bakery-Style
        Wild Maine Blueberry Muffin Mix
    1 egg
    1/2 cup dairy sour cream
    1/2 cup milk
    1 tablespoon grated lemon peel (see Tip)
    1/2 cup chopped pecans
GLAZE
    1/3 cup granulated sugar
    2 tablespoons lemon juice

1. Preheat oven to 350°F. Grease and flour 9×5-inch loaf pan.

2. Rinse blueberries from Mix with cold water and drain.

3. For bread, empty muffin mix into medium bowl. Break up any lumps. Add egg, sour cream, milk and grated lemon peel. Stir until moistened, about 50 strokes. Fold in blueberries and pecans. Pour into pan. Bake at 350°F 60 to 65 minutes or until toothpick inserted in center comes out clean. Poke holes in top of warm loaf with toothpick or long-tined fork.

4. For glaze, combine sugar and lemon juice in small saucepan. Cook on medium heat, stirring constantly, until sugar dissolves. Spoon hot glaze evenly over loaf. Cool in pan 15 minutes. Loosen loaf from pan. Invert onto cooling rack. Turn right side up. Cool completely.   *Makes 1 loaf (12 slices)*

Tip: When grating lemon peel, avoid the bitter white portion known as the pith.

Cinnamon-Pecan Pull-Apart Bread

Hot Rolls

Hot Rolls

(Pictured above)

**6 cups sifted PILLSBURY BEST® All-Purpose
      or Unbleached Flour**
1/2 cup sugar
1 teaspoon salt
1 egg
**3/4 CRISCO® Butter Flavor Stick or 3/4 cup
      CRISCO® Butter Flavor Shortening**
2 packages active dry yeast
2 cups lukewarm water (120° to 130°F)
1/2 cup (1 stick) butter

1. Sift flour, sugar and salt together; add egg and shortening. Dissolve yeast in 1 cup water; add to mixture. Add remaining 1 cup water. Mix with hands for 5 minutes or until thoroughly mixed. Cover with waxed paper and refrigerate overnight.

2. Melt butter. Roll out dough to 1/2-inch thickness on floured board; cut with 2-1/2-inch biscuit cutter. Dip in melted butter and fold over, pressing lightly. Place on ungreased baking sheet; let rise 1 to 2 hours.

3. Preheat oven to 400°F. Bake rolls 10 minutes.

Makes 3 dozen rolls

Toll House® Crumbcake

(Pictured on page 108)

TOPPING
  1/3 cup packed brown sugar
    1 tablespoon all-purpose flour
    2 tablespoons butter or margarine, softened
  1/2 cup chopped nuts
    **2 cups (12-ounce package) NESTLÉ®
        TOLL HOUSE® Semi-Sweet Chocolate
        Mini Morsels, *divided***

CAKE
  1-3/4 cups all-purpose flour
    1 teaspoon baking powder
    1 teaspoon baking soda
  1/4 teaspoon salt
  3/4 cup granulated sugar
  1/2 cup (1 stick) butter or margarine, softened
    1 teaspoon vanilla extract
    3 large eggs
    1 cup sour cream

PREHEAT oven to 350°F. Grease 13×9-inch baking pan.

FOR TOPPING
COMBINE brown sugar, flour and butter in small bowl with pastry blender or two knives until crumbly. Stir in nuts and *1/2 cup* morsels.

FOR CAKE
COMBINE flour, baking powder, baking soda and salt in small bowl. Beat granulated sugar, butter and vanilla extract in large mixer bowl until creamy. Add eggs, one at a time, beating well after each addition. Gradually add flour mixture alternately with sour cream. Fold in *remaining 1-1/2 cups* morsels. Spread into prepared baking pan; sprinkle with topping.

BAKE for 25 to 35 minutes or until wooden pick inserted in center comes out clean. Cool in pan on wire rack.　　*Makes 12 servings*

Helpful Hint

To soften butter quickly for baking, place 1 stick of butter on a microwavable plate and heat at LOW (30% power) about 30 seconds or just until softened.

Bayou Yam Muffins

(Pictured below)

1 cup flour
1 cup yellow cornmeal
1/4 cup sugar
1 tablespoon baking powder
1-1/4 teaspoons ground cinnamon
1/2 teaspoon salt
2 eggs
1 cup mashed yams or sweet potatoes
1/2 cup very strong cold coffee
1/4 cup butter or margarine, melted
1/2 teaspoon TABASCO® brand Pepper Sauce

Preheat oven to 425°F. Grease 12 (3×1-1/2-inch) muffin cups. Combine flour, cornmeal, sugar, baking powder, cinnamon and salt in large bowl. Beat eggs in medium bowl; stir in yams, coffee, butter and TABASCO® Sauce. Make a well in center of dry ingredients; add yam mixture and stir just to combine. Spoon batter into prepared muffin cups. Bake 20 to 25 minutes or until cake tester inserted in center of muffin comes out clean. Cool 5 minutes on wire rack. Remove from pans. Serve warm or at room temperature. *Makes 12 muffins*

Warm Focaccia Pizza Bread

1/2 cup HELLMANN'S® or BEST FOODS®
    Real Mayonnaise
1/4 cup plus 2 tablespoons shredded mozzarella
    cheese
2 tablespoons grated Parmesan cheese
1 tablespoon thinly sliced fresh basil leaves
6 ounces cooked chicken, sliced
    (about 1-1/3 cups)
6 slices tomato
2 (6-inch) prebaked pizza crusts

Preheat oven to 450°F.

In medium bowl, combine Hellmann's or Best Foods Real Mayonnaise, 1/4 cup mozzarella cheese, Parmesan cheese and basil. Stir in chicken.

Evenly spread on pizza crusts, then top with tomato and remaining 2 tablespoons mozzarella cheese. Arrange on baking sheet.

Bake 15 minutes or until crusts are golden brown and cheese is melted. *Makes 4 servings*

Bayou Yam Muffins

Southwestern Biscuits

2-1/4 cups all-purpose flour
  2 tablespoons granulated sugar
  1 tablespoon baking powder
1/2 teaspoon salt (optional)
  3 tablespoons butter or margarine, softened
  1 egg
  1 can (8 ounces) cream-style corn
  1 can (4 ounces) ORTEGA® Diced Green Chiles
  1 tablespoon chopped fresh cilantro (optional)

PREHEAT oven to 400°F.

COMBINE flour, sugar, baking powder and salt in large bowl. Add butter; cut in with pastry blender or two knives until mixture resembles coarse crumbs.

STIR in egg, corn, chiles and cilantro; combine just until mixture holds together. Knead dough 10 times on well-floured surface. Pat dough into 3/4-inch thickness. Cut into 3-inch biscuits. Place on greased baking sheets.

BAKE for 20 to 25 minutes or until wooden pick inserted in center comes out clean. Cool on baking sheets for 5 minutes; remove to wire racks to cool completely.   *Makes 8 biscuits*

Greek Flat Breads

(Pictured at right)

  Basic Yeast Bread (recipe follows)
8 ounces crumbled feta cheese
1 cup chopped kalamata olives
6 cloves garlic, minced
2 tablespoons olive oil
2 eggs
2 tablespoons water
  Coarse salt (optional)

1. Prepare Basic Yeast Bread through Step 4. Grease 2 baking sheets; set aside. Turn out dough onto lightly oiled work surface; divide in half. Keep one half of dough covered. Divide other half of dough into 16 equal pieces. Form each piece into ball. Cover with towel; let rest 5 minutes.

2. Combine cheese, olives, garlic and oil in medium bowl; set aside. Beat eggs and water in small bowl.

3. Flatten each ball of dough to 1/2-inch thickness. Place 2 inches apart on prepared baking sheet. Brush dough with beaten egg. Sprinkle each round of dough with half of olive mixture; press topping

into dough slightly. Cover with towel; let rise 45 minutes. Repeat with remaining half of dough.

4. Place heavy baking or roasting pan on lower rack of oven. Preheat oven to 400°F.

5. Sprinkle tops of dough with coarse salt, if desired. Place bread in oven. Carefully place 4 to 5 ice cubes in heavy pan below bread. Bake 15 minutes or until lightly browned. Immediately remove bread from baking sheets and place on wire rack to cool.
      Makes 32 flat breads

Basic Yeast Bread

  2 cups milk
1/4 cup (1/2 stick) unsalted butter, softened
6-1/2 to 7-1/2 cups bread or all-purpose flour, divided
1/4 cup sugar
  2 packages active dry yeast
  2 teaspoons salt
  2 eggs

1. Heat milk and butter in small saucepan over medium heat just until butter is melted. Remove from heat; cool to about 120° to 130°F.

2. Combine 4 cups flour, sugar, yeast and salt in large bowl. Add milk mixture and eggs. Beat vigorously 2 minutes. Add remaining flour, 1/4 cup at a time, until dough begins to pull away from side of bowl.

3. Turn out dough onto lightly floured work surface; flatten slightly. Knead 10 minutes or until smooth and elastic, adding flour if necessary to prevent sticking.

4. Shape dough into a ball. Place in large lightly oiled bowl; turn dough over once to oil surface. Cover with towel; let rise in warm place about 1 hour or until doubled in bulk.

5. Grease two 9×5-inch loaf pans; set aside. Turn out dough onto lightly oiled work surface; divide in half. Shape each half of dough into loaf; place in prepared pans. Cover with towel; let rise in warm place 45 minutes.

6. Preheat oven to 375°F. Bake 25 minutes or until loaves are golden and sound hollow when tapped. Immediately remove bread from pans and cool on wire rack.   *Makes 2 loaves*

Greek Flat Breads

Orange Marmalade Bread

(Pictured at right)

3 cups PILLSBURY BEST® All-Purpose or
    Unbleached Flour
4 teaspoons baking powder
1 teaspoon salt
1/2 cup chopped walnuts
3/4 cup milk
3/4 cup SMUCKER'S® Sweet Orange Marmalade
2 eggs, lightly beaten
1/4 cup honey
2 tablespoons CRISCO® Oil*

Use your favorite Crisco Oil.

1. Preheat oven to 350°F. Grease 9×5×3-inch loaf pan. Combine flour, baking powder and salt in large bowl. Stir in nuts. Combine milk, marmalade, eggs, honey and oil in medium bowl; stir until well blended. Add marmalade mixture to flour mixture; stir just until dry ingredients are moistened. (Batter will be lumpy.) Turn into prepared pan.

2. Bake at 350°F for 65 to 70 minutes or until lightly browned and toothpick inserted in center comes out clean.   *Makes 8 to 10 servings*

Baby Bran Muffins with Citrus Spread

(Pictured on page 108)

1 cup whole bran cereal
1 cup milk
1 egg, beaten
2 tablespoons butter, melted
1 cup all-purpose flour
1/4 cup packed brown sugar
2-1/2 teaspoons baking powder
1/2 teaspoon baking soda
1/4 teaspoon salt
1/4 teaspoon ground cinnamon
1/4 cup currants
1 (8-ounce) package cream cheese,
    at room temperature
3 tablespoons orange juice
1 teaspoon granulated sugar

1. Preheat oven to 375°F. Spray 24 miniature (1-3/4-inch) muffin pan cups with nonstick cooking spray. Set aside.

2. Combine cereal, milk, egg and butter in large bowl. Set aside 10 minutes. Combine flour, brown sugar, baking powder, baking soda, salt and cinnamon in large bowl. Add to bran mixture, stirring just until blended. Fold in currants.

3. Spoon batter into prepared muffin cups filling 3/4 full. Bake 15 minutes or until firm when lightly pressed. Let muffins stand 1 minute; remove to wire rack to cool.

4. For Citrus Spread, beat cream cheese, orange juice and granulated sugar in large bowl with electric mixer at high speed 1 minute or until cream cheese is light and fluffy. Split open muffins and spread lightly with Citrus Spread.   *Makes 24 muffins*

Tip: Leftover muffins can be frozen in resealable plastic food storage bag. Reheat in preheated 325°F oven for 5 minutes.

Golden Apricot Scones

2 cups flour
3 tablespoons sugar, divided
2 teaspoons baking powder
1/2 teaspoon salt
1/3 cup butter or margarine
1 cup diced fresh Washington apricots
1/4 cup milk, divided
2 eggs

Mix flour, 2 tablespoons sugar, baking powder and salt in large bowl. Add butter and cut into flour mixture until mixture resembles coarse cornmeal. Add apricots and toss until pieces are coated with flour mixture. Reserve 1 tablespoon milk; mix remaining milk and eggs. Add milk mixture to flour mixture and stir until moistened.

On lightly floured board, knead dough gently about 10 times. Pat dough into 3/4-inch-thick round; cut into 8 wedge-shaped pieces. Place dough on lightly oiled baking sheet; brush with reserved milk and sprinkle with remaining sugar.

Bake at 450°F 12 to 15 minutes or until golden brown and wooden pick inserted near center comes out clean.   *Makes 8 servings*

Favorite recipe from **Washington State Fruit Commission**

Orange Marmalade Bread

Mocha Walnut Crunch Coffeecake

(Pictured at right)

COFFEECAKE
> 1 package (16 ounces) hot roll mix
> 1 cup QUAKER® Oats (quick or old fashioned, uncooked)
> 1/4 teaspoon salt (optional)
> 3/4 cup milk
> 1/2 cup (1 stick) margarine or butter
> 1/2 cup granulated sugar
> 3 eggs, room temperature
> 1/2 cup semisweet chocolate pieces

TOPPING
> 1/2 cup all-purpose flour
> 1/2 cup granulated sugar
> 1/4 cup QUAKER® Oats (quick or old fashioned, uncooked)
> 1 tablespoon instant coffee granules or espresso powder
> 1/2 cup (1 stick) margarine or butter, chilled
> 1/2 cup semisweet chocolate pieces
> 1/2 cup chopped walnuts

1. Grease 10-inch tube pan or 12-cup Bundt pan. For coffeecake, in large mixing bowl, combine hot roll mix (including yeast packet), oats and salt; mix well. In small saucepan, heat milk and margarine over low heat until margarine is melted; remove from heat. Stir in sugar; cool mixture to 120°F to 130°F. Add to oat mixture; add eggs. Beat at low speed of electric mixer until well blended. Stir in chocolate pieces. Spoon into prepared pan.

2. For topping, combine flour, sugar, oats and coffee granules; cut in margarine with pastry blender or two knives until mixture is crumbly. Stir in chocolate pieces and nuts. Sprinkle evenly over top of dough. Cover loosely with plastic wrap. Let rise in warm place 30 to 40 minutes or until nearly double in size.

3. Heat oven to 350°F. Bake, uncovered, 45 to 50 minutes or until wooden pick inserted near center comes out clean. Cool in pan 10 minutes. Remove from pan, topping side up, onto wire rack. Cool completely. Store tightly covered.
Makes 16 servings

Note: If hot roll mix is not available, combine 3 cups all-purpose flour, two 1/4-ounce packages quick-rising yeast and 1-1/2 teaspoons salt; mix well. Continue as recipe directs.

Cheese Pull-Apart Bread

> 3 packages frozen bread dough dinner rolls, thawed to room temperature
> 1/3 cup butter, melted
> 1 cup freshly grated BELGIOIOSO® Parmesan Cheese
> 1 cup shredded BELGIOIOSO® Provolone Cheese

Roll each dinner roll in butter, and then roll in BelGioioso Parmesan Cheese to coat. Arrange half of rolls in well-greased fluted tube pan. Sprinkle with BelGioioso Provolone Cheese. Top with remaining half of coated rolls. Sprinkle with any remaining Parmesan. Let rise until doubled in size, about 1 hour. Bake in preheated 375°F oven 35 to 45 minutes or until golden brown. Use table knife to loosen edge of bread; remove from pan. Serve warm.
Makes 12 servings

Upside-Down Cornbread

> 3 plum tomatoes, thinly sliced
> 1-1/3 cups *French's®* French Fried Onions, divided
> 2 packages (6-1/2 ounces each) cornbread mix
> 2/3 cup milk
> 1/2 cup finely chopped zucchini
> 2 eggs
> 1/4 cup butter, melted
> 1 teaspoon *French's®* Bold n' Spicy Brown Mustard
> 1/2 teaspoon dried basil leaves

1. Preheat oven to 425°F. Coat 8-inch square baking dish with nonstick cooking spray. Layer tomatoes in bottom of dish and sprinkle with *1/3 cup* French Fried Onions.

2. Combine *1 cup* onions and remaining ingredients in medium bowl; mix just until dry ingredients are moistened. Pour over tomato layers. Bake 30 minutes or until toothpick inserted in center comes out clean. Cool 15 minutes; invert onto serving plate. Serve warm with tossed green salad.
Makes 6 servings

Mocha Walnut Crunch Coffeecake

Main Dishes

Bodacious Grilled Ribs

(Pictured at left)

        4 pounds pork loin back ribs
        2 tablespoons paprika
        2 teaspoons dried basil leaves
    1/2 teaspoon onion powder
    1/4 teaspoon garlic powder
    1/4 teaspoon cayenne pepper
    1/4 teaspoon black pepper
        2 sheets (24×18 inches) heavy-duty foil, lightly sprayed
            with nonstick cooking spray
        8 ice cubes
        1 cup barbecue sauce
    1/2 cup apricot all-fruit spread

1. Prepare grill for direct cooking. Cut ribs into 4- to 6-rib pieces.

2. Combine paprika, basil, onion powder, garlic powder, cayenne pepper and black pepper in small bowl. Rub on both sides of rib pieces. Place 2 pounds of ribs, in single layer, in center of each foil sheet. Place 4 ice cubes on top of each.

3. Double fold sides and ends of foil to seal packets, leaving head space for heat circulation. Place on baking sheet. Slide packets off baking sheet onto grill grid.

4. Grill, covered, over medium heat 45 to 60 minutes or until tender. Stir together barbecue sauce and jam. Carefully open one end of each packet to allow steam to escape.

5. Open packets and transfer ribs to grill rack. Brush with barbecue sauce mixture. Continue grilling 5 to 10 minutes, brushing with sauce and turning often.   *Makes 4 servings*

Clockwise from top left: *Garlic and Basil Halibut (p. 172), Easy Slow-Cooked Chili (p. 176), Bodacious Grilled Ribs and Skillet Pasta Roma (p. 144)*

Pantry Fruited Chicken

(Pictured at right)

3 pounds chicken parts
1 bottle (12 ounces) LAWRY'S® Lemon Pepper
   Marinade With Lemon Juice, divided
1 can (29 ounces) yams or sweet potatoes,
   drained
1 cup canned apple pie filling
1/2 cup dried cranberries

Preheat oven to 375°F. Spray broiler pan bottom
with nonstick cooking spray; arrange chicken skin
side down on pan. Pour 2/3 cup Lemon Pepper
Marinade over chicken. Bake for 30 minutes. Turn
chicken over. Arrange yams, apple pie filling and
cranberries around chicken. Pour remaining Marinade
over fruit and chicken. Return pan to oven and bake
30 minutes or until chicken is thoroughly cooked.
Spoon pan juices over chicken and fruit before
serving. *Makes 4 to 6 servings*

Meal Idea: Serve with warm crusty bread or rice
pilaf.

Variation: Try with LAWRY'S® Citrus Grill Marinade
with Orange Juice for another great flavor
combination!

Tuna Tacos

1 (3-ounce) STARKIST Flavor Fresh Pouch®
   Tuna (Albacore or Chunk Light)
1/3 cup chopped green onions
1/4 cup bottled salsa
2 cups shredded lettuce
8 corn taco shells*
1 cup garbanzo beans
1 cup chopped tomato
1/3 cup sliced pitted ripe olives
   Salsa, shredded cheese, diced avocado,
   chopped green chilies for toppings
   (optional)

*Substitute 8 (6-inch) flour tortillas for the taco shells if soft tacos are
preferred.*

In medium bowl toss together tuna, onions and
salsa until combined. To assemble tacos, sprinkle
lettuce into each taco shell. Divide tuna mixture
among tacos, along with garbanzo beans, tomato
and olives. Garnish as desired with toppings.
Makes 4 servings

Zesty Lamb Taco Skillet

1 tablespoon vegetable or olive oil
1 clove garlic, minced
1 pound boneless lamb (leg or shoulder),
   cut into 1/8-inch strips
1-1/2 cans (21 ounces) beef broth
1-1/2 cans (12 ounces) tomato sauce
1 package taco seasoning mix (about
   1-1/4 ounces)
2 cups green or red bell pepper strips
1-1/2 cups fresh or frozen corn
2 cups quick-cooking rice, white or brown
   Grated cheese (optional)
   Sliced ripe olives (optional)
   Crushed tortilla chips (optional)

Heat oil over medium-high heat in large skillet. Add
garlic and lamb strips. Cook and stir until lamb is no
longer pink. Add broth, tomato sauce and seasoning
mix. Bring to a boil; reduce heat. Cover and simmer
5 minutes. Add bell peppers and corn. Bring to a
boil; stir in rice. Remove from heat. Cover and let
stand 5 minutes or until moisture is absorbed.
Fluff with fork. Serve with grated cheese, sliced
ripe olives and crushed tortilla chips, if desired.
Makes 6 servings

Favorite recipe from **American Lamb Council**

BBQ Yogurt Marinated Chicken

1 cup STONYFIELD FARM® Yogurt
1/4 cup olive oil
2 tablespoons lemon juice
2 garlic cloves, chopped
1 tablespoon chopped fresh rosemary
1 tablespoon chopped fresh thyme
1 teaspoon salt
1 teaspoon black pepper
4 chicken breasts, skinless, boneless

Combine all ingredients except chicken in bowl; add
chicken breasts and allow to marinade for at least
2 hours. Grill chicken over medium-high heat and
serve with potato salad, grilled corn or any other
favorite summer side dishes. *Makes 4 servings*

Pantry Fruited Chicken

Pesto Lasagna Rolls

(Pictured at right)

2 cups fresh basil leaves
2 cloves garlic
3/4 cup (3 ounces) SARGENTO® Fancy Parmesan
    Shredded Cheese, divided
3/4 cup olive oil
2 cups (15 ounces) SARGENTO® Whole Milk
    Ricotta Cheese*
1 cup (4 ounces) SARGENTO® Reduced Fat
    Mozzarella Shredded Cheese
1 egg, beaten
1 cup diced zucchini
16 lasagna noodles, cooked, drained and cooled

SARGENTO® Part-Skim Ricotta, Light Ricotta or Fat Free Ricotta can also be used.

Prepare pesto sauce in covered blender or food processor by processing basil with garlic until chopped. Add 1/2 cup Parmesan cheese; process until well mixed. With machine running, slowly add oil and continue processing until smooth. Set aside. In medium bowl, combine Ricotta and Mozzarella cheeses, remaining 1/4 cup Parmesan cheese and egg; blend well. Fold in zucchini. Spread 2 heaping tablespoons cheese mixture on each lasagna noodle. Roll up each noodle individually and stand vertically in greased 11×7-inch baking dish. Pour pesto sauce over lasagna rolls; cover and bake at 350°F 40 minutes or until bubbly and heated through.

Makes 8 servings

Classic Turkey Pot Pie

2 cans (15 ounces each) VEG•ALL® Original
    Mixed Vegetables, drained
1 can (10-3/4 ounces) condensed cream of
    potato soup, undiluted
1/4 cup milk
1 pound (2 cups) cooked turkey, shredded
1/4 teaspoon thyme
1/4 teaspoon pepper
2 (9-inch) refrigerated ready-to-bake pie crusts

Preheat oven to 375°F. In medium bowl, combine first 6 ingredients; mix well. Place 1 pie crust into 9-inch pie pan; pour vegetable mixture into pie crust. Top with remaining crust, crimp edges to seal and slit top with knife. Bake for 50 to 60 minutes on lower oven rack or until crust is golden brown and filling is hot. Allow pie to cool slightly before cutting into wedges to serve. *Makes 8 servings*

Fajitas

1/2 cup chopped onion
1/4 cup GRANDMA'S® Molasses
1/4 cup oil
2 tablespoons ROSE'S® Lime Juice
2 tablespoons chili powder
2 cloves garlic, minced
1/2 teaspoon dried oregano leaves
1 pound boneless top round or sirloin steak,
    cut into thin strips
10 flour tortillas (8 to 10 inches), warmed
1/2 cup (2 ounces) shredded Monterey Jack cheese
2 cups refried beans
2 tomatoes, chopped
1-1/2 cups shredded lettuce
1 avocado, chopped
1 cup salsa
Sour cream

1. In medium plastic bowl, combine onion, molasses, oil, lime juice, chili powder, garlic and oregano. Mix well. Add steak; stir to coat. Cover; refrigerate 4 to 6 hours or overnight, stirring occasionally.

2. In large skillet, stir-fry meat mixture 5 minutes or until brown. To serve, place meat in center of each tortilla; top with cheese, refried beans, tomatoes, lettuce, avocado and salsa. Fold up tortilla. Serve with sour cream. *Makes 5 servings*

Grilled Ham Steaks with Apricot Glaze

1 pound boneless fully cooked ham,
    cut into 4 (1/2-inch-thick) slices
1/4 cup apricot jam
2 teaspoons Dijon mustard
2 teaspoons cider vinegar

Prepare grill. Combine jam, mustard and vinegar in small bowl; blend well. Grill ham slices over medium-hot coals 8 to 10 minutes or until browned, brushing with apricot sauce occasionally and turning once. Serve immediately.

Makes 4 servings

Favorite recipe from **National Pork Board**

Pesto Lasagna Rolls

Irish Stew in Bread

(Pictured at right)

1-1/2 pounds lean, boned American lamb shoulder,
    cut into 1-inch cubes
1/4 cup all-purpose flour
2 tablespoons vegetable oil
2 cloves garlic, crushed
2 cups water
1/4 cup Burgundy wine
5 medium carrots, chopped
3 medium potatoes, peeled and sliced
2 large onions, peeled and chopped
2 ribs celery, sliced
3/4 teaspoon black pepper
1 cube beef bouillon, crushed
1 cup frozen peas
1/4 pound sliced fresh mushrooms
    Round bread, unsliced*

*Stew can be served individually in small loaves or in one large loaf. Slice bread crosswise near top to form lid. Hollow larger piece, leaving 1-inch border. Fill "bowl" with hot stew; cover with "lid." Serve immediately.

Coat lamb with flour while heating oil over low heat in Dutch oven. Add lamb and garlic; cook and stir until brown. Add water, wine, carrots, potatoes, onions, celery, pepper and bouillon. Cover; simmer 30 to 35 minutes.

Add peas and mushrooms. Cover; simmer 10 minutes. Bring to a boil; adjust seasonings, if necessary. Serve in bread. *Makes 6 to 8 servings*

Favorite recipe from **American Lamb Council**

BelGioioso® Four Cheese Pasta

1/4 cup butter plus additional for greasing
1/4 cup all-purpose flour
1-1/2 cups milk
1 (28-ounce) can whole Italian tomatoes,
    drained and finely chopped, reserving
    1-1/4 cups juice
    Salt and pepper to taste
1 pound uncooked pasta
1-1/2 cups grated BELGIOIOSO® Parmesan Cheese
1/2 cup grated BELGIOIOSO® Asiago Cheese
1/2 cup grated BELGIOIOSO® Fontina Cheese
1-1/3 cups grated BELGIOIOSO® Romano Cheese,
    divided
1/2 cup chopped parsley leaves

Preheat oven to 375°F. Butter 3- to 4-quart shallow baking dish. In heavy saucepan over medium-low heat, melt 1/4 cup butter. Add flour and cook, whisking 3 minutes. Whisk milk and reserved tomato juice into flour mixture. Bring mixture to a boil. Stir in tomatoes, salt and pepper; simmer until thickened, about 3 minutes.

Cook pasta according to package directions; drain well. Combine milk mixture, BelGioioso® Parmesan, BelGioioso Asiago, BelGioioso Fontina, 1 cup BelGioioso Romano Cheese and parsley; transfer to serving dish. Sprinkle pasta with remaining 1/3 cup BelGioioso Romano Cheese. Serve immediately. *Makes 6 to 8 servings*

African Peanut Butter Chicken

6 skinless bone-in chicken breast halves
    (about 3 pounds)
1 tablespoon vegetable oil
1 large onion, peeled and thinly sliced
1 large red bell pepper, cut into thin strips
2 teaspoons salt
1 teaspoon curry powder
8 ounces (1 cup) NEWMAN'S OWN® Mild Salsa
1 large tomato, thinly sliced
1-1/2 cups uncooked rice
1/4 cup crunchy peanut butter
1/4 cup warm water

In 12-inch nonstick skillet over medium-high heat, cook chicken in batches in oil 5 minutes, turning once, until golden; remove and set aside.

Reduce heat to medium. Add onion, bell pepper, salt and curry powder; cook and stir 1 minute. Add salsa and tomato to skillet; cover and simmer 5 minutes.

Return chicken to skillet. Cover and simmer over medium-low heat 25 minutes or until chicken is cooked through. Meanwhile, cook rice according to package directions. Spoon onto large platter. Arrange chicken over rice; keep warm.

Whisk peanut butter with warm water in small bowl. Stir into vegetable mixture in skillet; heat to boiling. Spoon over chicken and rice. *Makes 6 servings*

Irish Stew in Bread

Springtime Pasta with Lemon Cream Sauce

(Pictured below)

1 (1-pound) package frozen ravioli
1 pound asparagus, cut into 1-1/2-inch pieces
1/2 cup milk
1 (3-ounce) package cream cheese, softened
1/4 cup butter or margarine
1 tablespoon freshly grated lemon peel
1 cup (6 ounces) diced CURE 81® ham
1/2 cup grated Parmesan cheese
1/8 teaspoon white pepper

In large saucepan, cook ravioli and asparagus in boiling water 7 minutes or until ravioli is tender. Drain. Meanwhile, in saucepan, combine milk, cream cheese, butter and lemon peel. Cook over medium heat 5 minutes. Stir in ham, Parmesan cheese and white pepper. Toss cream mixture with ravioli and asparagus. Serve immediately.   *Makes 4 servings*

Springtime Pasta with Lemon Cream Sauce

Zesty Steak Fajitas

3/4 cup *French's* Worcestershire Sauce, divided
1 pound boneless top round, sirloin or flank steak
3 tablespoons taco seasoning mix
2 red or green bell peppers, cut into quarters
1 to 2 large onions, cut into thick slices
3/4 cup chili sauce
8 (8-inch) flour or corn tortillas, heated
Sour cream and shredded cheese (optional)

Pour 1/2 cup Worcestershire over steak in deep dish. Cover and refrigerate 30 minutes or up to 3 hours. Drain meat and rub both sides with seasoning mix.

Grill meat and vegetables over medium-hot coals 10 to 15 minutes until meat is medium rare and vegetables are blackened but tender.

Thinly slice meat and vegetables. Place in large bowl. Add chili sauce and 1/4 cup Worcestershire. Toss to coat. Serve in tortillas and garnish with sour cream and cheese.   *Makes 4 servings*

Cornish Hens with New Potatoes, Artichokes and Peas

4 PERDUE® Fresh Cornish Hens, wings tucked under, legs tied together
3 lemons, halved
1/4 cup fresh basil, chopped
2 tablespoons olive oil
Salt and pepper, to taste
1 pound new potatoes, halved or quartered if large
2 (14-ounce) cans artichoke hearts in water, drained and halved
1 cup chicken broth
1 cup frozen peas, thawed

Preheat oven to 350°F. Set Cornish hens in a large roasting pan and squeeze lemons over them. Sprinkle with basil, olive oil, salt and pepper. Scatter potatoes and artichoke hearts around Cornish hens and add chicken broth. Season vegetables with salt and pepper. Roast until meat thermometer inserted into thickest part of thigh registers 180°F (approximately 1 hour).

Transfer Cornish hens to a serving platter. Stir peas into vegetables and transfer to a serving dish.
    Makes 4 servings

Creamy Pesto Chicken & Bow Ties

Creamy Pesto Chicken & Bow Ties

(Pictured above)

3 cups uncooked bow tie pasta
2 tablespoons butter *or* margarine
1 pound boneless chicken breasts, cubed
1 can (10-3/4 ounces) CAMPBELL'S® Cream of Chicken *or* 98% Fat Free Cream of Chicken Soup
1/2 cup pesto sauce
1/2 cup milk

1. **COOK** pasta according to package directions. Drain.

2. **MEANWHILE**, heat butter in skillet. Add chicken and cook until browned, stirring often.

3. **ADD** soup, pesto sauce and milk. Bring to a boil. Cook over low heat 5 minutes or until done. Stir in drained pasta and heat through.

Makes 4 servings

Moroccan Lamb or Beef

3/4 pound ground lamb or beef
1 cup chopped onion
1 can (14-1/2 ounces) DEL MONTE® Stewed Tomatoes - Original Recipe
1/3 cup chopped dried apricots
1/4 cup seedless raisins
1 teaspoon ground cinnamon
1/4 teaspoon ground cloves
1 banana, sliced
2 cups hot cooked rice, brown rice or bulgur

Brown meat in large skillet over medium-high heat.

Add onion and cook until tender; drain. Add tomatoes, apricots, raisins, cinnamon and cloves.

Cover and simmer 10 minutes. Season with salt and pepper, if desired. Add banana. Heat through. Serve over rice. Top with plain yogurt and chopped peanuts, if desired. *Makes 4 to 5 servings*

Sautéed Swordfish with Cherry Salsa

(Pictured at right)

SALSA

    2 cups coarsely chopped fresh tomatoes
    1 cup coarsely chopped green bell pepper
    1 cup coarsely chopped red bell pepper
  1/2 cup coarsely chopped onion
  1/2 cup SMUCKER'S® Cherry Preserves
  1/4 cup minced jalapeño or other hot chili
      peppers*
    1 teaspoon hot pepper sauce
  1/2 teaspoon salt

SWORDFISH

    3 to 4 tablespoons CRISCO® Vegetable Oil**
1-1/2 pounds fresh swordfish, cut into 4 portions
      about 1 inch thick
    Salt and black pepper to taste

When handling jalapeño peppers, be sure to wear rubber gloves and do not touch your face, nose, eyes or lips before thoroughly washing your hands.

**Or use your favorite Crisco Oil.*

1. Combine salsa ingredients in food processor; pulse 4 to 8 times or until salsa is slightly chunky.

2. Heat oil in heavy cast iron or nonstick skillet over medium-high heat. Lightly season swordfish with salt and pepper; place in skillet.

3. Cook swordfish for 5 to 7 minutes; turn and cook 8 minutes longer or until swordfish is slightly firm to the touch.

4. Place swordfish on serving plates; top each piece with several tablespoons salsa.

Makes 4 servings

Fusilli with Fresh Red & Yellow Tomato Sauce

  1/2 cup (1 stick) I CAN'T BELIEVE IT'S NOT
      BUTTER!® Spread
    1 medium onion, chopped
    2 cloves garlic, finely chopped (optional)
1-1/2 pounds red and/or yellow cherry tomatoes,
      halved
  1/3 cup chopped fresh basil leaves
    1 box (16 ounces) fusilli (long curly pasta)
      or linguine, cooked and drained
    Grated Parmesan cheese

In 12-inch nonstick skillet, melt I Can't Believe It's Not Butter!® Spread over medium heat and cook onion, stirring occasionally, 2 minutes or until softened. Stir in garlic and tomatoes and cook, stirring occasionally, 5 minutes or until tomatoes soften but do not lose their shape and sauce thickens slightly. Stir in basil and season, if desired, with salt and ground black pepper.

In large serving bowl, toss sauce with hot fusilli and sprinkle with cheese. *Makes 4 servings*

Ginger Apple Chicken

    4 boneless skinless chicken breast halves
      (1 pound)
    1 (16-ounce) jar MOTT'S® Apple Sauce
  1/4 cup apple-cider vinegar or white vinegar
    2 tablespoons soy sauce
    1 tablespoon grated fresh ginger
    1 tablespoon honey

1. Pound chicken breasts with meat mallet to 1/2-inch thickness. Place in single layer in large shallow glass dish.

2. In medium bowl, combine apple sauce, vinegar, soy sauce, ginger and honey. Reserve 1 cup apple sauce mixture. Pour remaining apple sauce mixture over chicken; turn to coat both sides. Cover and marinate in refrigerator at least 20 minutes or overnight.

3. Drain chicken; discard marinade from dish.

4. Broil chicken, on foil-lined baking sheet, 4 inches from heat, 10 minutes or until chicken is no longer pink in center, turning halfway through cooking time. Or, grill chicken, on covered grill over medium-hot coals, 10 minutes or until chicken is no longer pink in center, turning halfway through cooking time. Serve with reserved apple sauce mixture, warmed or at room temperature. Refrigerate leftovers. *Makes 4 servings*

Sautéed Swordfish with Cherry Salsa

Citrus Beef and Noodles

(Pictured at right)

8 ounces uncooked no-yolk or regular egg
   noodles
4 teaspoons cornstarch
3/4 cup orange juice
3 tablespoons LA CHOY® Reduced Sodium
   Soy Sauce (or regular soy sauce)
1 tablespoon packed brown sugar
1/2 teaspoon ground ginger
2 teaspoons WESSON® Vegetable Oil
1 pound boneless sirloin beef, cut across the
   grain into 1/4-inch-thick slices
1 can (14.5 ounces) HUNT'S® Diced Tomatoes
   in Juice, undrained
2 cups fresh or frozen snow peas, trimmed

COOK noodles according to package directions;
drain and keep warm.

COMBINE cornstarch, orange juice, soy sauce,
brown sugar and ginger; stir until cornstarch is
completely dissolved. Set aside.

HEAT oil in wok or large skillet over medium-high
heat. Add beef and cook until no longer pink, about
3 minutes. Remove from wok; keep warm.

WHISK orange juice mixture and add to skillet;
add tomatoes. Bring to a boil. Add snow peas;
simmer until crisp-tender, stirring frequently.

RETURN beef to wok; cook until heated through,
about 2 minutes.

SERVE over hot cooked noodles.

Makes 4 servings

Moo Shu Pork

2 teaspoons cornstarch
1 cup DOLE® Pineapple Juice
1 tablespoon soy sauce
2 teaspoons sesame oil
8 ounces pork tenderloin, cut into thin strips
1-1/2 cups Oriental-style mixed vegetables
1/4 cup hoisin sauce (optional)
8 (8-inch) flour tortillas, warmed
2 green onions, cut into thin strips

• Stir cornstarch, juice, soy sauce and sesame oil
in shallow, nonmetallic dish until blended; remove
1/2 cup mixture for sauce.

• Add pork to remaining juice mixture in shallow
dish. Cover and marinate 15 minutes in refrigerator.
Drain pork; discard marinade.

• Cook and stir pork in large, nonstick skillet
over medium-high heat 2 minutes or until pork
is lightly browned. Add vegetables; cook and stir
3 to 4 minutes or until vegetables are tender-crisp.
Stir in reserved 1/2 cup juice mixture; cook 1 minute
or until sauce thickens.

• Spread hoisin sauce onto center of each tortilla, if
desired; top with moo shu pork. Sprinkle with green
onions. Fold opposite sides of tortilla over filling;
fold remaining sides of tortilla over filling. Garnish
with slivered green onions, kumquats and fresh
herbs, if desired.   *Makes 4 servings*

Picadillo Stuffed
Pepper Casserole

1 pound ground beef
1 clove garlic, minced *or* 1/8 teaspoon garlic
   powder
1 can (about 14-1/2 ounces) stewed tomatoes
1/2 cup PACE® Picante Sauce
1 teaspoon ground cumin
1/4 teaspoon ground cinnamon
1/3 cup raisins
1/3 cup toasted slivered almonds
2 medium green peppers, seeded and cut into
   lengthwise quarters
1/2 cup shredded Cheddar cheese
   Fresh basil leaves

1. **COOK** beef and garlic in skillet until browned.

2. **ADD** tomatoes, picante sauce, cumin, cinnamon,
raisins and almonds. Heat through.

3. **ARRANGE** peppers in 2-quart casserole. Spoon
beef mixture over peppers. **Cover.**

4. **BAKE** at 400°F for 25 minutes or until peppers are
tender. Uncover. Top with cheese. Bake 5 minutes or
until cheese melts. Garnish with basil.

Makes 4 servings

Tip: To toast almonds, arrange almonds in single
layer in shallow-sided baking pan. Bake at 350°F
for 10 minutes or until lightly browned.

Citrus Beef and Noodles

Heartwarming Beef Stew Skillet

(Pictured at right and on back cover)

1 tablespoon WESSON® Vegetable Oil
1 pound boneless beef sirloin, seasoned with salt and black pepper, cut into 1-inch cubes
1 can (14.5 ounces) HUNT'S® Stewed Tomatoes, undrained
2 packages (0.87 ounces each) brown gravy mix
2 cups cold water
1 tablespoon Worcestershire sauce
1 bag (16 ounces) frozen stew vegetables, thawed

HEAT oil over medium-high heat in a large skillet. Add beef, in batches, if necessary, to brown. Remove beef; set aside.

ADD tomatoes, gravy mix blended with cold water, Worcestershire sauce and vegetables; bring to a boil.

RETURN beef to skillet; reduce heat. Cook, covered, 10 minutes or until vegetables are tender, stirring occasionally. *Makes 4 servings*

Roasted Vegetable Sausage Strudel

2 large heads garlic
3 tablespoons vegetable oil, divided
1 pound BOB EVANS® Savory Sage Roll Sausage
2 medium zucchini, cut lengthwise into 1/8-inch-thick slices
2 medium yellow squash, cut lengthwise into 1/8-inch-thick slices
1 large red onion, cut into wedges and separated into layers
  Salt and black pepper to taste
1 large red bell pepper, cored and seeded
1 (17-3/4-ounce) package frozen puff pastry sheets, thawed according to package directions
1/2 pound sliced Munster cheese

Preheat oven to 400°F. Place garlic in small shallow baking pan and drizzle with 1 tablespoon oil. Cover with foil and bake about 30 minutes or until lightly browned and soft. Crumble and cook sausage in medium skillet, making sure sausage does not dry out. Drain on paper towels and reserve.

Place zucchini, yellow squash and onion in large bowl; season lightly with salt and black pepper. Toss with remaining 2 tablespoons oil until evenly coated. Cook vegetables on grill or in oven 3 to 5 minutes or just until tender. Roast whole bell pepper on grill or in oven 25 minutes or until soft. Wrap in plastic wrap; let stand 10 minutes. Rinse pepper under running water, remove skin and cut into wedges.

To assemble strudel, press or roll out puff pastry sheets into 16×12-inch rectangles on lightly floured surface. Cut tops off roasted garlic heads. Squeeze garlic paste from cloves onto pastry sheets and spread evenly to cover, leaving border of 1/2 inch on short sides and 1 inch on long sides. Layer vegetables lengthwise down center of pastry. Cover with cooled sausage; top with cheese. Brush edges of pastry with water. Starting from long sides, wrap pastry around filling to form log, overlapping long edges of pastry by at least 1/2 inch. Seal ends of logs by folding under. Seal bottom seams and place strudels on lightly greased baking sheet about 2 inches apart.

Brush tops and sides of strudels with water for even browning. Cut 3 short slits on top of each strudel to allow steam to escape during baking. Place on center rack of oven and bake 35 to 40 minutes or until strudels are lightly browned. Let cool 5 minutes before cutting into 1-inch slices. Refrigerate leftovers.
Makes 6 to 8 servings (2 to 3 slices per main-dish serving)

Note: Cooking vegetables on a charcoal or gas grill adds the best flavor to this dish. (Scrape blackened skin off red pepper after grilling.) Or, use purchased roasted red peppers from a jar instead.

Helpful Hint

Puff pastry is a rich, delicate pastry made by layering chilled butter or shortening and pastry dough, then rolling out and folding the dough repeatedly. When baked, the pastry "puffs" as the moisture in the butter creates steam between the layers and causes them to separate.

Heartwarming Beef Stew Skillet

Hearty Shepherd's Pie

Black Bean & Pork Stew

2 (15-ounce) cans cooked black beans, rinsed and drained
2 cups water
1 pound boneless ham, cut into 3/4-inch cubes
3/4 pound BOB EVANS® Italian Dinner Link Sausage, cut into 1-inch pieces
3/4 pound BOB EVANS® Smoked Sausage, cut into 1-inch pieces
1 pint cherry tomatoes, stems removed
1 medium onion, chopped
6 cloves garlic, minced
1 teaspoon red pepper flakes
1/8 teaspoon grated orange peel
Cornbread or rolls (optional)

Preheat oven to 350°F. Combine all ingredients except cornbread in large Dutch oven. Bring to a boil over high heat, skimming foam off if necessary. Cover; transfer to oven. Bake 30 minutes; uncover and bake 30 minutes more, stirring occasionally. Serve hot with cornbread, if desired, or cool slightly, then cover and refrigerate overnight. Remove any fat from surface. Reheat over low heat. Refrigerate leftovers.   *Makes 8 servings*

Hearty Shepherd's Pie

(Pictured above)

1-1/2 pounds ground beef
2 cups *French's*® French Fried Onions, divided
1 can (10-3/4 ounces) condensed tomato soup, undiluted
1/2 cup water
2 teaspoons Italian seasoning
1/4 teaspoon salt
1/4 teaspoon pepper
1 package (10 ounces) frozen mixed vegetables, thawed
3 cups hot mashed potatoes

1. Preheat oven to 375°F. Cook meat in large ovenproof skillet until browned; drain. Stir in *1 cup* French Fried Onions, soup, water, Italian seasoning, salt and pepper.

2. Spoon vegetables over beef mixture. Top with mashed potatoes.

3. Bake 20 minutes or until hot. Sprinkle with remaining *1 cup* onions. Bake 2 minutes or until golden.   *Makes 6 servings*

Lemony Vegetable Salmon Pasta

1/2 pound salmon fillet
Juice of 1 SUNKIST® lemon, divided
2 cups broccoli florets
2 medium carrots, thinly sliced diagonally
1 cup chicken broth
1 teaspoon sesame oil
1 tablespoon cornstarch
1-1/2 cups (4 ounces) uncooked spiral-shaped pasta, cooked and drained

In large nonstick skillet, cover salmon with water. Add juice of 1/2 lemon. Bring to a boil; reduce heat and simmer 10 to 12 minutes or until fish flakes easily with fork. Remove salmon; cool enough to remove skin and flake fish. Discard liquid. In clean skillet, combine broccoli, carrots, chicken broth and sesame oil. Bring to a boil. Reduce heat; cover and briskly simmer 5 minutes or until vegetables are just tender. Combine cornstarch with remaining lemon juice; stir into vegetable mixture. Cook, stirring, until mixture thickens. Add cooked pasta and reserved salmon; heat. Serve with lemon wedges, if desired.   *Makes 4 servings*

Fabulous Fast Shrimp

(Pictured below)

1 tablespoon butter *or* margarine
2 stalks celery, chopped
1/4 cup chopped green pepper
1/4 cup sliced green onions
1 pound fresh large shrimp, shelled and
    deveined
1 can (10-3/4 ounces) CAMPBELL'S® Cream of
    Chicken *or* 98% Fat Free Cream of Chicken
    Soup
1/2 cup water
    Dash cayenne pepper
    Hot cooked rice
    Paprika

1. **HEAT** butter in skillet. Add celery, green pepper and green onions and cook until tender. Add shrimp and cook 3 to 5 minutes or until done.

2. **ADD** soup, water and cayenne pepper and heat through. Serve over rice. Sprinkle with paprika.

Makes 4 servings

Cheesy Chicken Pot Pie

1 pound boneless, skinless chicken breast halves,
    cut into 1/2-inch chunks
1 tablespoon all-purpose flour
1 jar (1 pound) RAGÚ® Cheesy! Double Cheddar
    Sauce
1 bag (16 ounces) frozen mixed vegetables,
    thawed
1 prepared pastry for single-crust pie

Preheat oven to 425°F. In 2-quart casserole, toss chicken with flour. Stir in Ragú Cheddar Sauce and vegetables. Cover casserole with prepared pastry. Press pastry around edge of casserole to seal; trim excess pastry, then flute edges. Cover with aluminum foil and bake 20 minutes. Remove foil and continue baking 20 minutes or until crust is golden and chicken is thoroughly cooked. Let stand 5 minutes before serving.

Makes 6 servings

Tip: This is the perfect dish for leftovers. Substitute cooked pork roast, turkey breast or even roast beef for the chicken.

Fabulous Fast Shrimp

Italian Sausage and Vegetable Stew

(Pictured at right)

1 pound hot or mild Italian sausage links, cut into 1-inch pieces
1 package (16 ounces) frozen vegetable blend, such as onions and green, red and yellow bell peppers
2 medium zucchini, sliced
1 can (14-1/2 ounces) diced Italian-style tomatoes, undrained
1 jar (4-1/2 ounces) sliced mushrooms, drained
4 garlic cloves, minced

1. Cook sausage in large saucepan, covered, over medium to medium-high heat 5 minutes or until browned; pour off drippings.

2. Add frozen vegetables, zucchini, tomatoes with juice, mushrooms and garlic; bring to a boil. Reduce heat and simmer, covered, 10 minutes. Cook uncovered 5 to 10 minutes or until thickened slightly.

Makes 6 servings

Skillet Pasta Roma

(Pictured on page 126)

1/2 pound Italian sausage, sliced or crumbled
1 large onion, coarsely chopped
1 large clove garlic, minced
2 cans (14-1/2 ounces each) DEL MONTE® Diced Tomatoes with Basil, Garlic & Oregano
1 can (8 ounces) DEL MONTE Tomato Sauce
1 cup water
8 ounces uncooked rotini or other spiral pasta
8 mushrooms, sliced (optional)
Grated Parmesan cheese and fresh parsley sprigs (optional)

1. Brown sausage in large skillet. Add onion and garlic. Cook until onion is soft; drain. Stir in undrained tomatoes, tomato sauce, water and pasta.

2. Cover and bring to a boil; reduce heat. Simmer, covered, 25 to 30 minutes or until pasta is tender, stirring occasionally.

3. Stir in mushrooms, if desired; simmer 5 minutes. Serve in skillet garnished with cheese and parsley, if desired.

Makes 4 servings

Pork Tenderloin with Orange Glaze

1 cup orange juice
1/4 cup cider vinegar
1 tablespoon finely grated fresh ginger
1 teaspoon finely grated orange peel
1 pork tenderloin (about 1 pound)
Salt and black pepper
Orange Glaze (recipe follows)

Combine orange juice, vinegar, ginger and orange peel in a shallow glass dish or large heavy plastic bag. Add pork tenderloin; cover dish or close bag. Marinate in refrigerator at least 4 hours, turning several times.

Meanwhile, prepare Orange Glaze. Reserve about 1/4 cup for brushing on meat. Remove pork from marinade; discard marinade. Season pork with salt and pepper.

Oil hot grid to help prevent sticking. Grill pork, on a covered grill, over medium KINGSFORD® Briquets, 18 to 25 minutes until a meat thermometer inserted in the thickest part registers 155°F. Brush with reserved Orange Glaze the last 5 to 10 minutes of cooking. Let pork stand 5 to 10 minutes to allow the internal temperature to rise to 160°F before slicing. Slice and serve with remaining Orange Glaze. Garnish, if desired.

Makes 4 servings

Orange Glaze

1 cup orange marmalade
2 tablespoons soy sauce
2 tablespoons cider vinegar
1 tablespoon finely grated ginger
1 tablespoon Dijon mustard
1/4 teaspoon salt
1/4 teaspoon black pepper

Melt orange marmalade in a small saucepan. Stir in remaining ingredients; reduce heat to low. Cook about 10 minutes. Reserve 1/4 cup of glaze for brushing pork; place remaining glaze in a small bowl to serve as accompaniment.

Makes about 1 cup

Italian Sausage and Vegetable Stew

Spicy Fish Tacos with Fresh Salsa

(Pictured at right)

3/4 cup plus 2 tablespoons *Frank's® RedHot® Chile 'n Lime™* Hot Sauce, divided
1 pound thick, firm white fish fillets, such as cod, halibut or sea bass, cut into 3/4-inch cubes
1/2 cup sour cream
1-1/2 cups finely chopped plum tomatoes
1/4 cup minced cilantro
2 tablespoons minced red onion
2 cups shredded iceberg lettuce
8 taco shells, warmed

1. Pour 1/2 cup *Chile 'n Lime™* Hot Sauce over fish in resealable plastic bag. Marinate in refrigerator 30 minutes.

2. Combine 1/4 cup *Chile 'n Lime™* Hot Sauce and sour cream in small bowl; chill until needed.

3. Combine tomatoes, cilantro, onion and remaining 2 tablespoons *Chile 'n Lime™* Hot Sauce. Reserve.

4. Drain fish and discard marinade. Heat large nonstick skillet until hot; coat with vegetable cooking spray. Stir-fry fish 3 to 5 minutes until just opaque and flakes with fork. Fill each taco shell with shredded lettuce, cooked fish and salsa. Drizzle with sour cream mixture.

Makes 4 to 6 servings

Variation: Substitute 1 pound peeled and deveined shrimp for fish.

Mexican Lasagna

1 jar (1 pound 10 ounces) RAGÚ® Old World Style® Pasta Sauce
1 pound ground beef
1 can (15-1/4 ounces) whole kernel corn, drained
4-1/2 teaspoons chili powder
6 (8-1/2-inch) flour tortillas
2 cups shredded Cheddar cheese (about 8 ounces)

1. Preheat oven to 350°F. Set aside 1 cup Ragú Pasta Sauce. In 10-inch skillet, brown ground beef over medium-high heat; drain. Stir in remaining Ragú Pasta Sauce, corn and chili powder.

2. In 13×9-inch baking dish, spread 1 cup sauce mixture. Arrange two tortillas over sauce, overlapping edges slightly. Layer half the sauce mixture and 1/3 of the cheese over tortillas; repeat layers, ending with tortillas. Spread tortillas with reserved sauce.

3. Bake 30 minutes, then top with remaining cheese and bake an additional 10 minutes or until sauce is bubbling and cheese is melted. *Makes 8 servings*

Tip: Substitute refried beans for ground beef for a meatless main dish.

Chicken Thai Stir-Fry

4 boneless, skinless chicken breast halves, cut into 1/2-inch strips
2 tablespoons vegetable oil
2 teaspoons grated fresh ginger
2 cloves garlic, minced
2 cups broccoli flowerets
1 medium yellow squash, cut into 1/4-inch slices
1 medium red bell pepper, cut into 2-inch strips
1/3 cup creamy peanut butter
1/4 cup soy sauce
2 tablespoons white vinegar
2 teaspoons brown sugar
1/2 teaspoon crushed red pepper
1/3 cup chicken broth, fat skimmed
8 ounces linguine, cooked according to package directions
2 green onions, white and green parts, thinly sliced

In large skillet, heat oil over medium-high heat. Add chicken, ginger and garlic; cook and stir about 5 minutes or until chicken is lightly browned and fork-tender. Remove chicken mixture to bowl; set aside. To drippings in same skillet, add broccoli, squash and red bell pepper strips. Cook, stirring, about 5 minutes or until vegetables are crisp-tender. Remove vegetables to bowl with chicken; set aside. To same skillet, add peanut butter, soy sauce, vinegar, brown sugar and crushed red pepper; stir in chicken broth. Return chicken and vegetables to pan; heat through. Serve over linguine. Sprinkle with green onions. *Makes 4 servings*

Favorite recipe from **Delmarva Poultry Industry, Inc.**

Spicy Fish Tacos with Fresh Salsa

Teriyaki Steak with Onions and Mushrooms

(Pictured at right)

1 boneless beef sirloin steak, about 1 inch thick (1-1/2 pounds)
3/4 cup teriyaki sauce, divided
1 tablespoon vegetable oil
1 can (8 ounces) sliced mushrooms, drained
1 small red or green bell pepper, cut into strips
1-1/3 cups *French's*® French Fried Onions, divided

1. Brush each side of steak with 1 tablespoon teriyaki sauce. Heat oil in grill pan or heavy skillet over medium-high heat. Cook steak for 3 to 4 minutes per side or until desired doneness. Remove steak; keep warm.

2. Add mushrooms and bell pepper to pan; cook until pepper is crisp-tender. Stir in remaining teriyaki sauce and *2/3 cup* French Fried Onions; heat through.

3. Serve mushroom mixture over steak. Sprinkle with remaining onions. *Makes 6 servings*

Grilled Salmon with Sweet Orange Salsa

1 tablespoon curry powder
1 teaspoon ground coriander
1 teaspoon powdered garlic
1 teaspoon dry mustard
6 salmon steaks (6 to 8 ounces each)
2 cups grape or cherry tomatoes, quartered
1 cup SMUCKER'S® Sweet Orange Marmalade
1 cup chopped peanuts
1/2 cup packed chopped cilantro leaves
1 to 2 tablespoons fresh lime juice
3 tablespoons peanut oil

1. In small bowl, stir together curry powder, coriander, garlic and dry mustard. Using clean hands, rub spice mixture on both sides of each salmon steak. Place salmon in resealable plastic bag; set bag on platter and refrigerate for 1 hour.

2. Meanwhile, in medium bowl, combine tomatoes, marmalade, peanuts, cilantro and lime juice; mix gently. Refrigerate salsa until serving time.

3. Remove salmon from refrigerator; brush each steak on both sides with oil. Transfer salmon

to heated grill; cook over medium-hot coals for 5 to 6 minutes on each side.

4. Serve each salmon steak with 1/2 cup salsa. (There will be leftover salsa.) *Makes 6 servings*

Spaghetti Squash with Tuna-Vegetable Sauce

1 spaghetti squash (about 1 pound), cut lengthwise into halves
1/4 cup water
1 medium zucchini, cut lengthwise into quarters and thinly sliced
1 cup chopped carrots
1/2 cup chopped onion
1 clove garlic, minced
1 large fresh tomato, chopped
2 cups tomato sauce
1 (7-ounce) STARKIST Flavor Fresh Pouch® Albacore Tuna
1 teaspoon dried basil, crushed
1 teaspoon dried rosemary, crushed
1/4 cup grated Parmesan or Romano cheese

Arrange squash, cut side up, in a shallow microwavable dish; add water. Cover loosely; micro-cook on HIGH power for 9 to 12 minutes, rotating dish once during cooking. Let stand, covered, while preparing sauce.

In a large microwavable bowl combine zucchini, carrots, onion and garlic. Micro-cook on HIGH power for 3 to 5 minutes or until tender, stirring once. Stir in tomato, tomato sauce, tuna, basil and rosemary. Cover loosely; micro-cook on HIGH power for 3 to 5 minutes or until sauce is heated through, stirring once. Using 2 forks, remove squash pulp by pulling it from the rind. Pile it onto a serving platter. Spoon tuna sauce over; sprinkle with cheese. Garnish with fresh basil, if desired. Serve immediately *Makes 4 to 5 servings*

Teriyaki Steak with Onions and Mushrooms

Spinach Lasagna Alfredo

(Pictured at right)

1 medium onion, diced
1 red or green pepper, diced
2 tablespoons olive oil
2 pounds cooked chicken breasts, diced
2 jars (16 ounces each) Alfredo sauce or roasted garlic Parmesan pasta sauce (such as RAGÚ®)
1/2 cup water
1 package (16 ounces) lasagna noodles, uncooked
1 can (27 ounces) *or* 2 cans (13.5 ounces each) POPEYE® Spinach, well drained
5 cups shredded mozzarella cheese
4 tablespoons Italian seasoning

Preheat oven to 375°F. Sauté onion and pepper in olive oil until tender. Place in large mixing bowl with diced chicken. Add pasta sauce and water to chicken mixture and mix well. Place 1 cup mixture in the bottom of a greased 13×9×2-inch baking dish. Top with 1 layer of uncooked lasagna noodles. Add 1/4 of the remaining mixture; layer with 1/4 of the spinach, 1 cup mozzarella cheese, 1 tablespoon Italian seasoning, and lasagna noodles. Repeat layers 3 times, ending with 1 cup mozzarella. Cover pan tightly with aluminum foil. Bake for 1-1/2 hours. Remove foil; bake an additional 30 minutes or until cheese browns. Let stand for 15 minutes before serving. *Makes 8 to 10 servings*

Tip: For a more traditional lasagna texture, two pounds of browned ground turkey can be substituted for diced chicken.

Country Roasted Chicken Dinner

1 envelope LIPTON® RECIPE SECRETS® Savory Herb with Garlic Soup Mix*
2 tablespoons honey
1 tablespoon water
1 tablespoon I CAN'T BELIEVE IT'S NOT BUTTER!® Spread, melted
1 roasting chicken (5 to 6 pounds)
3 pounds all-purpose and/or sweet potatoes, cut into chunks

Also terrific with Lipton® Recipe Secrets® Golden Onion Soup Mix.

Preheat oven to 350°F.

In small bowl, blend savory herb with garlic soup mix, honey, water and I Can't Believe It's Not Butter!® Spread.

In 18×12-inch roasting pan, arrange chicken, breast side up; brush with soup mixture. Cover loosely with aluminum foil. Roast 30 minutes; drain off drippings. Arrange potatoes around chicken and continue roasting covered, stirring potatoes occasionally, 1 hour or until meat thermometer inserted in thigh reaches 180°F and potatoes are tender. *If chicken reaches 180°F before potatoes are tender, remove chicken to serving platter and keep warm. Continue roasting potatoes until tender.*
Makes about 8 servings

Note: Insert meat thermometer into thickest part of thigh between breast and thigh. Make sure tip does not touch bone.

Garlic & Herb Chicken Sauté

1 pound boneless, skinless chicken,* cut into strips
1 cup KC MASTERPIECE™ Garlic & Herb Marinade, divided
1 tablespoon vegetable oil
6 cups assorted fresh vegetables,** such as broccoli florets, sliced mushrooms, sliced carrots, chopped onion and bell pepper
Hot cooked rice

Strips of lean pork can be substituted for chicken.

**For a quick and easy version, substitute 6 cups assorted frozen vegetables; cook as directed.*

Place chicken in bowl and add 1/2 cup Garlic & Herb Marinade; stir to coat. Marinate in refrigerator for 10 minutes. Heat oil in large nonstick skillet over high heat. Stir in vegetables and sauté until crisp-tender, about 7 minutes. Remove from skillet; set aside. Sauté marinated chicken in hot skillet until chicken is opaque, about 4 minutes. Add reserved vegetables and remaining 1/2 cup marinade to chicken; stir to combine. Heat thoroughly. Serve immediately with hot cooked rice.

Makes 4 servings

Triangle Tostadas

(Pictured below)

2 large (burrito size) flour tortillas
  Vegetable oil
1 package (about 1 pound) lean ground pork
1 package (1 ounce) LAWRY'S® Taco Spices &
  Seasonings
2/3 cup water
1 can (16 ounces) refried beans, warmed

TOPPINGS
  Shredded lettuce and cheese
  Chopped tomatoes

Preheat oven to 400°F. Cut each tortilla into
quarters, forming 4 triangles. Place triangles in
single layer on baking sheet. Brush each side of
triangles lightly with oil. Bake for 4 to 5 minutes or
until golden brown and crispy; let cool. Meanwhile,
in large skillet, brown ground pork over medium
high heat until crumbly; drain fat. Stir in Taco Spices
& Seasonings and water. Bring to a boil; reduce heat
to low and cook, uncovered for 7 minutes or until
pork is thoroughly cooked, stirring occasionally.
To assemble tostadas, evenly divide and spread

refried beans on each tortilla triangle. Spread about
1/4 cup seasoned pork on top of beans. Top with
shredded lettuce, cheese and tomatoes, as desired.
Makes 8 tostadas

Variations: Cut each tortilla into 8 pieces and make
mini appetizer tostadas. For additional toppings, try
sliced black olives, sour cream, guacamole, salsa or
jalapeños.

Layered Mexican Tortilla Cheese Casserole

1 can (14-1/2 ounces) salsa-style or Mexican-
  style stewed tomatoes, undrained
1/2 cup chopped fresh cilantro, divided
2 tablespoons fresh lime juice
  Nonstick vegetable cooking spray
6 (6-inch) corn tortillas, torn into 1-1/2-inch
  pieces
1 can (15 ounces) black beans, rinsed and
  drained
1 can (8 ounces) whole kernel corn, drained *or*
  1 cup frozen whole kernel corn, thawed
2 cups (8 ounces) SARGENTO® Mexican Blend
  Shredded Cheese

1. In small bowl, combine tomatoes, 1/4 cup cilantro
and lime juice; set aside.

2. Coat 8-inch square baking dish with cooking
spray. Arrange 1/4 of tortillas in bottom of dish;
spoon 1/4 of tomato mixture over tortillas. Top
with 1/4 of beans, 1/4 of corn and 1/4 of cheese.
Repeat layering 3 more times with remaining
tortillas, tomato mixture, beans, corn and cheese.

3. Bake uncovered at 375°F 25 minutes or until
cheese is melted and sauce is bubbly. Sprinkle
with remaining 1/4 cup cilantro. Let stand
10 minutes before serving. *Makes 4 servings*

Triangle Tostada

Helpful Hint

*Limes should be refrigerated,
although they may be kept at
room temperature for a few days,
if necessary. Keep them out of
the sunlight to prevent them
from turning yellow.*

Snappy Halibut Skillet

Snappy Halibut Skillet

(Pictured above)

1/2 teaspoon thyme, crushed
1-1/2 pounds halibut or other firm white fish
1 tablespoon olive oil
1 onion, chopped
1 clove garlic, minced
1 tablespoon cornstarch
1 can (14-1/2 ounces) DEL MONTE®
    Stewed Tomatoes, No Salt Added
1/4 cup sliced green onions

1. Sprinkle thyme over both sides of fish. In large skillet, cook fish in hot oil over medium-high heat until fish flakes easily when tested with fork. Remove fish to plate; keep warm.

2. Cook chopped onion and garlic in same skillet until tender. Stir cornstarch into tomatoes; pour into skillet. Cook, stirring frequently, until thickened. Return fish to skillet; top with green onions. Heat through.
Makes 4 servings

Quick Veg•All® Enchiladas

1 can (15 ounces) VEG•ALL® Original
    Mixed Vegetables, drained
1 can (15 ounces) refried beans
8 (6-inch) corn tortillas
1 can (10 ounces) enchilada sauce
1 cup shredded cheddar cheese
1 cup sour cream
1/2 cup chopped green onions
1/2 cup chopped ripe olives

Preheat oven to 350°F. Combine Veg•All and beans in medium bowl. Divide mixture and place in center of each tortilla; roll up. Place rolled tortillas in baking dish. Cover tortillas with enchilada sauce and cheese. Bake for 30 minutes. Top with sour cream, green onions and olives.
Makes 4 servings

Note: If the tortillas unfold as you are assembling them, turn them seam side down.

Hearty Chili Macaroni

(Pictured at right)

1 pound lean ground beef
1 medium onion, chopped
1 package (1.25 ounces) chili seasoning
1 can (14.5 ounces) HUNT'S® Petite Diced
    Tomatoes with Mild Green Chilies,
    undrained
1 can (15 ounces) kidney beans
1 cup cooked small elbow macaroni

COOK beef and onion in a large skillet until beef is
no longer pink; drain.

BLEND in next 3 ingredients; bring to a boil, cover
and simmer for 10 minutes.

STIR in macaroni; heat through.   *Makes 4 servings*

Tortellini Bake Parmesano

1 package (12 ounces) fresh or frozen cheese
    tortellini or ravioli
1/2 pound lean ground beef
1/2 medium onion, finely chopped
2 cloves garlic, minced
1/2 teaspoon dried oregano, crushed
1 can (26 ounces) DEL MONTE® Chunky
    Spaghetti Sauce with Garlic & Herb
2 small zucchini, sliced
1/3 cup (about 1-1/2 ounces) grated Parmesan
    cheese

1. Cook pasta according to package directions;
rinse and drain.

2. Meanwhile, brown beef with onion, garlic and
oregano in large skillet over medium-high heat;
drain. Season with salt and pepper, if desired.

3. Add spaghetti sauce and zucchini. Cook
15 minutes or until thickened, stirring occasionally.

4. Arrange half of pasta in oiled 2-quart microwavable
dish; top with half each of sauce and cheese. Repeat
layers ending with cheese; cover.

5. Microwave on HIGH 8 to 10 minutes or until
heated through, rotating dish halfway through
cooking time.   *Makes 4 servings*

Hint: For convenience, double the recipe and freeze
one for later use. The recipe can also be made
ahead, refrigerated and heated just before serving
(allow extra time in the microwave if dish is chilled).

Brunch Sausage Casserole

4 cups cubed day-old bread
2 cups (8 ounces) shredded sharp cheddar
    cheese
2 cans (12 fluid ounces *each*) NESTLÉ®
    CARNATION® Evaporated Milk
10 eggs, lightly beaten
1 teaspoon dry mustard
1/4 teaspoon onion powder
1 package (16 ounces) fresh breakfast sausage,
    cooked, drained and crumbled
    Ground black pepper to taste

GREASE 13×9-inch baking dish. Place bread in
prepared baking dish. Sprinkle with cheese.

COMBINE evaporated milk, eggs, dry mustard and
onion powder in medium bowl. Pour evenly over
bread and cheese. Sprinkle with sausage. Cover;
refrigerate overnight.

PREHEAT oven to 325°F.

BAKE for 55 to 60 minutes or until cheese is golden
brown. Cover with foil if top browns too quickly.
Season with ground black pepper.

Makes 8 to 10 servings

Grilled Citrus Halibut

1/4 cup lemon juice
3 tablespoons lime juice
3 tablespoons honey Dijon mustard
3 tablespoons olive oil
2 tablespoons MRS. DASH® Original
    Seasoning Blend
2 teaspoons MOLLY MC BUTTER® Natural
    Butter Flavor Sprinkles
1 pound halibut, cut into 4-ounce pieces

Combine all ingredients except halibut in resealable
plastic bag, mixing well. Add halibut and seal bag.
Marinate in refrigerator 30 to 60 minutes.

Remove halibut from bag and discard marinade.

Grill fish at medium high heat, 4 to 5 minutes per
side, or until fish flakes easily.   *Makes 4 servings*

Hearty Chili Macaroni

Italian Pork Chops

(Pictured at right)

2 cups uncooked long-grain white rice
4 large pork chops (1/2 inch thick)
1 teaspoon basil, crushed
1 can (26 ounces) DEL MONTE® Spaghetti Sauce
    with Mushrooms or Chunky Italian Herb
    Spaghetti Sauce
1 green bell pepper, cut into thin strips

1. Cook rice according to package directions.

2. Preheat broiler. Sprinkle meat with basil; season with salt and black pepper, if desired. Place meat on broiler pan. Broil 4 inches from heat about 6 minutes on each side or until no longer pink in center.

3. Combine sauce and green pepper in microwavable dish. Cover with plastic wrap; slit to vent. Microwave on HIGH 5 to 6 minutes or until green pepper is tender-crisp and sauce is heated through. Add meat; cover with sauce. Microwave 1 minute. Serve over hot rice. *Makes 4 servings*

Serving Suggestion: Serve with baked potatoes and vegetables instead of rice.

Spicy Tropical Shrimp

1-1/2 pounds Florida shrimp, peeled and deveined
1 cup diced pineapple
1/2 cup diced water chestnuts
2 tablespoons fresh Florida lime juice
2 tablespoons olive oil
2 tablespoons Florida honey
1 tablespoon minced garlic
2 teaspoons soy sauce

Combine all ingredients and toss well. Chill for 2 hours.

Drain and place on broiler pan.

Broil 3 to 4 inches from heat source for 3 to 4 minutes or until shrimp are opaque and pineapple begins to brown. *Makes 4 servings*

Favorite recipe from **Florida Department of Agriculture and Consumer Services, Bureau of Seafood and Aquaculture**

Green Dragon Stir-Fry

2 tablespoons vegetable oil, divided
1 pound beef flank steak, very thinly sliced
1 bunch asparagus *or* 8 ounces green beans,
    cut into 2-inch pieces
1 green bell pepper, cut into strips
1 cup julienned carrots
3 large green onions, sliced
1 tablespoon minced fresh ginger
1 clove garlic, minced
1/4 cup water
1 tablespoon soy sauce
1 tablespoon TABASCO® brand Green
    Pepper Sauce
1/2 teaspoon salt
2 cups hot cooked rice (optional)

Heat 1 tablespoon oil in 12-inch skillet over medium-high heat. Add flank steak; cook until well browned on all sides, stirring frequently. Remove steak to plate with slotted spoon.

Heat remaining 1 tablespoon oil in skillet over medium heat. Add asparagus, green bell pepper, carrots, green onions, ginger and garlic; cook about 3 minutes, stirring frequently. Add water, soy sauce, TABASCO® Green Pepper Sauce, salt and steak; heat to boiling over high heat.

Reduce heat to low; simmer, uncovered, 3 minutes, stirring occasionally. Serve with rice, if desired. *Makes 4 servings*

Note: Stir-fry is also delicious served over ramen or soba noodles.

Glazed Ham

1 cup KARO® Light or Dark Corn Syrup
1/3 cup brown sugar
1/4 cup brown mustard
1 (3- to 4-pound) boneless ham

In small bowl combine corn syrup, brown sugar and mustard. Brush glaze on meat during last 20 minutes of cooking. *Makes about 1 cup glaze*

Quick Chicken Jambalaya

(Pictured at right)

8 boneless, skinless chicken thighs, cut into
　　bite-size pieces
1/4 teaspoon garlic salt
1 tablespoon vegetable oil
2-1/2 cups 8-vegetable juice
1 bag (16 ounces) frozen pepper stir-fry mix
1/2 cup diced cooked ham
1 teaspoon hot pepper sauce
1-3/4 cups quick-cooking rice, uncooked

Sprinkle garlic salt over chicken. In large nonstick
skillet, heat oil over medium-high heat. Add chicken
and cook, stirring occasionally, 8 minutes or until
chicken is lightly browned. Add vegetable juice,
pepper stir-fry mix, ham and hot pepper sauce.
Heat to boiling; cover and cook over medium heat
4 minutes. Stir in rice; heat to boiling. Cover, remove
pan from heat and let stand 5 minutes or until rice
and vegetables are tender and liquid is absorbed.

Makes 4 servings

Favorite recipe from **Delmarva Poultry Industry, Inc.**

Harvest Pot Roast

(Pictured on front cover)

1 large (20×14-inch) oven cooking bag
1/4 cup all-purpose flour
1 (2-1/2- to 3-pound) ALWAYS TENDER®
　　boneless pork roast
1 pound medium new red potatoes, quartered
1 large onion, cut into thin wedges
1 cup baby carrots, cut in half
2 stalks celery, cut diagonally into 1-inch pieces
1 cup vegetable juice
1 tablespoon HERB-OX® reduced sodium beef
　　flavored bouillon
1 clove garlic, minced
1 bay leaf

Preheat oven to 350°F. Add flour to oven bag; twist
end of bag and shake to coat with flour. Place oven
bag into 13×9-inch baking dish. Add pork and
remaining ingredients. Gently squeeze bag to blend
ingredients. Close bag and secure with twist tie. Cut
six (1/2-inch) slits in top of bag. Bake 2 to 2-1/2 hours
or until pork has reached an internal temperature of
160°F and vegetables are fork-tender.

Makes 6 servings

57 & Honey Glazed Kabobs

2/3 cup HEINZ 57 Sauce®
1/3 cup honey
4 skinless boneless chicken breast halves, each
　　cut into 8 cubes (about 1 pound)
　　Fresh vegetables, cut into 1-1/2 inch pieces
　　(such as onions, mushrooms, bell peppers,
　　zucchini and yellow squash)
　　Cooking spray

Combine 57 Sauce and honey; set aside. Alternately
thread chicken and vegetables on skewers. Spray
with cooking spray. Grill over medium heat 12 to
15 minutes, turning often, until chicken is no longer
pink. Brush liberally with 57 Sauce mixture. Grill
until kabobs are brown and glazed, about 5 minutes.

Makes 4 servings

Vegetable Cheese Frittata

1/2 cup fresh green beans, cut into 1-inch pieces
1 small onion, chopped
3 tablespoons butter or margarine
1/4 red bell pepper, chopped
1/4 cup sliced fresh mushrooms
1/4 cup dry bread crumbs
1/2 cup prepared HIDDEN VALLEY®
　　The Original Ranch® Dressing
6 eggs, beaten
1/3 cup shredded Cheddar cheese
1/4 cup grated Parmesan cheese

Preheat oven to 350°F. In medium saucepan, steam
green beans over boiling water until crisp-tender,
about 4 minutes. In medium skillet, sauté onion in
butter until onion is softened; stir in beans, red
pepper and mushrooms. Fold vegetables, bread
crumbs and salad dressing into eggs. Pour into
buttered quiche dish. Sprinkle with cheeses. Bake
until set, about 25 minutes.　　*Makes 6 servings*

Note: Substitute chopped tomatoes, diced green
chili peppers, sliced black olives, chopped zucchini
or any vegetable combination for green beans,
onion and mushrooms.

Quick Chicken Jambalaya

Chicken & Roasted Garlic Risotto

Savory Onion Cheese Tart

1 envelope LIPTON® RECIPE SECRETS®
    Golden Onion Soup Mix
1 cup milk
1 egg, lightly beaten
1/2 teaspoon dried rosemary leaves
1 package (8 ounces) shredded mozzarella cheese
1 package (15 ounces) refrigerated pie crusts
    for 2 (9-inch) crusts

In small bowl, thoroughly blend soup mix, milk, egg and rosemary. Stir in cheese. Freeze 1 hour or refrigerate at least 2 hours until mixture is slightly thickened and not runny.

Preheat oven to 375°F. On two aluminum-foil-lined baking sheets, unfold crusts. Fold crust edges over 1 inch to form rim. Brush, if desired, with 1 egg yolk beaten with 2 tablespoons water. Fill center of each prepared crust with 1/2 of soup mixture; spread evenly to rim. Bake 25 minutes or until crusts are golden brown. To serve, cut into wedges.

Makes 2 tarts

Freezing/Reheating Directions: Tarts can be baked, then frozen. Simply wrap in heavy-duty aluminum foil; freeze. To reheat, unwrap and bake at 350°F until heated through.

Chicken & Roasted Garlic Risotto

(Pictured above)

4 boneless chicken breast halves
1 tablespoon butter or margarine
1 can (10-3/4 ounces) CAMPBELL'S® Cream
    of Chicken Soup *or* 98% Fat Free
    Cream of Chicken Soup
1 can (10-3/4 ounces) CAMPBELL'S® Creamy
    Mushroom and Roasted Garlic Soup
2 cups water
2 cups uncooked instant white rice
1 cup frozen peas and carrots

1. **SEASON** chicken.

2. **HEAT** butter in skillet. Add chicken and cook until browned. Remove chicken.

3. **ADD** soups and water. Heat to a boil. Stir in rice and vegetables. Top with chicken. Cover and cook over low heat 5 minutes or until done. Remove from heat. Let stand 5 minutes. *Makes 4 servings*

Cornmeal-Crusted Drums

3/4 cup buttermilk
1/4 cup finely chopped onion
1 package (about 1-1/4 pounds) PERDUE®
    Fresh Skinless Chicken Drumsticks
1/2 cup yellow cornmeal
1/2 cup fresh bread crumbs, lightly toasted
1/4 cup grated Parmesan cheese
1 tablespoon chopped fresh thyme or
    1-1/2 teaspoons dried thyme leaves
Dash ground red pepper
Salt and ground black pepper to taste
1 to 2 tablespoons vegetable oil

In medium bowl, combine buttermilk and onion. Add chicken; cover and marinate in refrigerator 2 to 3 hours.

Preheat oven to 425°F. On plate, combine cornmeal, bread crumbs, cheese, thyme, red pepper, salt and black pepper. Dredge chicken in crumbs, coating all sides. Place chicken on baking sheet; drizzle with oil. Bake 20 to 30 minutes until chicken is crisp and cooked through. *Makes 2 to 3 servings*

Pacific Rim Honey-Barbecued Fish

(Pictured below)

1/4 cup honey
1/4 cup chopped onion
2 tablespoons lime juice
2 tablespoons soy sauce
2 tablespoons hoisin sauce
2 cloves garlic, minced
1 jalapeño pepper, seeded and minced
1 teaspoon minced fresh gingerroot
4 swordfish steaks or other firm white fish
   (4 ounces each)

Combine all ingredients except swordfish in small bowl; mix well. Place fish in shallow baking dish; pour marinade over fish. Cover and refrigerate 1 hour. Remove fish from marinade. Grill over medium-hot coals or broil fish about 10 minutes per inch of thickness or until fish turns opaque and flakes easily when tested with fork.

Makes 4 servings

Favorite recipe from **National Honey Board**

Reuben Casserole

1 can (10-3/4 ounces) condensed cream of
   mushroom soup, undiluted
3/4 cup milk
1/4 cup chopped onion
1-1/2 teaspoons prepared mustard
1 can (16 ounces) sauerkraut, rinsed and drained
1 package (8 ounces) uncooked noodles
1 pound HILLSHIRE FARM® Polska Kielbasa,
   cut into 1/2-inch pieces
1 cup (4 ounces) shredded Swiss cheese
1/2 cup bread crumbs
2 tablespoons butter, melted

Preheat oven to 350°F.

Grease 13×9-inch baking dish. Combine soup, milk, onion and mustard in medium bowl. Spread sauerkraut onto bottom of prepared dish, pressing firmly. Add noodles. Spoon soup mixture evenly over noodles; cover with Polska Kielbasa. Top with cheese. Combine bread crumbs and butter in small bowl; sprinkle over cheese. Cover tightly. Bake 1 hour or until noodles are tender.

Makes 6 servings

Pacific Rim Honey-Barbecued Fish

Southwestern Beef Stew

(Pictured at right)

1 tablespoon plus 1 teaspoon BERTOLLI®
   Olive Oil, divided
1-1/2 pounds boneless beef chuck, cut into 1-inch
   cubes
1 can (4 ounces) chopped green chilies, drained
2 large cloves garlic, finely chopped
1 teaspoon ground cumin (optional)
1 can (14 to 16 ounces) whole or plum
   tomatoes, undrained and chopped
1 envelope LIPTON® RECIPE SECRETS® Onion
   or Beefy Onion Soup Mix
1 cup water
1 package (10 ounces) frozen cut okra or
   green beans, thawed
1 large red or green bell pepper, cut into
   1-inch pieces
4 frozen half-ears corn-on-the-cob, thawed
   and each cut into 3 round pieces
2 tablespoons chopped fresh cilantro (optional)

In 5-quart Dutch oven or heavy saucepot, heat
1 tablespoon oil over medium-high heat and
brown 1/2 of beef; remove and set aside. Repeat
with remaining beef; remove and set aside. In
same Dutch oven, heat remaining 1 teaspoon oil
over medium heat and cook chilies, garlic and
cumin, stirring constantly, 3 minutes. Return beef
to Dutch oven. Stir in tomatoes and onion soup mix
blended with water. Bring to a boil over high heat.
Reduce heat to low and simmer covered, stirring
occasionally, 1 hour. Stir in okra, red pepper and
corn. Bring to a boil over high heat. Reduce heat
to low and simmer covered, stirring occasionally,
30 minutes or until meat is tender. Sprinkle with
cilantro. *Makes about 6 servings*

Chicken Puttanesca-Style

2 tablespoons olive oil
1 (2-1/2- to 3-pound) chicken, cut into pieces
1 medium onion, sliced
1/4 cup balsamic vinegar
1 jar (1 pound 10 ounces) RAGÚ® Old World
   Style® Pasta Sauce
1 cup pitted ripe olives
1 tablespoon drained capers

In 12-inch skillet, heat olive oil over medium-high
heat and brown chicken. Remove chicken and set
aside; drain.

In same skillet, add onion and vinegar and cook
over medium heat, stirring occasionally, 3 minutes.
Stir in Ragú Pasta Sauce. Return chicken to skillet
and simmer covered 25 minutes or until chicken is
thoroughly cooked. Stir in olives and capers; heat
through. Serve, if desired, over hot cooked rice and
garnish with chopped fresh parsley.

Makes 4 servings

Tip: Be sure to use the best quality balsamic vinegar
you can afford. In general, the longer it's been aged,
the deeper and tastier the flavor.

Vegetarian Chili with Cornbread Topping

1 tablespoon oil
1 pound zucchini, halved and cut into 1/2-inch
   slices (about 4 cups)
1 red or green bell pepper, cut into 1-inch pieces
1 rib celery, thinly sliced
1 clove garlic, minced
2 cans (15 to 19 ounces each) kidney beans,
   rinsed and drained
1 can (28 ounces) crushed tomatoes in purée,
   undrained
1/4 cup *Frank's® RedHot®* Original Cayenne Pepper
   Sauce
1 tablespoon chili powder
1 package (6-1/2 ounces) cornbread mix plus
   ingredients to prepare mix

1. Preheat oven to 400°F. Heat oil in 12-inch
heatproof skillet* over medium-high heat. Add
zucchini, bell pepper, celery and garlic. Cook
and stir 5 minutes or until tender. Stir in beans,
tomatoes, *Frank's RedHot* Sauce and chili
powder. Heat to boiling, stirring.

2. Prepare cornbread mix according to package
directions. Spoon batter on top of chili mixture,
spreading to 1/2 inch from edges. Bake 30 minutes
or until cornbread is golden brown and mixture is
bubbly. *Makes 6 servings*

*If handle of skillet is not heatproof, wrap in foil.

Southwestern Beef Stew

Polynesian Pork Chops

(Pictured at right)

4 boneless pork chops, 3/4-inch thick each
1 teaspoon garlic powder
1 tablespoon vegetable oil
1 medium onion, chopped
1 can (10-3/4 ounces) CAMPBELL'S® Golden
    Mushroom Soup
1 can (8 ounces) pineapple chunks
1/4 cup water
3 tablespoons soy sauce
1 tablespoon honey
2 cups cooked instant white rice
    Sliced green onions

1. **SEASON** chops with garlic powder.

2. **HEAT** oil in skillet. Add chops and cook until browned. Add onion, soup, pineapple with juice, water, soy sauce and honey. Heat to a boil. Cook over low heat 10 minutes or until done.

4. **SERVE** with rice and garnish with green onions.

Makes 4 servings

Serving Suggestion: Serve with steamed snow peas and carrots, and mixed fruit salad for dessert.

Speed Way Soufflé

1 pound bulk Italian sausage
2 cups fresh sliced mushrooms
1/2 cup chopped green or red bell peppers
1/3 cup chopped onion
1/2 cup finely shredded Parmesan cheese
1 cup NEWMAN'S OWN® Roasted Garlic
    with Peppers Pasta Sauce
3 large eggs
3/4 cup baking mix
3/4 cup milk
1 cup shredded mozzarella cheese
    Chopped green onion and sliced ripe olives
    for garnish

Preheat oven to 400°F. Grease 10×1-1/2-inch deep-dish pie plate.

In 10-inch skillet, brown sausage over medium-high heat 7 minutes, stirring to break up sausage. Remove meat with slotted spoon and drain on paper towels. Drain all but 1 teaspoon fat from skillet. Add mushrooms, peppers and onion to skillet; cook 5 to 7 minutes or until tender.

In pie plate, layer sausage, mushroom mixture, Parmesan cheese and pasta sauce. In bowl, with wire whisk, beat together eggs, baking mix and milk until well blended. Pour and spread mixture over layered ingredients. *Do not stir.* Sprinkle with mozzarella cheese.

Bake 30 to 35 minutes or until set. Remove from oven; cool 5 minutes. Top with chopped green onion and sliced olives. *Makes 6 servings*

Texas Beef Stew

1 pound lean ground beef
1 small onion, chopped
1 can (28 ounces) crushed tomatoes with
    roasted garlic
1-1/2 cups BIRDS EYE® frozen Broccoli, Cauliflower
    & Carrots
1 can (14-1/2 ounces) whole new potatoes,
    halved
1 cup BIRDS EYE® frozen Sweet Corn
1 can (4-1/2 ounces) chopped green chilies,
    drained
1/2 cup water

• In large saucepan, cook beef and onion over medium-high heat until beef is well browned, stirring occasionally.

• Stir in tomatoes, vegetables, potatoes with liquid, corn, chilies and water; bring to a boil.

• Reduce heat to medium-low; cover and simmer 5 minutes or until heated through.

Makes 4 servings

Serving Suggestion: Serve over rice with warm crusty bread.

Tip: The smell of onions and garlic can penetrate into your cutting boards. Keep a separate cutting board exclusively for these vegetables.

Polynesian Pork Chop

Summer Quiche

Summer Quiche

(Pictured above)

    6 eggs
3/4 cup plain STONYFIELD FARM® Yogurt
    2 tablespoons grated Parmesan cheese
1/2 tablespoon chopped fresh basil
1/2 tablespoon chopped fresh thyme
1/4 teaspoon black pepper
    1 small Vidalia onion, diced
    1 small zucchini, diced
    1 small yellow squash, diced
    3 Roma tomatoes, diced
    1 unbaked 9-inch pie shell

Preheat oven to 375°F. In large bowl, combine eggs, yogurt, Parmesan cheese, herbs and pepper. Beat well. Add onion, zucchini, yellow squash and tomatoes; mix well. Pour mixture into pie shell; bake for 35 to 45 minutes or until cooked through (quiche should be firm to the touch). Let cool for 10 minutes before serving.

Makes 6 to 8 servings

Ham Asparagus Gratin

    1 can (10-3/4 ounces) CAMPBELL'S® Cream of
        Asparagus Soup
1/2 cup milk
1/4 teaspoon onion powder
1/8 teaspoon pepper
    3 cups hot cooked corkscrew pasta
1-1/2 cups cubed cooked ham
1-1/2 cups cooked cut asparagus
    1 cup shredded Cheddar *or* Swiss cheese

MIX soup, milk, onion powder and pepper in 2-quart casserole. Stir in pasta, ham, asparagus and **1/2 cup** cheese.

BAKE at 400°F for 25 minutes or until hot.

STIR and sprinkle with remaining cheese. Bake 5 minutes or until cheese melts.   *Makes 4 servings*

Substitution: Substitute 1-1/2 cups cubed cooked chicken for cubed cooked ham.

Salmon with Citrus-Tomato Salsa

    4 salmon fillets (about 1-1/2 pounds)
    4 tablespoons I CAN'T BELIEVE IT'S NOT
        BUTTER!® Spread, melted and divided
    2 cans (14-1/2 ounces each) diced tomatoes,
        drained
    2 large navel oranges, peeled, sectioned and
        coarsely chopped
2/3 cup finely sliced green onions
1/3 cup chopped fresh cilantro
    2 teaspoons finely chopped seeded jalapeño
        pepper (optional)

Preheat oven to 400°F.

In 13×9-inch glass baking dish, arrange salmon. Brush with 2 tablespoons I Can't Believe It's Not Butter! Spread and season, if desired, with salt and ground black pepper; set aside.

In large bowl, combine remaining 2 tablespoons I Can't Believe It's Not Butter!® Spread, tomatoes, oranges, green onions, cilantro and jalapeño pepper. Season, if desired, with salt and ground black pepper; spoon over salmon.

Bake 25 minutes or until salmon is opaque and salsa is heated through.   *Makes 4 servings*

Note: Recipe can be halved.

Tomato and Green Chilie Fajitas

(Pictured below)

1 pound flank steak, cut into 1/4-inch strips
1 can (14.5 ounces) HUNT'S® Petite Diced
   Tomatoes with Mild Green Chilies, drained
2 teaspoons chili powder
2 teaspoons ground cumin
1/2 teaspoon salt
3 tablespoons WESSON® Vegetable Oil, divided
1 medium green bell pepper, cut into thin strips
1 medium red bell pepper, cut into thin strips
1 medium onion, cut into thin strips
12 flour tortillas (fajita size), warmed
   Sour cream, cilantro, salsa (optional)

COMBINE steak, drained tomatoes, chili powder, cumin and salt in a large plastic resealable bag. Mix ingredients in the bag to coat steak pieces.

HEAT 1 tablespoon oil in a large skillet over high heat. Add half of the steak mixture and cook to desired doneness, stirring often. Remove from skillet; keep warm. Repeat with remaining batch of steak. Remove from skillet; keep warm.

ADD remaining 1 tablespoon oil to skillet; add peppers and onions. Stir-fry until tender, about 3 to 4 minutes. Return steak to skillet; heat through, about 1 minute. Serve in warm tortillas with toppings, if desired. *Makes 6 servings*

Chicken Marsala

1 tablespoon butter
2 boneless skinless chicken breasts, halved
1 cup sliced carrots
1 cup sliced fresh mushrooms
1/3 cup chicken broth
1/3 cup HOLLAND HOUSE® Marsala
   Cooking Wine

Melt butter in skillet over medium-high heat. Add chicken; cook 5 minutes. Turn chicken over; add remaining ingredients. Bring to a boil; simmer 15 to 20 minutes until juices run clear. Serve over cooked fettuccine, if desired. *Makes 4 servings*

Tomato and Green Chilie Fajitas

Southwestern Meat Loaf

(Pictured at right)

1 envelope LIPTON® RECIPE SECRETS®
    Onion Soup Mix*
2 pounds ground beef
2 cups (about 3 ounces) cornflakes or bran
    flakes cereal, crushed
1-1/2 cups frozen or drained canned whole kernel
    corn
3/4 cup water
1 small green bell pepper, chopped
2 eggs
1/3 cup ketchup

*Also terrific with LIPTON® RECIPE SECRETS® Onion Mushroom or Beefy Onion Soup Mix.

1. Preheat oven to 350°F. In large bowl, combine all ingredients.

2. In 13×9-inch baking or roasting pan, shape into loaf.

3. Bake uncovered 1 hour or until meat thermometer registers 160°F. Let stand 10 minutes before serving. Serve, if desired, with salsa.   *Makes 8 servings*

Tip: For a great lunchbox treat, wrap leftover meat loaf slices in a tortilla and top with your favorite taco toppings such as salsa, sour cream, grated cheese and shredded lettuce.

Mama's Best Ever Spaghetti & Meatballs

1 pound lean ground beef
1/2 cup Italian seasoned dry bread crumbs
1 egg
1 jar (1 pound 10 ounces) RAGÚ® Old World
    Style® Pasta Sauce
8 ounces spaghetti, cooked and drained

1. In medium bowl, combine ground beef, bread crumbs and egg; shape into 12 meatballs.

2. In 3-quart saucepan, bring Ragú Pasta Sauce to a boil over medium-high heat. Gently stir in meatballs.

3. Reduce heat to low and simmer covered, stirring occasionally, 20 minutes or until meatballs are no longer pink in center. Serve over hot spaghetti; sprinkle with shredded Parmesan cheese if desired.
   Makes 4 servings

Monterey Chicken and Rice Quiche

4 boneless, skinless chicken tenderloins,
    cut into 1-inch pieces
1-3/4 cups water
1 box UNCLE BEN'S® COUNTRY INN®
    Chicken & Vegetable Rice
1 cup frozen mixed vegetables
1 (9-inch) deep-dish ready-to-use frozen
    pie crust
3 eggs
1/2 cup milk
1/2 cup (2 ounces) shredded Monterey Jack cheese

1. Heat oven to 400°F.

2. In large skillet, combine chicken, water, rice, contents of seasoning packet and frozen vegetables. Bring to a boil. Cover; reduce heat and simmer 10 minutes. Spoon mixture into pie crust.

3. In small bowl, beat eggs and milk. Pour over rice mixture in pie crust; top with cheese. Bake 30 to 35 minutes or until knife inserted in center comes out clean.   *Makes 6 servings*

Serving Suggestion: A fresh fruit compote of orange sections and green grapes or blueberries is the perfect accompaniment to this delicious quiche.

Very Berry Pork Chops

4 pork chops, 3/4 inch thick
2 teaspoons vegetable oil
1/4 cup strawberry preserves
1 tablespoon mustard
1/4 cup cider vinegar

Heat oil in large skillet over medium-high heat. Add pork chops, cook and turn until brown on both sides. Reduce heat to low. In small bowl, stir together strawberry preserves, mustard and vinegar. Pour sauce over pork chops. Cover pan. Cook pork chops for 10 minutes or until sauce has thickened. To serve, spoon sauce over each chop.
   Makes 4 servings

Favorite recipe from **National Pork Board**

Southwestern Meat Loaf

Savory Roasted Vegetables & Pasta

(Pictured at right)

4 carrots, thinly sliced
2 red bell peppers, cut into strips
2 zucchini, cut into 1/2-inch chunks
2 yellow squash, cut into 1/2-inch chunks
4 cloves garlic, peeled
2 tablespoons olive oil
1 teaspoon salt
1/4 teaspoon black pepper
1/2 cup half-and-half
3 tablespoons *French's®* Honey Dijon Mustard
2 tablespoons water
8 ounces penne pasta, cooked
    Shaved Parmesan cheese

1. Preheat oven to 425°F. Toss vegetables, garlic, oil, salt and pepper in roasting pan. Bake, uncovered, 20 minutes or until tender, stirring occasionally.

2. Spoon half of vegetables into blender or food processor. Add half-and-half, mustard and water. Blend until mixture is smooth.

3. Toss pasta with vegetable purée in large serving bowl. Spoon remaining vegetables on top. Sprinkle with Parmesan cheese.   *Makes 4 servings*

Swanson® Balsamic Glazed Salmon

1 tablespoon olive oil
4 salmon fillets, 3/4 inch thick
    (about 1-1/2 pounds)
    Lemon pepper seasoning
1 can (14 ounces) SWANSON® Seasoned
    Chicken Broth with Italian Herbs
3 tablespoons balsamic vinegar
1-1/2 tablespoons cornstarch
4 cups hot cooked rice

HEAT oil in skillet. Add salmon, skin side up, and cook until browned, about 5 minutes. Turn salmon and season with lemon pepper.

ADD 1/2 cup broth. Heat to a boil. Cover and cook over low heat 5 minutes or until done. Remove salmon and keep warm.

MIX remaining broth, vinegar and cornstarch. Add to skillet; cook and stir until mixture boils and thickens. Place rice in bowls and top with salmon. Spoon sauce over all.   *Makes 4 servings*

Apricot Glazed Pork Roast

1 can (10-1/2 ounces) CAMPBELL'S® Condensed
    Chicken Broth
1 jar (18 ounces) apricot preserves
1 large onion, chopped
2 tablespoons Dijon mustard
4 pounds boneless pork loin roast

1. **MIX** broth, preserves, onion and mustard in slow cooker. Add pork and turn to coat.

2. **COVER** and cook on LOW 8 to 9 hours or until done.   *Makes 8 servings*

For thicker sauce: After cooking pork, remove from cooker. Mix 2 tablespoons cornstarch and 2 tablespoons water. Stir into cooker. Cover and cook on HIGH 10 minutes or until mixture boils and thickens.

Chicken Curry Bombay

1 medium onion, cut into wedges
2 cloves garlic, minced
2 teaspoons curry powder
1 tablespoon olive oil
2 boneless, skinless chicken breast halves,
    sliced 1/4 inch thick
1 can (14-1/2 ounces) DEL MONTE® Stewed
    Tomatoes - Original Recipe
1/3 cup seedless raisins
1 can (14-1/2 ounces) DEL MONTE Whole New
    Potatoes, drained and cut into chunks
1 can (14-1/2 ounces) DEL MONTE Cut Green
    Beans, drained

1. Cook onion, garlic and curry in oil in large skillet until tender, stirring occasionally.

2. Stir in chicken, tomatoes and raisins; bring to a boil.

3. Cover and simmer over medium heat 8 minutes. Add potatoes and green beans.

4. Cook, uncovered, 5 minutes, stirring occasionally. Season with salt and pepper, if desired.
        Makes 4 servings

Savory Roasted Vegetables & Pasta

Hot and Spicy Thai Ginger Noodles

(Pictured at right)

1 bottle (12 ounces) LAWRY'S® Thai Ginger
    Marinade With Lime Juice, divided
4 boneless, skinless chicken breasts
    (about 1 pound)
6 ounces Asian or linguine noodles, cooked
1 package (16 ounces) frozen stir-fry vegetable
    mix, cooked just until tender
1/4 cup peanuts

In large resealable plastic bag, add 1 cup Thai
Ginger Marinade and chicken; seal bag. Marinate
in refrigerator at least 30 minutes. Remove chicken
from bag, discarding used marinade. Grill or broil
chicken, brushing with 1/4 cup Marinade, for
10 minutes or until thoroughly cooked. Cool
chicken slightly and slice. In large bowl, combine
chicken with noodles, vegetables, peanuts and
remaining Marinade. Serve warm or chilled.

Makes 4 to 5 servings

Garlic and Basil Halibut

(Pictured on page 126)

1/2 teaspoon garlic powder
1/2 teaspoon dried thyme leaves
1/4 teaspoon ground black pepper
1-1/2 pounds halibut fillets or any firm white fish
    (6 pieces)
1 tablespoon margarine or butter
1 can (15 ounces) HUNT'S® Tomato Sauce
1 can (6 ounces) HUNT'S® No Salt Added
    Tomato Paste
1/2 cup chopped fresh basil leaves
1/4 cup water

COMBINE garlic powder, thyme and pepper in a
small bowl. Sprinkle on both sides of each fish fillet.
Melt margarine in a medium skillet over medium
heat. Place fish in skillet; cook both sides until
lightly golden, about 2 minutes per side. Remove
from skillet; keep warm.

ADD remaining ingredients to skillet; blend well.
Return fish to skillet; do not let sauce cover the
top of the fillets. Simmer, covered, over low heat
until thoroughly heated, about 5 minutes.

Makes 6 servings

Easiest-Ever Fish Steaks in Foil

1 pound salmon, halibut, swordfish or shark
    steaks (1 inch thick)
Grated peel and juice of 1/2 SUNKIST® lemon
Paprika and/or salt *or* seafood herb blend
    or Cajun seasoning *or* dried or chopped
    fresh dill
1/2 tablespoon butter or margarine

Spray 18-inch square of heavy-duty aluminum foil
with nonstick cooking spray. Arrange fish steaks
in center of foil. Sprinkle with lemon juice, then
grated peel. Lightly sprinkle with seasoning; dot
with butter. Bring 2 sides of foil together above
fish; fold down several times to seal. Fold in short
ends of foil to seal. Place on baking sheet. Bake at
450°F 11 to 12 minutes or until fish is opaque and
flakes easily with fork. Remove from foil and spoon
pan drippings over fish. Serve with lemon wedges,
if desired. *Makes 3 to 4 servings*

Overnight Ham and Cheese Strata

12 slices white bread, crust removed
 1 (10-ounce) package frozen chopped broccoli,
    thawed and drained
 2 (5-ounce) cans HORMEL® chunk ham, drained
    and flaked
 6 eggs, beaten
 2 cups milk
1/4 cup minced onion
1/4 teaspoon dry mustard
 3 cups shredded Cheddar cheese

Cut bread into small cubes. Layer half of bread
cubes, broccoli and chunk ham in buttered
13×9-inch baking dish. Top with remaining bread
cubes. Beat together eggs, milk, onion and dry
mustard. Pour over bread. Sprinkle top with
cheese. Cover and refrigerate overnight. Heat
oven to 325°F. Bake 55 to 60 minutes or until eggs
are set. *Makes 12 servings*

Hot and Spicy Thai Ginger Noodles

Chili Mole

1 pound ground beef
1 Spanish onion, diced
1 green bell pepper, diced
1 banana pepper, finely chopped
2 jalapeño peppers,* finely chopped
2 garlic cloves, minced
2 cans (15 ounces each) kidney beans, rinsed and drained
2 cans (14-1/2 ounces each) diced tomatoes, undrained
1 can (4 ounces) tomato paste
1 packet (2 ounces) chili seasoning
3 tablespoons unsweetened cocoa powder
2 tablespoons chili powder
1 tablespoon brown sugar
1 tablespoon lime juice

Jalapeño peppers can sting and irritate the skin. Wear rubber gloves when handling peppers and do not touch eyes. Wash hands after handling peppers.

Brown ground beef in large Dutch oven over medium-high heat, stirring to separate meat. Drain fat.

Add onion and bell pepper to Dutch oven; cook and stir until onion is translucent. Add banana pepper, jalapeños and garlic; cook and stir 3 minutes.

Add beans and tomatoes with liquid. Stir in tomato paste, chili seasoning, cocoa, chili powder, brown sugar and lime juice. Cover; simmer 1 hour.

Makes 6 servings

Pennsylvania Dutch Chicken Bake

1 package (about 1-3/4 pounds) PERDUE® Fresh Skinless Chicken Thighs
Salt and pepper to taste
1 to 2 tablespoons canola oil
1 can (14 to 16 ounces) sauerkraut, undrained
1 can (14 to 15 ounces) whole onions, drained
1 tart red apple, unpeeled and sliced
6 to 8 dried whole apricots
1/2 cup raisins
1/4 cup brown sugar, or to taste

Preheat oven to 350°F. Season thighs with salt and pepper. In large nonstick skillet over medium-high heat, heat oil. Cook thighs 6 to 8 minutes per side until browned. Meanwhile, in 13×9-inch shallow baking dish, mix sauerkraut, onions, apple, apricots, raisins and brown sugar until blended. Arrange thighs in sauerkraut mixture. Cover and bake 30 to 40 minutes or until chicken is cooked through and a meat thermometer inserted in thickest part of thigh registers 180°F.

Makes 6 servings

Variation: If desired, substitute other fresh or dried fruit in this recipe, such as pears or pitted prunes.

Greek-Style Kale and Sausage Stew with Egg-Lemon Sauce

(Pictured at right)

1 tablespoon olive oil
1 small onion, diced
1 pound uncooked Portuguese or hot Italian sausage
6 cups (4 ounces) coarsely chopped kale leaves (trimmed of thick stems)
1-1/4 cups hot chicken broth, divided
2 eggs, beaten
3 tablespoons fresh lemon juice

Heat oil in deep skillet. Add onion and cook over medium heat 5 minutes or until tender. Break sausage into bite-size pieces and add to skillet. Cook sausage about 5 minutes over medium heat or until browned on all sides, stirring frequently. Stir in kale and 1/2 cup chicken broth. Reduce heat to low; cover and simmer 20 minutes or until kale is tender.

Beat eggs with lemon juice in heatproof bowl. Gradually add remaining 3/4 cup hot chicken broth to egg mixture while beating constantly so eggs do not scramble. Pour egg mixture into kale and sausage mixture. Simmer over low heat 1 to 2 minutes or until egg mixture is slightly thickened. (Do not bring mixture to a boil or eggs will scramble.)

Makes 4 servings

Greek-Style Kale and Sausage Stew with Egg-Lemon Sauce

Caribbean Pork Kabobs and Rice

Caribbean Pork Kabobs and Rice

(Pictured above)

1 cup UNCLE BEN'S® ORIGINAL CONVERTED® Brand Rice
1-1/2 cups peeled, diced sweet potato
2 tablespoons plus 2 teaspoons Caribbean seasoning, divided
1 can (8 ounces) pineapple chunks in juice
1 (12-ounce) pork tenderloin, cut into 1-1/2-inch cubes
1 red bell pepper, cut into 1-inch squares
1 green bell pepper, cut into 1-inch squares
1/4 cup dry-roasted peanuts

1. In medium pan, heat 2 cups water to a boil. Add rice, sweet potato and 2 teaspoons Caribbean seasoning. Cover, reduce heat and simmer 10 minutes or until rice and sweet potato are tender.

2. Drain pineapple chunks, reserving juice. Add pineapple chunks to rice mixture.

3. Preheat broiler. Place remaining 2 tablespoons Caribbean seasoning into large resealable plastic food storage bag. Add pork; seal bag and turn to coat pork with seasoning. Thread pork and bell peppers onto skewers.

4. Broil kabobs 4 minutes on each side. Turn and brush with reserved pineapple juice. Continue cooking 2 minutes on each side until pork is no longer pink.

5. Top rice with peanuts and serve with kabobs.

Makes 4 servings

Easy Slow-Cooked Chili

(Pictured on page 126)

2 pounds lean ground beef
2 tablespoons chili powder
1 tablespoon ground cumin
1 can (28 ounces) crushed tomatoes in purée, undrained
1 can (15 ounces) red kidney beans, rinsed and drained
1 cup water
2 cups *French's*® French Fried Onions, divided
1/4 cup *Frank's*® *RedHot*® Original Cayenne Pepper Sauce
Sour cream and shredded Cheddar cheese

SLOW COOKER DIRECTIONS

1. Cook ground beef, chili powder and cumin in large nonstick skillet over medium heat until browned, stirring frequently; drain. Transfer to slow cooker.

2. Stir in tomatoes with juice, beans, water, *1/2 cup* French Fried Onions and ***Frank's RedHot*** Sauce.

3. Cover; cook on LOW setting for 6 hours (or on HIGH for 3 hours). Serve chili topped with sour cream, cheese and remaining onions.

Makes 8 servings

Variation: For added Cheddar flavor, substitute ***French's*® Cheddar French Fried Onions** for the original flavor.

Sweet and Sour Ham Steaks

(Pictured below)

- **1 cup peach jam**
- **2 tablespoons cider vinegar**
- **1 tablespoon chopped fresh parsley**
- **1 tablespoon brown sugar**
- **2 garlic cloves, minced**
- **1/2 teaspoon black pepper**
- **4 ham steaks (about 5 ounces each)**

1. Prepare grill for direct cooking.

2. Combine jam, vinegar, parsley, brown sugar, garlic and pepper in small bowl; mix well.

3. Place ham steaks on grid. Brush with jam mixture. Grill over medium-high heat 4 minutes. Turn ham steaks and brush with jam mixture. Grill 4 minutes.

4. Serve ham steaks with remaining jam mixture on the side. *Makes 4 servings*

Paris Pasta

- **2 tablespoons margarine or butter**
- **2 cloves garlic, minced**
- **1/2 cup milk**
- **2 cups 1-inch asparagus pieces or very thin green beans**
- **1/4 teaspoon ground black pepper**
- **1 (4.7-ounce) package PASTA RONI® Parmesano**
- **1/2 cup diced roasted red bell peppers**
- **1/2 cup chopped muenster cheese**
- **1/4 cup chopped fresh basil or parsley**

1. In large saucepan over medium-high heat, melt margarine. Add garlic; sauté 1 minute.

2. Stir in 1-1/3 cups water, milk, asparagus and black pepper. Bring to a boil.

3. Stir in pasta and Special Seasonings. Reduce heat to low. Gently boil uncovered, 5 to 6 minutes or until pasta is tender, stirring occasionally.

4. Stir in bell peppers and cheese. Let stand 3 minutes or until cheese is melted. Top with basil. *Makes 4 servings*

Sweet and Sour Ham Steaks

Sweet and Sour Fish

(Pictured at right)

1/3 cup GRANDMA'S® Molasses

1/4 cup cider vinegar

1/4 cup plus 2 tablespoons cornstarch, divided

2 tablespoons pineapple juice, reserved from chunks

2 tablespoons ketchup

2 tablespoons soy sauce

1 pound swordfish or red snapper, cut into 1-inch cubes

3 tablespoons vegetable oil, divided

1 green, red or yellow bell pepper, cut into strips

2 green onions, chopped

1 (8-ounce) can pineapple chunks in its own juice, drained, reserving 2 tablespoons juice for sauce

Cherry tomatoes, cut into halves

Hot cooked rice or noodles

In medium bowl, combine molasses, vinegar, 2 tablespoons cornstarch, pineapple juice, ketchup and soy sauce; blend well. Set aside. Coat swordfish with remaining 1/4 cup cornstarch. In large skillet, heat 2 tablespoons oil. Stir-fry fish 5 minutes or until fish flakes easily with fork. Remove from skillet. Heat remaining 1 tablespoon oil in skillet. Stir-fry bell pepper and onions 2 minutes or until crisp-tender. Add molasses mixture; cook until thickened. Add fish, pineapple and tomatoes; cook until heated through. Serve with rice. *Makes 4 servings*

Ham and Potato au Gratin

3 tablespoons butter or margarine

3 tablespoons all-purpose flour

2 cups milk

1-1/2 cups (6 ounces) shredded Cheddar cheese

1 tablespoon Dijon mustard

2 cups HILLSHIRE FARM® Ham, cut into thin strips

1 package (24 ounces) frozen shredded hash brown potatoes, thawed

1 package (10 ounces) frozen chopped spinach, thawed and drained

Preheat oven to 350°F.

Melt butter in large saucepan over medium heat; stir in flour. Add milk. Cook and stir until bubbly; cook 1 minute more. Remove from heat. Stir in cheese and mustard; set aside.

Place 1/2 of Ham in ungreased medium casserole. Top with 1/2 of potatoes and 1/2 of milk mixture. Spoon spinach over top. Repeat layers with remaining ham, potatoes and milk mixture.

Bake, uncovered, 30 minutes or until heated through. *Makes 8 servings*

Mustard-Crusted Pork Roast

1 boneless pork loin roast, about 2 pounds

2 tablespoons spicy mustard

1 cup garlic croutons, crushed*

Place croutons in plastic bag; roll with rolling pin until crushed.

Heat oven to 400°F. Season roast with salt and pepper; place in shallow pan and roast for 30 minutes. Remove from oven; spread surface with mustard and sprinkle with crouton crumbs. Return to oven and continue to roast for 10 to 15 minutes longer, until meat thermometer registers 155°F. *Makes 4 to 6 servings*

Favorite recipe from **National Pork Board**

Quick 'n' Easy Pasta Bolognese

1/2 pound ground beef

2 cloves garlic, finely chopped

1 jar (1 pound 10 ounces) RAGÚ® Chunky Pasta Sauce

1/4 cup light cream or half-and-half

3 tablespoons dry white wine (optional)

8 ounces penne or ziti pasta, cooked and drained

In 12-inch skillet, brown ground beef with garlic over medium-high heat; drain. Stir in Ragú Pasta Sauce, cream and wine. Simmer uncovered, stirring occasionally, 15 minutes. Serve over hot pasta and sprinkle, if desired, with grated Parmesan cheese. *Makes 4 servings*

Sweet and Sour Fish

Peach-Pepper Chicken

(Pictured at right)

1 (4-pound) broiler chicken, cut into
    serving pieces
1/2 teaspoon salt
1/4 cup butter or margarine
3/4 cup SMUCKER'S® Peach Preserves
1 medium onion, sliced
1 medium green or red bell pepper,
    cut into strips
1 tablespoon lemon juice
1/2 teaspoon ground ginger
1 teaspoon cornstarch
2 tablespoons water

1. Sprinkle chicken with salt. Melt butter in large skillet. Add chicken pieces and brown lightly on all sides.

2. Combine preserves, onion, bell pepper, lemon juice and ginger in small bowl; stir until well blended. Pour over chicken; cover and simmer for 25 minutes.

3. Blend cornstarch and water in small bowl. Stir into sauce; cook until sauce is slightly thickened. Serve with rice. *Makes 4 servings*

Hungarian Beef Goulash

1/4 cup all-purpose flour
1 tablespoon Hungarian sweet paprika
1-1/2 teaspoons salt
1/2 teaspoon Hungarian hot paprika
1/2 teaspoon black pepper
2 pounds beef for stew, cut into 1-1/4-inch
    pieces
1/4 cup vegetable oil, divided
1 large onion, chopped
4 garlic cloves, minced
2 cans (about 14 ounces each) beef broth
1 can (14-1/2 ounces) stewed tomatoes,
    undrained
1 cup water
1 tablespoon dried marjoram
1 large green bell pepper, chopped
3 cups uncooked thin egg noodle twists
    Sour cream

1. Combine flour, sweet paprika, salt, hot paprika and black pepper in large resealable food storage bag. Add half of beef. Seal bag; shake to coat well.

Remove beef and set aside. Repeat with remaining beef.

2. Heat 4-1/2 teaspoons oil in Dutch oven over medium heat until hot. Add half of beef; brown on all sides. Transfer to large bowl. Repeat with 4-1/2 teaspoons oil and remaining beef; transfer to same bowl.

3. Heat remaining 1 tablespoon oil in same Dutch oven. Add onion and garlic; cook 8 minutes or until tender, stirring often.

4. Return beef and any juices to Dutch oven. Add broth, tomatoes with juice, water and marjoram. Bring to a boil over medium-high heat. Reduce heat to medium-low; cover and simmer 1-1/2 hours or until meat is tender, stirring once.

5. Stir in bell pepper and noodles. Cover and simmer about 8 minutes or until noodles are tender, stirring once. To serve, ladle into 8 soup bowls. Dollop with sour cream. *Makes 8 servings*

Lemon-Basil Pasta

8 ounces linguine or other pasta
2 tablespoons butter or margarine, melted
1 tablespoon lemon juice
1-1/2 teaspoons McCORMICK® Basil Leaves
3/4 teaspoon McCORMICK® Garlic Salt
1/4 teaspoon McCORMICK® Ground Black Pepper
1/4 cup grated Parmesan cheese

1. Cook pasta in unsalted water according to package directions. Drain pasta and return to pot.

2. Combine melted butter, lemon juice, basil, garlic salt and pepper in small bowl. Add to cooked pasta and toss gently.

3. Spoon into serving dish and sprinkle with cheese. Garnish with lemon slices and fresh basil leaves, if desired. *Makes 4 servings*

Peach-Pepper Chicken

Desserts

Blueberry Yogurt Cake

(Pictured at left)

1 cup applesauce
1/2 cup granulated sugar
1/4 cup (1/2 stick) butter, softened
2 eggs
1 teaspoon vanilla extract
1-1/2 cups cake flour
1 teaspoon baking powder
1/4 teaspoon baking soda
1/2 cup plain or vanilla-flavored yogurt
1 cup fresh blueberries
1 teaspoon all-purpose flour
1 cup chopped walnuts
1/2 cup packed brown sugar
1 teaspoon ground cinnamon

1. Preheat oven to 350°F. Line 8-inch square baking pan with foil and spray with nonstick cooking spray.

2. Beat applesauce, granulated sugar and butter in medium bowl with electric mixer at medium speed 2 minutes. Beat in eggs and vanilla. Sift cake flour, baking powder and baking soda into small bowl. Add to applesauce mixture with yogurt; beat until smooth. Toss blueberries with all-purpose flour; gently fold into batter.

3. Combine walnuts, brown sugar and cinnamon in small bowl. Sprinkle layer of walnut mixture over bottom of prepared pan. Pour batter over walnut mixture. Sprinkle remaining walnut mixture over batter.

4. Bake 30 to 35 minutes or until toothpick inserted into center comes out clean. Cool completely on wire rack. Garnish as desired. *Makes 9 servings*

Clockwise from top left: *Blueberry Yogurt Cake, Chocolate Almond Biscotti (p. 196), Mixed Berry Pie (p. 208) and Frozen Peppermint Cheesecake (p. 203)*

Winterfruit Cobbler

(Pictured at right)

FILLING

    2 cups SUN•MAID® Raisins
    2 cups fresh or frozen cranberries
3/4 cup sugar
    2 teaspoons cornstarch
1/2 teaspoon ground allspice
    1 cup orange juice

TOPPING

    1 cup all-purpose flour
    2 tablespoons sugar
    2 teaspoons baking powder
1/4 teaspoon salt
1/4 cup butter or margarine
1/2 cup milk
    Sugar
    Ground cinnamon

TO PREPARE FILLING

In medium saucepan, combine raisins, cranberries, sugar, cornstarch and allspice. Gradually stir in orange juice. Bring to boil over high heat; reduce heat to low and simmer, stirring until cranberries begin to pop and mixture thickens slightly. Pour into shallow 1-1/2-quart baking dish.

TO PREPARE TOPPING

In small bowl, combine flour, sugar, baking powder and salt. Cut in butter until mixture resembles coarse crumbs. Mix in milk lightly with fork. Drop spoonfuls of batter over filling; sprinkle lightly with additional sugar mixed with a little cinnamon. Bake in preheated 400°F oven about 25 minutes or until golden. Serve warm with ice cream or whipped cream. *Makes 6 servings*

Chewy Red Raspberry Bars

    1 cup firmly packed light brown sugar
1/2 cup butter or margarine, at room temperature
1/2 teaspoon almond extract
    1 cup all-purpose flour
    1 cup quick-cooking or old-fashioned oats
    1 teaspoon baking powder
1/2 cup SMUCKER'S® Red Raspberry Preserves

Combine brown sugar and butter in large bowl; beat until fluffy. Beat in almond extract. Mix in flour, oats and baking powder until crumbly. Reserve 1/4 cup

mixture; pat remaining mixture into bottom of greased 8-inch square baking pan. Dot preserves over crumb mixture in pan; sprinkle with reserved crumb mixture.

Bake at 350°F for 30 to 40 minutes or until brown. Cool on wire rack. Cut into bars. *Makes 12 bars*

Rustic Honey Polenta Cake

2-1/2 cups all-purpose flour
    1 cup yellow cornmeal
    2 tablespoons baking powder
    1 teaspoon salt
    1 cup (2 sticks) butter or margarine, melted
1-3/4 cups milk
3/4 cup honey
    2 eggs, slightly beaten
    Honey-Orange Syrup (recipe follows)
    Sweetened whipped cream and orange
      segments for garnish (optional)

In large bowl, combine flour, cornmeal, baking powder and salt; mix well. In small bowl, combine melted butter, milk, honey and eggs; mix well. Stir into flour mixture, mixing until just blended. Pour into lightly greased 13×9-inch baking pan.

Bake at 325°F for 25 to 30 minutes or until toothpick comes out clean. Meanwhile, prepare Honey-Orange Syrup. When cake is done, remove from oven to wire rack. Pour hot syrup evenly over top of cake, spreading if necessary to cover entire surface. Cool completely. Garnish with dollop of whipped cream and orange segments, if desired. *Makes 12 servings*

Honey-Orange Syrup: In small saucepan, whisk together 1/2 cup honey, 3 tablespoons orange juice concentrate and 1 tablespoon freshly grated orange peel. Heat over medium-high heat until mixture begins to boil; remove from heat.

Favorite recipe from **National Honey Board**

Winterfruit Cobbler

Brown Sugar Shortbread

(Pictured at right)

**1 cup (2 sticks) I CAN'T BELIEVE IT'S NOT
    BUTTER!® Spread
3/4 cup firmly packed light brown sugar
2 cups all-purpose flour
1/3 cup semisweet chocolate chips, melted**

Preheat oven to 325°F. Grease 9-inch round cake
pan; set aside.

In large bowl, with electric mixer, beat I Can't
Believe It's Not Butter!® Spread and brown sugar
until light and fluffy, about 5 minutes. Gradually
add flour and beat on low until blended. Spread
mixture into prepared pan and press into even layer.
With knife, score surface into 16 pie-shaped wedges.

Bake 45 minutes or until lightly golden. On wire
rack, cool 20 minutes; remove from pan and cool
completely. To serve, pour melted chocolate into
small plastic storage bag. Snip corner and drizzle
chocolate over shortbread. Cut into wedges.

Makes 16 servings

Chocolate Orange Marble
Chiffon Cake

(Pictured on front cover)

**1/3 cup HERSHEY'S Cocoa
1/4 cup hot water
3 tablespoons plus 1-1/2 cups sugar, divided
2 tablespoons plus 1/2 cup vegetable oil, divided
2-1/4 cups all-purpose flour
1 tablespoon baking powder
1 teaspoon salt
3/4 cup cold water
7 egg yolks
1 cup egg whites (about 8)
1/2 teaspoon cream of tartar
1 tablespoon freshly grated orange peel
Orange Glaze (recipe follows)**

1. Remove top oven rack; move other rack to lowest
position. Heat oven to 325°F.

2. Stir together cocoa and hot water in medium bowl.
Stir in 3 tablespoons sugar and 2 tablespoons oil; set
aside. Stir together flour, remaining 1-1/2 cups sugar,
baking powder and salt in large bowl. Add cold water,
remaining 1/2 cup oil and egg yolks; beat with spoon
until smooth.

3. Beat egg whites and cream of tartar in another
large bowl on high speed of mixer until stiff peaks
form. Pour egg yolk mixture in a thin stream over
egg white mixture, gently folding just until blended.
Remove 2 cups batter; add to chocolate mixture,
gently folding until well blended. Fold orange peel
into remaining batter.

4. Spoon half the orange batter into ungreased 10-inch
tube pan; drop half the chocolate batter on top by
spoonfuls. Repeat layers of orange and chocolate
batters. Gently swirl with knife for marbled effect,
leaving definite orange and chocolate areas.

5. Bake 1 hour and 15 to 20 minutes or until top
springs back when lightly touched. Immediately
invert cake onto heatproof funnel; cool cake
completely. Remove cake from pan; invert onto
serving plate. Prepare Orange Glaze; spread over
top of cake, allowing glaze to run down sides.
Garnish as desired. *Makes 12 to 16 servings*

Orange Glaze

**1/3 cup butter or margarine
2 cups powdered sugar
2 tablespoons orange juice
1/2 teaspoon freshly grated orange peel**

Melt butter in medium saucepan over low heat.
Remove from heat; gradually stir in powdered
sugar, orange juice and orange peel, beating until
smooth and of desired consistency. Add additional
orange juice, 1 teaspoon at a time, if needed.

Makes about 1 cup glaze

Helpful Hint

*One medium orange yields 1/3 to
1/2 cup juice and 1 to 2 tablespoons
grated peel. When the peel will be
used, scrub the orange thoroughly to
remove any pesticide residues as
well as the wax coating. The peel
can then be grated with the fine side
of a box grater. Grate the peel first,
then squeeze the orange for juice.*

Brown Sugar Shortbread

Bananas with Caramel Sauce

3 to 4 bananas, peeled
2 tablespoons orange or lemon juice
2 tablespoons butter
1/4 cup whipping cream
1/4 cup GRANDMA'S® Molasses
1/4 teaspoon ground cinnamon
1/4 teaspoon ground nutmeg
1/4 cup walnut halves

1. Slice bananas in half lengthwise, then crosswise. Place bananas in large bowl; brush with orange juice. Set aside.

2. Place butter in 9-inch microwave-safe pie plate. Microwave at HIGH power for 30 seconds or until melted. Stir in cream, molasses, cinnamon and nutmeg. Microwave at HIGH for 1-1/2 to 2 minutes or until thickened, stirring once. Add bananas and walnuts; mix well to coat. Microwave at HIGH for 30 seconds or until bananas are tender. Serve immediately over waffles, ice cream or orange slices. *Makes 4 servings*

Raisin Spice Drops

3/4 cup (1-1/2 sticks) margarine, softened
2/3 cup granulated sugar
2/3 cup firmly packed brown sugar
2 eggs
1 teaspoon vanilla
2-1/2 cups QUAKER® Oats (quick or old fashioned, uncooked)
1-1/4 cups all-purpose flour
1 teaspoon ground cinnamon
1/2 teaspoon baking soda
1/2 teaspoon salt (optional)
1/4 teaspoon ground nutmeg
2/3 cup raisins
1/2 cup chopped nuts

Preheat oven to 350°F. In large bowl, beat margarine and sugars until fluffy. Blend in eggs and vanilla. Add remaining ingredients; mix well. Drop dough by rounded teaspoonfuls onto ungreased cookie sheets. Bake 8 to 10 minutes or until light golden brown. Cool on wire racks. Store tightly covered.
Makes about 4-1/2 dozen cookies

Apple Crisp Cookies

(Pictured at right)

COOKIES

1 CRISCO® Butter Flavor Stick or 1 cup CRISCO® Butter Flavor shortening plus additional for greasing
1 cup firmly packed light brown sugar
1 teaspoon vanilla
2-1/2 cups oats (quick or old-fashioned, uncooked)
2-1/4 cups PILLSBURY BEST® All-Purpose Flour
1/2 teaspoon baking soda
1/2 teaspoon salt
6 to 8 tablespoons water

TOPPING

1 can (21 ounces) apple pie filling, finely chopped
1 cup reserved crumb mixture
1/2 cup finely chopped pecans or walnuts

1. Heat oven to 375°F. Grease baking sheet with shortening. Place sheets of foil on countertop for cooling cookies.

2. For cookies, combine 1 cup shortening, brown sugar and vanilla in large bowl. Beat at medium speed of electric mixer until well blended.

3. Combine oats, flour, baking soda and salt. Add alternately with water to creamed mixture stirring with spoon. Mix well after each addition. (Mixture will be crumbly, but will hold together when shaped into small ball.) Add additional water if necessary. Reserve 1 cup dough for topping. Shape remaining dough into 1-inch balls. Place 2 inches apart on prepared baking sheet. Flatten to 1/8-inch thickness with floured bottom of glass. Smooth edges.

4. Bake at 375°F for 5 to 7 minutes or until light brown around edges and firm. *Do not overbake.* Remove from oven. Cool on baking sheet about 5 minutes.

5. For topping, place 1 measuring teaspoonful of pie filling in center of each cookie. Spread carefully to cover.

6. Combine 1 cup reserved crumbs and nuts in small bowl. Toss until mixed. Sprinkle over apple filling.

7. Return cookies to oven. Bake 5 minutes or until topping is light brown. *Do not overbake.* Cool 2 minutes on baking sheet. Remove cookies to foil to cool completely.
Makes about 3 dozen cookies

Apple Crisp Cookies

S'more Pie

1 (12-ounce) chocolate candy bar, broken
    into pieces
30 regular marshmallows
3/4 cup milk
2-1/2 cups whipped cream, divided
1 (6-ounce) jar hot fudge topping, warmed
1 (9-ounce) READY CRUST® 2 Extra Servings
    Graham Cracker Pie Crust
Chocolate syrup, for garnish

1. Place chocolate bar, marshmallows and milk in medium saucepan. Cook over low heat, stirring constantly, until marshmallows and chocolate are melted. Cool to room temperature.

2. Fold 1-1/2 cups whipped cream into chocolate mixture. Spread thin layer of warm hot fudge over bottom of crust. Gently spoon chocolate mixture into crust. Top with remaining 1 cup whipped cream and garnish with chocolate syrup.

3. Refrigerate 3 hours or until set. Refrigerate leftovers. *Makes 8 servings*

Variation: Use a chocolate almond or chocolate peanut candy bar in place of a plain chocolate bar.

Candy Crunch

4 cups (half of 15-ounce bag) pretzel sticks or
    pretzel twists
1 (14-ounce) can EAGLE BRAND® Sweetened
    Condensed Milk (NOT evaporated milk)
2 (10- to 12-ounce) packages premium white
    chocolate chips
1 cup dried fruit, such as dried cranberries,
    raisins or mixed dried fruit bits

1. Line 15×10-inch baking pan with foil. Place pretzels in large mixing bowl.

2. In large saucepan over medium-low heat, heat EAGLE BRAND® until warm, about 5 minutes. Remove from heat and immediately stir in white chocolate chips until melted. Pour over pretzels, stirring to coat.

3. Immediately spread mixture in prepared pan. Sprinkle with dried fruit; press down lightly with back of spoon.

4. Chill 1 to 2 hours or until set. Break into chunks. Store loosely covered at room temperature.
Makes about 1-3/4 pounds

Hershey's Kisses® Birthday Cake

(Pictured at right)

2 cups sugar
1-3/4 cups all-purpose flour
3/4 cup HERSHEY'S Cocoa or HERSHEY'S
    SPECIAL DARK® Cocoa
1-1/2 teaspoons baking powder
1-1/2 teaspoons baking soda
1 teaspoon salt
2 eggs
1 cup milk
1/2 cup vegetable oil
2 teaspoons vanilla extract
1 cup boiling water
Vanilla Buttercream Frosting (recipe follows)
HERSHEY'S KISSES® Brand Milk Chocolates

1. Heat oven to 350°F. Grease and flour two 9-inch round baking pans or one 13×9×2-inch baking pan.

2. Stir together sugar, flour, cocoa, baking powder, baking soda and salt in large bowl. Add eggs, milk, oil and vanilla; beat with electric mixer on medium speed for 2 minutes. Stir in boiling water (batter will be thin). Pour batter into prepared pans.

3. Bake 30 to 35 minutes for round pans, 35 to 40 minutes for rectangular pan or until wooden pick inserted in center comes out clean. Cool 10 minutes; turn out onto wire racks. Cool completely.

4. Frost with Vanilla Buttercream Frosting. Remove wrappers from chocolates. Garnish top and side of cake with chocolates. *Makes 10 to 12 servings*

Vanilla Buttercream Frosting

1/3 cup butter or margarine, softened
4 cups powdered sugar, divided
3 to 4 tablespoons milk
1-1/2 teaspoons vanilla extract

Beat butter with electric mixer on medium speed in large bowl until creamy. With mixer running, gradually add about 2 cups powdered sugar, beating until well blended. Slowly beat in milk and vanilla. Gradually add remaining powdered sugar, beating until smooth. Add additional milk, if necessary, until frosting is desired consistency.
Makes about 2-1/3 cups frosting

Hershey's Kisses® Birthday Cake

Cinnamon Chips Gems

Cinnamon Chips Gems

(Pictured above)

> 1 cup (2 sticks) butter or margarine, softened
> 2 packages (3 ounces each) cream cheese, softened
> 2 cups all-purpose flour
> 1/2 cup sugar
> 1/3 cup ground toasted almonds
> 2 eggs
> 1 can (14 ounces) sweetened condensed milk
> 1 teaspoon vanilla extract
> 1-1/3 cups HERSHEY'S Cinnamon Chips, divided

1. Beat butter and cream cheese in large bowl until well blended; stir in flour, sugar and almonds. Cover; refrigerate about 1 hour.

2. Divide dough into 4 equal parts. Shape each part into 12 smooth balls. Place each ball in small muffin cup (1-3/4 inches in diameter); press evenly on bottom and up side of each cup.

3. Heat oven to 375°F. Beat eggs in small bowl. Add sweetened condensed milk and vanilla; mix well. Place 7 cinnamon chips in bottom of each cookie shell; fill a generous 3/4 full with sweetened condensed milk mixture.

4. Bake 18 to 20 minutes or until tops are puffed and just beginning to turn golden brown. Cool 3 minutes. Sprinkle about 15 chips on top of each cookie. Cool completely in pan on wire rack. Remove from pan using small metal spatula or sharp knife. Store tightly covered at room temperature.

Makes 4 dozen cookies

Easy Upside Down Cake

> 1 can (20 ounces) DOLE® Pineapple Slices
> 1/4 cup butter or margarine, melted
> 2/3 cup packed brown sugar
> 10 maraschino cherries
> 1 package (18.25 ounces) yellow or pineapple-flavored cake mix

• Drain pineapple, reserving 3/4 cup juice.

• Stir together melted butter and brown sugar in 12-inch skillet with heatproof handle. Arrange pineapple slices in sugar mixture. Place cherry in center of each pineapple slice.

• Prepare cake mix according to package directions, replacing water with reserved 3/4 cup juice. Pour batter evenly over pineapple.

• Bake at 350°F 40 to 45 minutes or until toothpick inserted in center comes out clean.

• Cool 5 minutes. Loosen edges and invert onto serving platter. *Makes 10 servings*

Note: Cake can be baked in 13×9-inch baking pan instead of skillet. Prepare and assemble cake as above except cut two pineapple slices in half and place whole slices along edges of pan and halved slices in center. Place cherries in center of slices. Bake and cool as above.

Mini Upside Down Cakes: Drain 1 can (20 ounces) DOLE® Crushed Pineapple, reserving juice. Grease 24 muffin cups. **Stir** 1/3 cup melted butter with 2/3 cup packed brown sugar. Evenly spoon mixture into bottoms of cups; spoon about 1 tablespoon crushed pineapple over sugar mixture. Top with cherry. **Prepare** cake mix as above. Evenly pour batter into cups. **Bake** 20 to 25 minutes. Invert onto serving platter. Makes 24 servings.

Strawberry Bonbons

1 (14-ounce) can EAGLE BRAND® Sweetened Condensed Milk (NOT evaporated milk)
4 (3-1/2-ounce) cans flaked coconut
1 (6-ounce) package strawberry-flavored gelatin
1 cup ground blanched almonds
1 teaspoon almond extract
  Red food coloring
2 cups sifted powdered sugar
1/2 cup whipping cream
  Green food coloring

1. In large bowl, combine EAGLE BRAND®, coconut, 1/3 cup gelatin, almonds, almond extract and enough red food coloring to tint mixture to desired strawberry red shade. Transfer mixture to food processor and pulse several times to form paste. Chill until firm enough to handle. Shape spoonfuls of coconut mixture (about 3/4 tablespoon) into strawberry shapes.

2. Sprinkle remaining gelatin into flat dish; roll each strawberry in gelatin to coat. Place on baking sheet lined with waxed paper; refrigerate.

3. To make frosting "hulls," combine powdered sugar, cream and green food coloring until well blended. Fill pastry bag fitted with open star tip with frosting, and pipe small amount on top of each strawberry to form hull. Store tightly covered in refrigerator.

Makes about 2-1/2 pounds or about 4 dozen candies

Snowballs

1/2 cup DOMINO® Confectioners 10-X Sugar
1/4 teaspoon salt
  1 cup butter or margarine, softened
  1 teaspoon vanilla extract
2-1/4 cups all-purpose flour
1/2 cup chopped pecans
  DOMINO® Confectioners 10-X Sugar

In large bowl, combine 1/2 cup confectioners sugar, salt and butter; mix well. Add vanilla. Gradually stir in flour. Work nuts into dough. Chill well. Form into 1-inch balls. Place on ungreased cookie sheets. Bake at 400°F for 8 to 10 minutes or until set but not brown. Roll in confectioners sugar immediately. Cool on rack. Roll in sugar again. Store in airtight container.

Makes 5 dozen cookies

Strawberry Bonbons

Strawberry Banana Sorbet

1 pint strawberries, hulled
2 medium-size ripe bananas, cut into chunks
1 cup KARO® Light Corn Syrup
1 cup orange juice
1/2 cup sugar
2 tablespoons lemon juice

1. In blender or food processor purée strawberries until almost smooth. Add bananas, corn syrup, orange juice, sugar and lemon juice. Process until smooth.

2. Pour into container of ice cream maker and freeze according to manufacturer's directions.

Makes about 1-1/2 quarts

"M&M's"® Jam Sandwiches

1/2 cup (1 stick) butter, softened
3/4 cup granulated sugar
1 large egg
1 teaspoon almond extract
1/2 teaspoon vanilla extract
1-1/3 cups all-purpose flour
1/4 teaspoon baking powder
1/4 teaspoon salt
Powdered sugar
1/2 cup seedless raspberry jam
1/2 cup "M&M's"® Chocolate Mini Baking Bits

In large bowl cream butter and sugar until light and fluffy; beat in egg, almond extract and vanilla. In small bowl combine flour, baking powder and salt; blend into creamed mixture. Wrap and refrigerate dough 2 to 3 hours. Preheat oven to 375°F. Working with half the dough at a time on lightly floured surface, roll to 1/8-inch thickness. Cut into desired shapes using 3-inch cookie cutters. Cut out equal numbers of each shape. (If dough becomes too soft, refrigerate several minutes before continuing.) Cut 1-1/2- to 2-inch centers out of half the cookies of each shape. Reroll trimmings and cut out more cookies. Using rigid spatula, carefully transfer shapes to ungreased cookie sheets. Bake 7 to 9 minutes. Cool on cookie sheets 1 to 2 minutes; cool completely on wire racks. Sprinkle powdered sugar on cookies with holes. Spread about 1 teaspoon jam on flat side of whole cookies, spreading almost to edges. Place cookies with holes, flat side down, over jam. Place "M&M's"® Chocolate Mini Baking Bits over jam in holes.

Store between layers of waxed paper in tightly covered container.

Makes 1 dozen sandwich cookies

Peach Yogurt Pie with Raspberry Sauce

(Pictured at right)

CRUST
1 cup graham cracker crumbs
1/4 cup sugar
3 tablespoons CRISCO® Oil*
1-1/4 teaspoons water

FILLING
1 quart peach flavor frozen yogurt, softened

SAUCE
1 package (12 ounces) frozen unsweetened raspberries, thawed
1/3 cup sugar
1 teaspoon cornstarch
1/8 teaspoon salt
1/4 teaspoon almond extract

*Use your favorite Crisco Oil.

1. Heat oven to 350°F. Place cooling rack on countertop.

2. For crust, combine graham cracker crumbs, sugar, oil and water in 9-inch pie plate. Mix with fork. Press firmly against bottom and up side of pie plate.

3. Bake at 350°F for 8 minutes. *Do not overbake.* Remove pie plate to cooling rack. Cool completely.

4. For filling, spread softened yogurt into cooled crust. Freeze 2-1/2 to 3 hours or until firm.

5. For sauce, combine raspberries, sugar, cornstarch and salt in small saucepan. Cook and stir over medium heat until mixture comes to a boil and is thickened. Press through sieve to remove seeds. Stir in almond extract. Cool to room temperature. Refrigerate. Drizzle over pie just before serving. Garnish, if desired.

Makes 1 (9-inch) pie (8 servings)

Kitchen Hint: For a richer version of this pie, try substituting chocolate flavor frozen yogurt for the peach flavor frozen yogurt.

Peach Yogurt Pie with Raspberry Sauce

Chocolate Almond Biscotti

(Pictured on page 182)

> 1 package DUNCAN HINES® Moist Deluxe®
> Dark Chocolate Cake Mix
> 1 cup all-purpose flour
> 1/2 cup butter or margarine, melted
> 2 eggs
> 1 teaspoon almond extract
> 1/2 cup chopped almonds
> White chocolate, melted (optional)

1. Preheat oven to 350°F. Line 2 baking sheets with parchment paper.

2. Combine cake mix, flour, butter, eggs and almond extract in large bowl. Beat at low speed with electric mixer until well blended; stir in almonds. Divide dough in half. Shape each half into 12×2-inch log; place logs on prepared baking sheets. (Bake logs separately.)

3. Bake at 350°F for 30 to 35 minutes or until toothpick inserted in center comes out clean. Remove logs from oven; cool on baking sheets 15 minutes. Using serrated knife, cut logs into 1/2-inch slices. Arrange slices on baking sheets. Bake biscotti 10 minutes. Remove to cooling racks; cool completely.

4. Dip one end of each biscotti in melted white chocolate, if desired. Allow white chocolate to set at room temperature before storing biscotti in airtight container

Makes about 2-1/2 dozen cookies

Chocolate Peanutty Crumble Bars

> 1/2 cup butter or margarine
> 1 cup all-purpose flour
> 3/4 cup quick-cooking oats, uncooked
> 1/3 cup firmly packed brown sugar
> 1/2 teaspoon baking soda
> 1/2 teaspoon vanilla extract
> 4 SNICKERS® Bars (2.07 ounces each),
> cut into 8 slices each

Preheat oven to 350°F. Grease bottom of 8-inch square baking pan. Melt butter in large saucepan. Remove from heat and stir in flour, oats, brown sugar, baking soda and vanilla. Blend until crumbly. Press 2/3 of mixture into prepared pan. Arrange SNICKERS® Bar slices in pan about 1/2 inch from

edge of pan. Finely crumble remaining mixture over sliced SNICKERS® Bars. Bake for 25 minutes or until edges are golden brown. Cool in pan on wire rack. Cut into bars or squares to serve.

Makes 24 bars

Ginger Pear Upside-Down Cake

(Pictured at right)

> 8 tablespoons (1 stick) softened margarine,
> divided
> 3/4 cup KARO® Dark Corn Syrup, divided
> 1/2 cup plus 2 tablespoons packed brown sugar,
> divided
> 1 can (16 ounces) pear halves, well drained
> 1/2 cup walnut halves
> 1-1/3 cups flour
> 1 teaspoon ground ginger
> 1/2 teaspoon baking soda
> 1/2 teaspoon cinnamon
> 1/4 teaspoon salt
> 1 egg
> 1/2 cup buttermilk

1. Preheat oven to 350°F. In small saucepan melt 2 tablespoons margarine. Stir in 1/4 cup corn syrup and 2 tablespoons brown sugar. Spread evenly in ungreased 9-inch round cake pan. Arrange pear halves and walnuts, rounded sides down, over corn syrup mixture.

2. In medium bowl combine flour, ginger, baking soda, cinnamon and salt; set aside.

3. In large bowl with mixer at medium speed, beat remaining 6 tablespoons margarine, 1/2 cup corn syrup and 1/2 cup brown sugar. Add egg and buttermilk; beat until well blended. Add flour mixture; beat 1 minute or until thoroughly combined. Carefully spoon batter over pears and walnuts, smoothing top.

4. Bake 55 to 60 minutes or until toothpick inserted into center comes out clean. Immediately run spatula around edge of pan and invert cake onto serving plate. *Makes 8 servings*

Note: Well-drained canned peaches, pineapple or apricots are excellent substitutes for pears. They all complement the spicy flavor of this tender cake.

Ginger Pear Upside-Down Cake

Lemon Curd Tartlets with Fresh Raspberries

(Pictured at right)

     3 egg yolks
 1/2 cup sugar
 1/3 cup fresh lemon juice
     1 teaspoon grated lemon peel
     6 tablespoons I CAN'T BELIEVE IT'S NOT
          BUTTER!® Spread, cut into pieces
    24 frozen mini phyllo dough shells, thawed
 1/2 cup whipped cream or non-dairy whipped
          topping
    24 fresh raspberries

In top of double boiler, with wire whisk, beat egg yolks, sugar, lemon juice and lemon peel until blended. Stir in I Can't Believe It's Not Butter!® Spread. Cook over medium heat, stirring frequently, 10 minutes or until mixture thickens and reaches 160°F.

Turn into large bowl and cover with plastic wrap, pressing wrap on surface of lemon curd; refrigerate to chill completely, about 2 hours.

To serve, evenly fill shells with lemon curd. Garnish with whipped cream and raspberries.

Makes about 2 dozen tartlets

Libby's® Pumpkin Roll

(Pictured on back cover)

CAKE
          Powdered sugar
 3/4 cup all-purpose flour
 1/2 teaspoon baking powder
 1/2 teaspoon baking soda
 1/2 teaspoon ground cinnamon
 1/2 teaspoon ground cloves
 1/4 teaspoon salt
     3 large eggs
     1 cup granulated sugar
 2/3 cup LIBBY'S® 100% Pure Pumpkin
     1 cup chopped walnuts (optional)

FILLING
     1 package (8 ounces) cream cheese, softened
     1 cup sifted powdered sugar
     6 tablespoons butter or margarine, softened
     1 teaspoon vanilla extract
          Powdered sugar (optional)

FOR CAKE
PREHEAT oven to 375°F. Grease 15×10-inch jelly-roll pan; line with wax paper. Grease and flour paper. Sprinkle clean towel with powdered sugar.

COMBINE flour, baking powder, baking soda, cinnamon, cloves and salt in small bowl. Beat eggs and granulated sugar in large mixer bowl until thick. Beat in pumpkin. Stir in flour mixture. Spread evenly into prepared pan. Sprinkle with nuts.

BAKE for 13 to 15 minutes or until top of cake springs back when touched. Immediately loosen and turn cake onto prepared towel. Carefully peel off paper. Roll up cake and towel together, starting with narrow end. Cool on wire rack.

FOR FILLING
BEAT cream cheese, powdered sugar, butter and vanilla extract in small mixer bowl until smooth. Carefully unroll cake; remove towel. Spread cream cheese mixture over cake. Reroll cake. Wrap in plastic wrap and refrigerate at least one hour. Sprinkle with powdered sugar before serving.

Makes 10 servings

Plantation Gingerbread

       2 cups all-purpose flour
       2 teaspoons cinnamon
 1-1/2 teaspoons ginger
       1 teaspoon baking powder
   1/2 teaspoon baking soda
   1/2 teaspoon salt
   1/3 cup melted shortening
       1 cup GRANDMA'S® Molasses
   1/2 cup buttermilk
       1 egg
   1/2 cup MOTT'S® Apple Sauce
   1/2 cup raisins

Heat oven to 350°F. In large bowl, combine dry ingredients. In another large bowl, combine shortening and molasses until well blended. Add molasses mixture, buttermilk and egg to flour mixture. Stir in apple sauce and raisins. Bake in greased 9-inch square pan for about 35 minutes or until toothpick inserted in center comes out clean.

Makes 4 servings

Lemon Curd Tartlets with Fresh Raspberries

Milk Chocolate Florentine Cookies

(Pictured at right)

2/3 **cup butter**
2 **cups quick oats**
1 **cup granulated sugar**
2/3 **cup all-purpose flour**
1/4 **cup light or dark corn syrup**
1/4 **cup milk**
1 **teaspoon vanilla extract**
1/4 **teaspoon salt**
1-3/4 **cups (11.5-ounce package) NESTLÉ® TOLL HOUSE® Milk Chocolate Morsels**

PREHEAT oven to 375°F. Line baking sheets with foil.

MELT butter in medium saucepan; remove from heat. Stir in oats, sugar, flour, corn syrup, milk, vanilla extract and salt; mix well. Drop by level teaspoon, about 3 inches apart, onto prepared baking sheets. Spread thinly with rubber spatula.

BAKE for 6 to 8 minutes or until golden brown. Cool completely on baking sheets on wire racks. Peel foil from cookies.

MICROWAVE morsels in medium, uncovered, microwave-safe bowl on MEDIUM-HIGH (70%) power for 1 minute. Stir. Morsels may retain some of their original shape. If necessary, microwave at additional 10- to 15-second intervals, stirring just until morsels are melted. Spread thin layer of melted chocolate onto flat side of *half* the cookies. Top with *remaining* cookies.

Makes about 3-1/2 dozen sandwich cookies

Cream Cheese Raisin Pound Cake

1 **cup (2 sticks) butter, softened**
1 **(8-ounce) package cream cheese,* softened**
1-1/2 **cups granulated sugar**
4 **eggs, at room temperature**
2 **teaspoons vanilla**
2 **teaspoons baking powder**
1/4 **teaspoon salt**
2-1/4 **cups all-purpose flour**
1-1/2 **cups SUN-MAID® Raisins**

*Use brick-style cream cheese for this recipe, but not a low-fat or fat-free variety.

HEAT oven to 325°F. Generously butter 2-piece angel food cake pan (10×4-inch) or 12-cup (10-inch)bundt pan.

BEAT butter and cream cheese until blended, about 30 seconds on medium-high speed.

GRADUALLY add in sugar; beat about 2 minutes until mixture is light and fluffy. Scrape side of bowl.

ADD eggs, one at a time, beating on medium speed just until incorporated. Beat in vanilla, baking powder and salt just until blended.

FOLD in flour in 2 additions by hand with rubber spatula just until blended. Gently fold in raisins.

POUR batter into prepared pan and gently smooth top. Bake 50 to 60 minutes or until wooden pick inserted near center comes out clean. Edges should be golden brown, top lightly browned and just firm to the touch, but not yet shrunken from sides. Cool completely in pan on wire rack.

LOOSEN cake from side of pan with thin knife. Dust with powdered sugar if desired.

Makes 12 to 16 slices

Berry Crumb Tarts

1 **package PEPPERIDGE FARM® Frozen Puff Pastry Shells**
1/3 **cup all-purpose flour**
2 **tablespoons sugar**
1/4 **teaspoon ground cinnamon**
2 **tablespoons butter or margarine, melted**
1 **can (21 ounces) fruit pie filling (blueberry, cherry or strawberry)**

1. **BAKE** pastry shells according to package directions. Let cool. Remove and discard pastry tops.

2. **MIX** flour, sugar, cinnamon and butter.

3. **SPOON** about **1/3 cup** pie filling into **each** pastry shell. Top with crumb mixture. Bake 5 minutes Remove from baking sheet and cool on wire rack 10 minutes. Serve warm or at room temperature.

Makes 6 servings

Milk Chocolate Florentine Cookies

Fudgey Coconut Clusters

Fudgey Coconut Clusters

(Pictured above)

5-1/3 cups MOUNDS® Sweetened Coconut Flakes
1 can (14 ounces) sweetened condensed milk
   (not evaporated milk)
2/3 cup HERSHEY'S Cocoa
1/4 cup (1/2 stick) butter, melted
2 teaspoons vanilla extract
1-1/2 teaspoons almond extract
   HERSHEY'S MINI KISSES® Brand Milk
   Chocolates or candied cherry halves
   (optional)

1. Heat oven to 350°F. Line cookie sheets with aluminum foil; generously grease foil with vegetable shortening.

2. Combine coconut, sweetened condensed milk, cocoa, melted butter, vanilla and almond extract in large bowl; mix well. Drop by rounded tablespoons onto prepared cookie sheets.

3. Bake 9 to 11 minutes or just until set; press 3 milk chocolates or candied cherry halves in center of each cookie, if desired. Immediately remove cookies to wire rack and cool completely.
   Makes about 2-1/2 dozen cookies

Chocolate Chip Macaroons: Omit melted butter and cocoa; stir together other ingredients. Add 1 cup HERSHEY'S MINI CHIPS™ Semi-Sweet Chocolate Chips. Bake 9 to 11 minutes or just until set. Immediately remove to wire racks and cool completely.

Sugar Cookies

2-1/2 cups all-purpose flour
1/2 teaspoon baking soda
1/2 teaspoon cream of tartar
1/4 teaspoon salt
1 cup (2 sticks) IMPERIAL® Spread, softened
3/4 cup granulated sugar, divided
1/2 cup confectioners' sugar
1 egg
1/2 teaspoon vanilla extract

In medium bowl, combine flour, baking soda, cream of tartar and salt; set aside.

In large bowl, with electric mixer, beat Imperial Spread, 1/2 cup granulated sugar and confectioners' sugar until light and fluffy, about 5 minutes. Beat in egg and vanilla until blended. Gradually beat in flour mixture until blended. Cover with plastic wrap and chill until firm, several hours or overnight.

Preheat oven to 375°F. Shape dough into 1-inch balls, then roll in remaining 1/4 cup granulated sugar. Arrange on ungreased baking sheets about 2 inches apart. Flatten each with bottom of glass.

Bake 8 minutes or until centers are set. On wire rack, let stand 2 minutes; remove from sheets and cool completely.   *Makes 2-1/2 dozen cookies*

Helpful Hint

For even baking and browning, place only one baking sheet at a time in the center of the oven. When baking more than one sheet of cookies at a time, rotate them from the top rack to the bottom rack halfway through the baking time.

Englishman's Trifle

(Pictured below)

1 box (10 ounces) BIRDS EYE® frozen
   Strawberries*
1 package (3.4 ounces) vanilla instant pudding
1-1/2 cups milk
1 cup thawed frozen whipped topping
8 thin slices fresh or thawed frozen pound cake
1/2 cup toasted sliced almonds
1/4 cup mini semisweet chocolate chips (optional)

Or, substitute Birds Eye® frozen Raspberries.

• Thaw strawberries according to package
directions.

• Prepare pudding with 1-1/2 cups milk according
to package directions. Let stand 5 minutes; gently
stir in whipped topping.

• Place 1 slice cake in each of 4 individual serving
bowls. Spoon half the strawberries over cake. Top
with half the pudding mixture, almonds and
chocolate chips.

• Repeat layers of cake, strawberries, pudding,
almonds and chips. Cover and chill until ready
to serve.   *Makes 4 servings*

Frozen Peppermint Cheesecake

(Pictured on page 182)

2 cups chocolate wafer cookie or sandwich
   cookie crumbs, divided
1/4 cup sugar
1/4 cup butter or margarine, melted
1 (8-ounce) package cream cheese, softened
1 (14-ounce) can EAGLE BRAND® Sweetened
   Condensed Milk (NOT evaporated milk)
2 teaspoons peppermint extract
   Red food coloring (optional)
2 cups whipping cream, whipped
   Fudge ice cream topping (optional)

1. Combine cookie crumbs and sugar. Add butter;
mix well. Line 9-inch round cake or springform pan
with foil. Press 2 cups crumb mixture firmly on
bottom and halfway up side of prepared pan. Chill.

2. In large bowl, beat cream cheese with electric
mixer on low speed until fluffy. Gradually beat in
EAGLE BRAND® until smooth. Stir in extract and
food coloring, if desired; mix well. Fold in whipped
cream. Pour filling into prepared crust. Cover; freeze
6 hours or until firm. Garnish with topping. Store
unused portions in freezer.

Makes one (9-inch) cheesecake

Englishman's Trifle

Deep-Dish Peach Custard Pie

    1 *unbaked* 9-inch (4-cup volume) deep-dish
        pie shell
3-1/2 cups (about 7 medium) peeled, pitted and
        sliced peaches
    1 can (14 ounces) NESTLÉ® CARNATION®
        Sweetened Condensed Milk
    2 large eggs
  1/4 cup butter or margarine, melted
    1 to 3 teaspoons lemon juice
  1/2 teaspoon ground cinnamon
        Dash ground nutmeg
        Streusel Topping (recipe follows)

PREHEAT oven to 425°F.

ARRANGE peaches in pie shell. Combine sweetened
condensed milk, eggs, butter, lemon juice, cinnamon
and nutmeg in large mixer bowl; beat until smooth.
Pour over peaches.

BAKE for 10 minutes. Sprinkle with Streusel
Topping. Reduce oven temperature to 350°F.;
bake for additional 55 to 60 minutes or until knife
inserted near center comes out clean. Cool on wire
rack.   *Makes 8 servings*

Streusel Topping: COMBINE 1/3 cup all-purpose
flour, 1/3 cup packed brown sugar and 1/3 cup
chopped walnuts in medium bowl. Cut in
2 tablespoons butter or margarine with pastry
blender or two knives until mixture resembles
coarse crumbs.

Easy Fudgy Mayo Brownies

3/4 cup all-purpose flour
1/2 teaspoon baking powder
1/4 teaspoon salt
  1 cup (6 ounces) semi-sweet chocolate chips,
      melted
  1 cup sugar
1/2 cup HELLMANN'S® or BEST FOODS®
      Real Mayonnaise
  2 eggs
  1 teaspoon vanilla extract
1/2 cup chopped walnuts (optional)

1. Preheat oven to 350°F. Grease 8-inch square
baking pan with nonstick cooking spray or line
with aluminum foil; set aside.

2. In small bowl, combine flour, baking powder and
salt; set aside.

3. In large bowl, combine melted chocolate chips,
sugar, Hellmann's or Best Foods Real Mayonnaise,
eggs and vanilla until smooth. Stir in flour mixture
just until blended. Gently stir in walnuts. Spread
into prepared pan.

4. Bake 35 minutes or until toothpick inserted
1 inch from edge comes out clean. On wire rack,
cool completely. To serve, cut into squares.
                   Makes 16 servings

Upside-Down German Chocolate Cake

(Pictured at right)

1-1/2 cups flaked coconut
1-1/2 cups chopped pecans
    1 package DUNCAN HINES® Moist Deluxe®
        German Chocolate or Classic Chocolate
        Cake Mix
    1 package (8 ounces) cream cheese, softened
  1/2 cup butter or margarine, melted
    1 pound (3-1/2 to 4 cups) confectioners' sugar

1. Preheat oven to 350°F. Grease and flour 13×9-inch
baking pan.

2. Spread coconut evenly on bottom of prepared
pan. Sprinkle with pecans. Prepare cake mix as
directed on package. Pour over coconut and
pecans. Combine cream cheese and melted
butter in medium mixing bowl. Beat at low speed
with electric mixer until creamy. Add sugar; beat
until blended and smooth. Drop by spoonfuls evenly
over cake batter. Bake at 350°F for 45 to 50 minutes
or until toothpick inserted halfway to bottom of
cake comes out clean. Cool completely in pan. To
serve, cut into individual pieces; turn upside down
onto plate.   *Makes 12 to 16 servings*

Tip: This cake can be served warm, if desired. Also,
store leftover coconut in the refrigerator and use
within four weeks.

Upside-Down German Chocolate Cake

Butter Pecan Sweet Potato Crunch

(Pictured at right)

2 cans (15 ounces each) PRINCELLA® or
   SUGARY SAM® Cut Sweet Potatoes,
   drained and mashed
1 can (12 ounces) evaporated milk
1 cup sugar
3 eggs
1 tablespoon cinnamon
1 teaspoon vanilla
1/2 regular-size package yellow cake mix (dry)
1 cup chopped pecans
1/2 cup (1 stick) butter or margarine, melted
   Whipped topping

Preheat oven to 350°F. In large bowl, combine first six ingredients. Pour sweet potato mixture into greased 13×9-inch cake pan. Sprinkle dry cake mix on top. Cover with chopped pecans. Drizzle melted butter over pecans. Bake for about 1 hour or until center is firm. Chill well. Cut into squares. Serve with whipped topping.   *Makes 15 to 20 servings*

Hint of Lemon Bread Pudding

4 cups day-old bread cubes (about 6 slices)
3 cups milk
3 eggs, slightly beaten
1/2 cup sugar
1/2 cup raisins
2 tablespoons butter or margarine, melted
   Grated peel of 1 SUNKIST® lemon
1/4 teaspoon salt
   Ground nutmeg

In large shallow baking pan, arrange bread cubes in single layer; bake at 350°F 10 minutes to lightly dry bread. Meanwhile, combine remaining ingredients except nutmeg; stir to dissolve sugar.

In large bowl, pour milk mixture over dried bread cubes and stir well. Let soak 10 minutes. Pour into well-buttered 1-1/2-quart casserole. Sprinkle with nutmeg. Set casserole in shallow baking pan filled with 1 inch hot water. Bake, uncovered, at 350°F 1 hour or until knife inserted in center comes out clean. Remove from water bath and cool 10 minutes. Serve warm. Refrigerate leftovers.

Makes 6 servings (about 4-1/2 cups)

Chocolate Buttercream Cherry Candies

About 48 maraschino cherries with stems,
   well drained
1/4 cup (1/2 stick) butter, softened
2 cups powdered sugar
1/4 cup HERSHEY'S Cocoa or HERSHEY'S
   SPECIAL DARK® Cocoa
1 to 2 tablespoons milk, divided
1/2 teaspoon vanilla extract
1/4 teaspoon almond extract
   White Chip Coating (recipe follows)
   Chocolate Chip Drizzle (recipe follows)

1. Cover tray with wax paper. Lightly press cherries between paper towels to remove excess moisture.

2. Beat butter, powdered sugar, cocoa and 1 tablespoon milk in small bowl until well blended; stir in vanilla and almond extract. If necessary, add remaining milk, one teaspoon at a time, until mixture will hold together but is not wet.

3. Mold scant teaspoon mixture around each cherry, covering completely; place on prepared tray. Cover; refrigerate 3 hours or until firm.

4. Prepare White Chip Coating. Holding each cherry by stem, dip into coating. Place on tray; refrigerate until firm.

5. About 1 hour before serving, prepare Chocolate Chip Drizzle; with tines of fork drizzle randomly over candies. Refrigerate until drizzle is firm. Store in refrigerator.   *Makes about 48 candies*

White Chip Coating: Place 2 cups (12-ounce package) HERSHEY'S Premier White Chips in small microwave-safe bowl; drizzle with 2 tablespoons vegetable oil. Microwave at HIGH (100%) 1 minute; stir. If necessary, microwave at HIGH an additional 15 seconds at a time, stirring after each heating just until chips are melted and mixture is smooth. If mixture thickens while coating, microwave at HIGH 15 seconds; stir until smooth.

Chocolate Chip Drizzle: Place 1/4 cup HERSHEY'S Semi-Sweet Chocolate Chips and 1/4 teaspoon shortening (do not use butter, margarine, spread or oil) in another small microwave-safe bowl. Microwave at HIGH (100%) 30 seconds to 1 minute; stir until chips are melted and mixture is smooth.

Butter Pecan Sweet Potato Crunch

Double Delicious Cookie Bars

(Pictured at right)

1/2 cup (1 stick) butter or margarine
1-1/2 cups graham cracker crumbs
1 (14-ounce) can EAGLE BRAND® Sweetened
    Condensed Milk (NOT evaporated milk)
1 cup (6 ounces) semi-sweet chocolate chips*
1 cup (6 ounces) peanut butter-flavored chips*

Butterscotch-flavored chips or white chocolate chips can be substituted for the semi-sweet chocolate chips and/or the peanut butter-flavored chips.

1. Preheat oven to 350°F (325°F for glass dish). In 13×9-inch baking pan, melt butter in oven.

2. Sprinkle crumbs evenly over butter; pour EAGLE BRAND® evenly over crumbs. Top with remaining ingredients; press down firmly.

3. Bake 25 to 30 minutes or until lightly browned. Cool. Cut into bars. Store covered at room temperature.   *Makes 2 to 3 dozen bars*

Mixed Berry Pie

(Pictured on page 182)

CRUST
    9-inch Classic Crisco® Double Crust
    (recipe follows)

FILLING
    5 cups assorted fresh or frozen berries such as
        blackberries, blueberries or raspberries,
        thawed and well drained
    1/8 teaspoon almond extract
    1/2 cup granulated sugar
    3 tablespoons cornstarch

1. For crust, prepare as directed. Do not bake. Heat oven to 425°F.

2. For filling, combine blackberries, blueberries, raspberries and almond extract in large bowl. Combine sugar and cornstarch; add to berries. Toss well to mix. Spoon into unbaked pie crust.

3. Cut top crust into leaf shapes and arrange on top of pie, or cover pie with top crust. Flute edge. Cut slits into top crust, if using, to allow steam to escape.

4. Bake at 425°F for 40 minutes or until filling in center is bubbly and crust is golden brown. Cover with foil if necessary to prevent overbrowning. Cool until barely warm or room temperature before serving.   *Makes 1 (9-inch) pie (8 servings)*

9-inch Classic Crisco® Double Crust

2 cups PILLSBURY BEST® All-Purpose Flour
1 teaspoon salt
3/4 CRISCO® Stick or 3/4 cup CRISCO shortening
5 tablespoons cold water

1. Spoon flour into measuring cup and level. Combine flour and salt in medium bowl.

2. Cut in shortening using pastry blender or 2 knives until flour is blended to form pea-size chunks.

3. Sprinkle with water, 1 tablespoon at a time. Toss lightly with fork until dough forms a ball.

4. Divide dough in half. Press half of dough between hands to form a 5- to 6-inch "pancake." Flour rolling surface and rolling pin lightly. Roll dough into circle. Trim circle 1 inch larger than upside-down pie plate. Carefully remove trimmed dough. Set aside to reroll and use for pastry cut-out garnish, if desired. Repeat with remaining half of dough.

Makes 2 (9-inch) crusts

Hot Stuff Ice Cream

1/2 cup milk
1 medium cinnamon stick
1 strip orange peel (from 1 small orange)
4 whole cloves
1 (14-ounce) can sweetened condensed milk
2 teaspoons vanilla extract
1-1/2 teaspoons TABASCO® brand Pepper Sauce
2 cups heavy cream, whipped
    Cinnamon sticks and orange peel twists
    (optional)

Heat milk, cinnamon stick, orange peel and cloves to boiling in small saucepan over medium heat. Reduce heat to low; cover and simmer 5 minutes to blend flavors. Set aside to cool to room temperature. Strain mixture.

Combine milk mixture, sweetened condensed milk, vanilla and TABASCO® Sauce in large bowl. Gently fold in whipped cream. Cover and freeze until firm, stirring once.

To serve, scoop ice cream into glasses or dessert dishes. Garnish with cinnamon sticks and orange peel twists, if desired.   *Makes 6 servings*

Double Delicious Cookie Bars

Peanut Butter Fudge Brownie Bars

(Pictured at right)

1 cup (2 sticks) butter or margarine, melted
1-1/2 cups sugar
2 eggs
1 teaspoon vanilla extract
1-1/4 cups all-purpose flour
2/3 cup HERSHEY'S Cocoa
1/4 cup milk
1-1/4 cups chopped pecans or walnuts, divided
1/2 cup (1 stick) butter or margarine
1-2/3 cups (10-ounce package) REESE'S® Peanut Butter Chips
1 can (14 ounces) sweetened condensed milk (not evaporated milk)
1/4 cup HERSHEY'S Semi-Sweet Chocolate Chips

1. Heat oven to 350°F. Grease 13×9×2-inch baking pan.

2. Beat melted butter, sugar, eggs and vanilla in large bowl with electric mixer on medium speed until well blended. Add flour, cocoa and milk; beat until blended. Stir in 1 cup nuts. Spread in prepared pan.

3. Bake 25 to 30 minutes or just until edges begin to pull away from sides of pan. Cool completely in pan on wire rack.

4. Melt 1/2 cup butter and peanut butter chips in medium saucepan over low heat, stirring constantly. Add sweetened condensed milk; stirring until smooth; pour over baked layer.

5. Place chocolate chips in small microwave-safe bowl. Microwave at HIGH (100%) 45 seconds or just until chips are melted when stirred. Drizzle bars with melted chocolate; sprinkle with remaining 1/4 cup nuts. Refrigerate 1 hour or until firm. Cut into bars. Cover; refrigerate leftover bars.

Makes 36 bars

Chocolate-Caramel Fondue

3 (1-ounce) squares unsweetened chocolate, chopped
1 (14-ounce) can EAGLE BRAND® Sweetened Condensed Milk (NOT evaporated milk)
1 (12-1/4-ounce) jar caramel ice cream topping
Dippers: Fresh fruit, cookies, pound cake pieces or angel food cake pieces

1. In medium saucepan, melt chocolate with EAGLE BRAND® and caramel topping.

2. Pour into serving bowl or individual cups. Serve with desired dippers.   *Makes 2-1/2 cups*

Fresh Orange Cookies

1-1/2 cups all-purpose flour
1/2 teaspoon baking soda
1/4 teaspoon salt
1/2 cup (1 stick) butter or margarine, softened
1/2 cup granulated sugar
1/2 cup packed light brown sugar
1 egg
1 unpeeled SUNKIST® orange, finely chopped*
1/2 cup chopped walnuts
Orange Glaze (recipe follows)

*Chop SUNKIST® orange in blender or food processor, or by hand, to equal 3/4 cup chopped fruit.

Sift together flour, baking soda and salt. In large bowl, beat butter and sugars until light and fluffy. Add egg and chopped orange; beat well. Gradually blend in dry ingredients. Stir in walnuts. Cover and chill at least 1 hour. Drop dough by teaspoons onto lightly greased cookie sheets. Bake at 375°F for 10 to 12 minutes. Cool on wire racks. Spread cookies with Orange Glaze.

Makes about 4 dozen cookies

Orange Glaze

1 cup confectioners' sugar
1 to 2 tablespoons fresh SUNKIST® orange juice
1 tablespoon butter or margarine, softened
1 teaspoon grated SUNKIST® orange peel

In small bowl, combine all ingredients until smooth.
Makes about 1/2 cup

Peanut Butter Fudge Brownie Bars

The publisher would like to thank the companies and organizations listed below for the use of their recipes and photographs in this publication.

ACH Food Companies, Inc.

Allen Canning Company

American Lamb Council

Bays English Muffin Corporation

Alouette® Cheese, Chavrie® Cheese, Saladena®

BelGioioso® Cheese, Inc.

Birds Eye Foods

Bob Evans®

California Olive Industry

Campbell Soup Company

COLLEGE INN® Broth

ConAgra Foods®

Crisco is a registered trademark of The J.M. Smucker Company

Delmarva Poultry Industry, Inc.

Del Monte Corporation

Dole Food Company, Inc.

Domino® Foods, Inc.

Duncan Hines® and Moist Deluxe® are registered trademarks of Pinnacle Foods Corp.

EAGLE BRAND®

Filippo Berio® Olive Oil

Florida Department of Agriculture and Consumer Services, Bureau of Seafood and Aquaculture

The Golden Grain Company®

Grandma's® is a registered trademark of Mott's, LLP

Heinz North America

The Hershey Company

The Hidden Valley® Food Products Company

Hillshire Farm®

Holland House® is a registered trademark of Mott's, LLP

Hormel Foods, LLC

Jennie-O Turkey Store®

JOLLY TIME® Pop Corn

Keebler® Company

The Kingsford® Products Co.

Lawry's® Foods

© Mars, Incorporated 2005

MASTERFOODS USA

McCormick®

McIlhenny Company (TABASCO® brand Pepper Sauce)

Minnesota Cultivated Wild Rice Council

Mott's® is a registered trademark of Mott's, LLP

Mrs. Dash®

Mushroom Information Center

National Honey Board

National Pork Board

Nestlé USA

Newman's Own, Inc.®

North Dakota Wheat Commission

Ortega®, A Division of B&G Foods, Inc.

Parkay® is a registered trademark of ConAgra Brands, Inc.

Perdue Farms Incorporated

The Quaker® Oatmeal Kitchens

Reckitt Benckiser Inc.

Riviana Foods Inc.

Sargento® Foods Inc.

Smucker's® is a trademark of The J.M. Smucker Company

Sonoma® Dried Tomatoes

Southeast United Dairy Industry Association, Inc.

StarKist Seafood Company

Stonyfield Farm®

Sun•Maid® Growers of California

Reprinted with permission of Sunkist Growers, Inc.

Unilever Foods North America

USA Dry Pea & Lentil Council

USA Rice Federation

Veg•All®

Walnut Marketing Board

Washington State Fruit Commission

Watkins Incorporated

General Index

Alphabetical Index

METRIC CONVERSION CHART

VOLUME MEASUREMENTS (dry)

$^1/_8$ teaspoon = 0.5 mL
$^1/_4$ teaspoon = 1 mL
$^1/_2$ teaspoon = 2 mL
$^3/_4$ teaspoon = 4 mL
1 teaspoon = 5 mL
1 tablespoon = 15 mL
2 tablespoons = 30 mL
$^1/_4$ cup = 60 mL
$^1/_3$ cup = 75 mL
$^1/_2$ cup = 125 mL
$^2/_3$ cup = 150 mL
$^3/_4$ cup = 175 mL
1 cup = 250 mL
2 cups = 1 pint = 500 mL
3 cups = 750 mL
4 cups = 1 quart = 1 L

VOLUME MEASUREMENTS (fluid)

1 fluid ounce (2 tablespoons) = 30 mL
4 fluid ounces ($^1/_2$ cup) = 125 mL
8 fluid ounces (1 cup) = 250 mL
12 fluid ounces (1$^1/_2$ cups) = 375 mL
16 fluid ounces (2 cups) = 500 mL

WEIGHTS (mass)

$^1/_2$ ounce = 15 g
1 ounce = 30 g
3 ounces = 90 g
4 ounces = 120 g
8 ounces = 225 g
10 ounces = 285 g
12 ounces = 360 g
16 ounces = 1 pound = 450 g

DIMENSIONS

$^1/_{16}$ inch = 2 mm
$^1/_8$ inch = 3 mm
$^1/_4$ inch = 6 mm
$^1/_2$ inch = 1.5 cm
$^3/_4$ inch = 2 cm
1 inch = 2.5 cm

OVEN TEMPERATURES

250°F = 120°C
275°F = 140°C
300°F = 150°C
325°F = 160°C
350°F = 180°C
375°F = 190°C
400°F = 200°C
425°F = 220°C
450°F = 230°C

BAKING PAN SIZES

Utensil	Size in Inches/Quarts	Metric Volume	Size in Centimeters
Baking or Cake Pan (square or rectangular)	8×8×2	2 L	20×20×5
	9×9×2	2.5 L	23×23×5
	12×8×2	3 L	30×20×5
	13×9×2	3.5 L	33×23×5
Loaf Pan	8×4×3	1.5 L	20×10×7
	9×5×3	2 L	23×13×7
Round Layer Cake Pan	8×1½	1.2 L	20×4
	9×1½	1.5 L	23×4
Pie Plate	8×1¼	750 mL	20×3
	9×1¼	1 L	23×3
Baking Dish or Casserole	1 quart	1 L	—
	1½ quart	1.5 L	—
	2 quart	2 L	—